The Disintegration
of Community

The Disintegration of Community

On Jorge Portilla's Social and Political Philosophy, With Translations of Selected Essays

CARLOS ALBERTO SÁNCHEZ

and

FRANCISCO GALLEGOS

Published by State University of New York Press, Albany

For information, contact State University of New York Press, Albany, NY
www.sunypress.edu

Library of Congress Cataloging-in-Publication Data

Names: Sánchez, Carlos Alberto, 1975– author. | Gallegos, Francisco, 1983–
author. | Portillo, Jorge, 1919–1963. Works. Selections. English.
Title: The disintegration of community : on Jorge Portilla's social and political
philosophy, with translations of selected essays / Carlos Alberto Sánchez
and Francisco Gallegos.
Description: Albany, NY : State University of New York Press, 2020. |
Series: SUNY series in Latin American and Iberian thought and culture |
Includes bibliographical references and index.
Identifiers: LCCN 2020018353 | ISBN 9781438480091 (hardcover) |
ISBN 9781438480107 (pbk.)
Subjects: LCSH: Portillo, Jorge, 1919–1963. | Philosophy, Mexican—20th century.
Classification: LCC B1019.P674 D57 2020 | DDC 199/.72—dc23
LC record available at https://lccn.loc.gov/2020018353

10 9 8 7 6 5 4 3 2 1

For Tricia Rodrillo Ryan,
for her unwavering love and unrelenting support.
—CAS

For Petra Salazar,
whose love is the condition of all my possibilities.
—FG

Contents

Acknowledgments   ix

Introduction
On Thinking *with* Portilla about Politics   1
   Carlos Alberto Sánchez & Francisco Gallegos

Part I
On "Critique of Criticism"

Chapter 1
Terrorism of the Social   17
   Carlos Alberto Sánchez

Chapter 2
Portilla's Conceptual Framework: Phenomenological Nationalism   43
   Francisco Gallegos

Part II
On "The Spiritual Crisis of the United States"

Chapter 3
The Politics of Innocence   71
   Carlos Alberto Sánchez

Chapter 4
Portilla's Method: A Phenomenological Social Theory   93
   Francisco Gallegos

PART III
ON "THOMAS MANN AND GERMAN IRRATIONALISM"

CHAPTER 5
From Irrationalism to Complacency for the Death of the Other   123
    Carlos Alberto Sánchez

CHAPTER 6
Portilla's Hope: Phenomenological Flourishing and
Affective Liberation   145
    Francisco Gallegos

APPENDIX
Critique of Criticism   165
    Jorge Portilla, translated by Francisco Gallegos and
    Carlos Alberto Sánchez

The Spiritual Crisis of the United States   175
    Jorge Portilla, translated by Francisco Gallegos and
    Carlos Alberto Sánchez

Thomas Mann and German Irrationalism   191
    Jorge Portilla, translated by Francisco Gallegos and
    Carlos Alberto Sánchez

BIBLIOGRAPHY   207

INDEX   213

Acknowledgments

This book would not be possible without the support of many. The authors wish to thank the Fondo de Cultura Económica in Mexico City for permission to publish our translations of Portilla's essays, which are included in the appendix; the Society for Mexican American Philosophy for creating spaces to present early versions of the essays contained here; and those who have supported our efforts throughout, but especially Robert Eli Sanchez, Lori Gallegos de Castillo, Manuel Vargas, Clinton Tolley, Amy Oliver, Guillermo Hurtado, José Mendoza, and Jorge Gracia. We are particularly grateful to Rebecca Colesworthy, our editor at State University of New York Press, who believed in our project from the beginning.

Carlos would like to thank the Department of Philosophy at San José State University for their constant support, as well as his children, Julian, Pascual, and Ethan, his friends, and his colleagues for making it all worthwhile.

Francisco would like to thank Wake Forest University for supporting this research, as well as all those who have worked to help Latin American and Latinx philosophy thrive in the US.

Introduction

On Thinking with *Portilla about Politics*

Carlos Alberto Sánchez and
Francisco Gallegos

Jorge Portilla's (1919–1963) single most important contribution to Mexican philosophy is undoubtedly his essay "Phenomenology of Relajo," a rich and fascinating meditation on values, nihilism, and the disruptive nature of *relajo* as a complex intersubjective mood or attitude.[1] This relatively lengthy text was published posthumously in 1966, three years after Portilla's death, in a book titled *Femenología del relajo y otros ensayos,* which also included other, shorter works making up the entirety of Portilla's known oeuvre.[2] Sánchez's translation of "Phenomenology of Relajo," included as an appendix to his 2012 book, *The Suspension of Seriousness,* introduced the English-speaking philosophical community to this remarkable essay and to Portilla as a value theorist and philosopher of culture.[3]

The translation of "Phenomenology of Relajo," as well as Sánchez's analysis of it, have been widely discussed and have given rise to questions surrounding the content of Portilla's other works, the *"otros ensayos"* referenced in the title of Portilla's anthology.[4] Overshadowed by Portilla's masterpiece, these other essays have been largely ignored both in Spanish and in English-speaking treatments of Portilla's work. In this book, we attend to these forgotten *"otros ensayos"* in the hopes of, one, highlighting a contribution that, while rooted in its own time, is both timely and relevant to our own, and two, completing a picture of a philosophical project that benefits the history of philosophy, and, in particular, the history of Latin American philosophy.

What we find is that Portilla's other essays are primarily concerned with social and cultural issues. We would like to suggest that, in their content and intention, these essays constitute Portilla's "politics." In the three essays that are translated here for the first time, Portilla discusses the allure and dangers of nationalism and the weaponization of political correctness, especially in cultural criticism ("Critique of Criticism"), the cultural and political life of the United States from the Mexican point of view, and the existential roots of US American exceptionalism and xenophobia ("The Spiritual Crisis of the United States"), and the nihilistic worldview that gave rise to Nazism and still threatens to give rise to fascism today ("Thomas Mann and German Irrationalism").[5] These political meditations are unified by Portilla's central concern with community and its disintegration through attitudes that destroy communities from within.

The kind of community that most fascinates Portilla in these essays is that of the *nation*. Like many of his contemporaries, Portilla sought to understand the ways that nationality influences people, for good and ill. But Portilla's work stands out for both its philosophical sophistication and the extraordinary quality of his writing. Indeed, readers who are new to Portilla will be delighted to discover that his prose seems to leap off the page with one thought-provoking idea after another. Portilla's work also stands out for its deeply humane perspective. His essays are driven by a palpable anxiety concerning the possibility of experiencing genuine solidarity with one's fellow citizens, despite their differences and even their character flaws. The thread that ties these essays together is a question that is as urgent today as ever: Under what conditions does that which sustains our communities *disintegrate*? It is our belief that Portilla's post-War anxieties, as manifested in these "other essays," motivate deep and illuminating reflections that can help us answer this timely question.

In the chapters that follow, we approach Portilla's work from different angles in order to shed light on his insights and oversights, the historical context of his work, and its significance to contemporary debates on a wide range of topics—including the politics of social and cultural identity, the nature of community and nationality, and the phenomenology of moods. The chapters authored by Sánchez focus on Portilla as a *political thinker*, drawing out the political implications of his views and comparing them to a wide range of figures in social and political philosophy. The chapters authored by Gallegos focus on Portilla as a *phenomenologist* and *social theorist*, extracting and assessing the general principles, arguments, and methodologies that underlie his intriguing views about how various kinds of "affective attunements" (emotions, moods, character traits, and so on) can profoundly shape people's everyday lives and even alter the destinies of nations. Our different approaches reflect some differences in our interpretation of Portilla—differences that we intentionally leave unresolved in order to provide the reader with a richer understanding of Portilla's work. At the root of our differing interpretations are questions about Portilla's methodology and the systematicity of his thinking. Gallegos argues that in Portilla's essays, we can discern a largely implicit but fairly well-developed philosophical system that is grounded in his commitment to phenomenology. In contrast, Sánchez views Portilla's work as less systematically developed and less committed to any particular methodology, yet more concerned with the importance of offering rational perspectives that can battle the chaos of the world around him. But despite these divergences, the authors engage Portilla in the spirit of critique and dialog.

In a more overarching sense, the analyses contained here attempt to think *with* Portilla about our contemporary crises. This approach to Portilla's work can be distinguished from two alternatives that are perhaps more common when discussing a figure in the history of philosophy. The first is a strictly exegetical approach that is subservient to the original texts; the second is an approach that exploits the original texts as a mere resource for the authors' own philosophical agenda. In order to approach Portilla in a way that is neither subservient nor exploitative, we have endeavored to think of him as though he were a deeply respected colleague who has begun a philosophical investigation to which we are also committed. We thus make every effort to translate and interpret his texts accurately, but at the same time, we take liberties to agree and disagree with Portilla as we see fit, to abandon some of his lines of thought and develop or embellish others, according to our own (inevitably biased and partial) philosophical interests. For this reason, we find that thinking *with* Portilla occasionally involves thinking *after* him, pursuing independent considerations about philosophical and political themes that, while not addressed by Portilla himself, are addressed by us in his critical spirit. All of this is done with the hope that Portilla's thinking, always so vibrant on the page, may once again animate a living philosophical investigation.

1. Portilla's Disquiet

Who was Jorge Portilla? His biography is sketchy. He never taught philosophy and never received a graduate degree in the field. Although he was a respected member of the famed but short-lived philosophical Grupo Hiperión, he did not produce, during his lifetime, the sort of celebrated academic texts that cemented the philosophical status of his contemporaries Octavio Paz, Emilio Uranga, Leopoldo Zea, or Luis Villoro.[6] What we know is that he was anxious and uneasy, an alcoholic, a Catholic, a depressive who, apparently, succeeded in taking his own life in 1963.[7] We know also that he had a formidable intellectual acuity. Juan José Reyes, whose father, Salvador Reyes Nevárez, was also a member of the Grupo Hiperión, describes Portilla as "brilliant and profound, attentive and loquacious, focused and expansive."[8] Reyes reports that Portilla was feared for his ability to engage in practical and abstract criticism with anyone, anytime, but also that he was "generous with his friends," and kind.[9] Although Portilla's intensity could be unnerving, it appeared to spring from a sincere search for "his own salvation and the salvation of others on the margins . . . he was given over fully to others but always inclined toward his own spiritual salvation [*al recogimiento*]."[10]

By all accounts, Portilla was, at heart, a remarkable and caring thinker who despised chaos, irrationalism, and the political games that separated and alienated people from one another, from themselves, and from the truth. His untimely death in 1963 left many questions unanswered, both about his person and about his philosophy. Here, our aim is to answer some of those questions about his philosophy and to solidify as much as possible his somewhat unusual philosophical orientation. As Portilla himself confessed to his friends: "I do not fit into any of the frames that make up Mexican philosophy."[11] To us, this confession is an invitation to venture into his work without the burden of any orthodoxy or rigid interpretations getting in our way. And, thus, we venture beyond the usual interpretation of Portilla as phenomenologist of *relajo*, to speak about his social and political thought.

Portilla's core political values are perhaps most evident in his manner of philosophizing. It could be said that his philosophical labor was always a labor for others—or, more specifically, that it was always labor for Mexico and for Mexicans, labor that he hoped would make things better, or serve, in some way, the betterment of his countrymen. His critique of *relajo*, for instance, is motivated by the hope that analyzing this issue would serve his community. As he puts it,

> [it is] worth the effort to examine this issue, not so much because of a Pharisee-like desire to warn the youth of the dangers of the lack of seriousness [*relajo*], but rather because of the desire to understand . . . an issue that is alive and well in our community and—so to speak—to take philosophy out into the streets (which is its natural place) by stripping it as much as possible of the "technical" shell that sometimes conceals it.[12]

The idea that the "natural place" of philosophy is "the streets" or the community is tied to the pragmatic notion that philosophy should be in the service of human life itself—that if it is not in the service of the community or not performing a practical and liberating labor in the streets, among people, then it is not operating according to its nature. Portilla held firm to this conviction, even in his daily life, where he "never ceased to point out, to denounce, to reveal, those traps that get in the way of liberation."[13]

Taking philosophy "out in to the streets" also meant that Portilla would not publish much in academic or professional journals or presses, thus restricting his output and largely confining his voice to conversations, magazines, and newspaper columns.[14] In order to gain a better sense of Portilla as a philosopher, then, let us consider a sampling of his columns, which originally appeared as supplements between 1958 and 1962 in the Mexico City newspapers *Excélsior* and *Siempre!*, and were collected in his posthumous anthology under the title "Quinta Columna" (or "Fifth Column") and "Cuaderno de Notas" (or "Notebook"). In these columns, Portilla sets as his goal the philosophical education of the masses for the sake of Mexico, based on his conviction that "philosophy is useful for understanding" [January 18, 1959; 200].[15] We see in these writings philosophy, disguised as the journalistic exercises of a restless yet agile mind, unapologetically broadcasted in the streets—specifically, in newsstands, bookstores, libraries, and waiting rooms, sold at intersections or dragged listlessly by the wind through the avenues—and, thus broadcasted, sought to enlighten and edify the passersby, the factory worker, the thief, the detective, the doctor, the everyday reader who knows nothing of Marx, Hegel, or the philosophy of *lo mexicano*, but who cares about Mexico, his community, and his fellows.

A quick study of these columns reveals that the greatest influences on Portilla's political views are Marxism and Catholicism, and that Portilla is committed to a kind of socialist humanism that puts truth before ideology, community before the individual, and brotherly solidarity before nation. In many of these seemingly hurried pieces, Portilla also touches on themes that he examines in more detail in his scholarly texts. Thus, time and again Portilla targets what he views as the negative and destructive forms of human conviviality that have historically kept Mexicans from recognizing and pursuing their own excellence. Even in his first column, Portilla laments the lack of "great . . . public virtues" in the Mexican community, and he argues that this "lack" is generated by a "skepticism, to which we, Mexican intellectuals, are especially inclined," rooted in the belief that Mexico is helplessly inferior to the industrialized world, both economically and politically [December 14, 1958; 199].

Over time, Portilla comes to view this form of alienation as a symptom of a larger sickness that he refers to as "skeptical nihilism" [September 5, 1962; 201]. Skeptical nihilism is a cultural and political disease; indeed, it the polar opposite of everything Portilla cherishes. Skeptical nihilism holds that universal values do not exist, and that the larger human community is an abstraction and thus of no value. It emphasizes a historicism bordering on relativism that says that only one's specifically situated community should matter, if anything is to matter at all. And, moreover, it says that any value that does not directly contribute to the empowerment of the individual is of no use. As such, skeptical nihilism is the closing of the mind, an abandonment of understanding for the sake of tribalism and individualism.

What is the antidote for the refusal of transcendence and understanding? By the late 1950s, Portilla is preaching a variation of Marxist Catholicism that he thinks can help in the effort to combat the closing of the mind and the disintegration of community. The effort, he suggests, ought to target the dangerous emotional dispositions of *fear* and *hate*. "Fear of man," he writes, "engenders hate and contempt, which are characteristic passions of the right and the petite bourgeoisie" [October 10, 1962; 206]. This hate—hatred of the new, of the foreign, of the other, of the strange—justifies an individual's or a community's skepticism toward the other; it justifies the nihilism of values that would otherwise promote progress and growth; it justifies, finally, *relajo*, corruption, and the lazy politics of nationalists who would rather close their ranks than understand other ways of being. Portilla insists, however, that philosophy can serve as a tool for the clarification and ultimate dissolution of hate. Thus, Portilla entreats the reader, "we must comprehend our own hate. We can literally drown in indignation and hate. So long as we do not clarify the origin or the meaning of this passion, we cannot be of help in anything or help anyone" [September 5, 1962; 203]. This view of the role of philosophy reflects what we could call Portilla's basic philosophical principle, announced in one of the earliest columns: "reality is only accessible with the truth, yet only if one is in truth can we modify reality" [January 18, 1959; 200].

One of Portilla's greatest strengths as a writer is his ability to identify and describe the *character types* that he encounters on the streets of Mexico City. Almost like a contemporary stand-up comedian, Portilla calls attention to "*that guy*—you know, the guy who . . . ," naming and describing a familiar type of person in a surprising, insightful, and humorous way. By doing so, he gently admonishes his audience not to be like the person he is criticizing, while also shedding light on aspects of our social space that we may have understood intuitively but could not articulate explicitly. In one column, for example, he targets the *mocho*, a caricature of the modern individual, or, better, of the radical individualism of the modern age [November 21, 1962; 210–211]. The *mocho* fetishizes production but ultimately seeks only his own advancement, pushing forward without respect for traditional values, cultural mores, rules, and logic. He is a narcissist, and for this reason, he is boring, pretentious, racist, closed-minded, hypocritical, and deceitful.

Portilla's final column appeared at the end of 1962, less than a year before his death in the fall of 1963. In it, he expresses hope that individualism will be overcome. Retreating into his Marxist humanism, he proclaims that "individualism's moment has passed," and that a return to reason is possible [December 12, 1962; 211]. Echoing Emiliano Zapata's famous dictum in his "Plan de Ayala" that what is important is to follow principles rather than personalities, Portilla writes, "Our time is no longer the time of 'personality,' but, perhaps, of 'truth'" [211]. Here, hope is inscribed in three words, "*sino, tal vez*,"—"but, perhaps"—a rare confirmation of what careful readers already know, that, after all, Portilla's philosophy is a philosophy of hope. His deconstructive critiques are meant to be uplifting, to help lay the groundwork for new kinds of intersubjective arrangements, or, at least, to help undo ways of thinking that obscure the possibility of new forms of being-with-others, communities grounded in trust, solidarity, and truth.

2. A Note on *Filósofas Mexicanas*

One salient feature common to Portilla's work, both the scholarly essays and his journalistic contributions, is his silence about issues related to gender. In fact, Portilla rarely discusses women at all. In his critiques of various character types (the *relajiento*, the *mocho*, the critic, etc.), for example, he consistently assumes that the individual he is criticizing is a man (*"el" hombre mexicano*). We find this assumption in his analysis of the *relajo individual* in the "Phenomenology of Relajo," where the *relajiento* is described as someone who is comfortable standing outside the rules of propriety, someone who is allowed by Mexican society to be disruptive and rebellious—social allowances made only for *men* in a traditionally patriarchal culture such that of Mexico.[16] The same holds true of the *mocho* and the critic he discusses in "Critique of Criticism" (see appendix). In fact, none of the character types that Portilla discusses are specifically female, and Portilla appears to overlook the possibility that women might participate in the roles and practices he describes (for example, as literary critics or even as *relajientas*).

Portilla's silence about gender, to some extent, reflected social, political, and academic attitudes typical of his time and place. In fact, most, if not all, established or recognized[17] Mexican philosophers in the first half of the twentieth century were complicit in this silence. Whether the writer was José Vasconcelos, Samuel Ramos, José Gaos, Emilio Uranga, Leopoldo Zea, or Luis Villoro, the perspective was masculine and, more-over, metropolitan, that is, related to *mestizo* males from Mexico City. One clearly sees, in the texts of these authors, that a single, relatively dominant perspective is taken for granted as the most legitimate and authoritative, a practice that although not a matter of policy was certainly adopted as a sort of implicit default. This, of course, adds a problematic layer to our discussion of Portilla's thinking regarding society's disintegration. Although we touch only briefly upon these and related issues in the chapters that follow, we are convinced that it should be the focus of future research, because retrieving diverse voices that speak about social and political issues during this period of Mexican history would certainly enrich Mexican philosophy as a whole.

When faced with Portilla's silence about issues related to gender, some readers might assume that women philosophers were simply missing from the spaces where these conversations were taking place, or that these issues were irrelevant to the topics of his inquiries. Neither of these assumptions would be correct. While there were relatively few Mexican women contributing to the philosophical conversation in Portilla's time, they were not insignificant. (A popular positive response to those who question whether or not there were any female Mexican philosophers in the first half of the twentieth century goes like this: *¡de que las hay, las hay!* In other words, there *certainly were* female Mexican philosophers, we just haven't looked hard enough to find them!) In fact, the first comprehensive study and commentary of Portilla's own work was by Rosa Krauze (1923–2003), a friend and contemporary of Portilla, student of the famed Mexican philosopher Antonio Caso, and prolific historian of twentieth-century Mexican philosophy. Krauze was one of a handful of interlocutors capable of approaching Portilla without hesitation. If her account is any indication, their conversations were mutually enriching, philosophically and psychologically, to the point that Krauze's influence on Portilla should not be hard to spot.[18]

Portilla would have had many such encounters with women philosophers of his day. During his time of philosophical production (1948–1963), several women philosophers had either already left their stamp on the intellectual life of Mexico or were in the process of doing so. Among them was Krauze, but also Rosario Castellanos (1925–1974), whose *Sobre cultura femenina* [*On Feminine Culture*] sought to avoid the assumptions of the male perspective in philosophy while making a case for the place of women in the production and maintenance of culture.[19] This work, published in 1950, had been written under the direction of José Gaos, and it was in Gaos' seminars that Mexican women philosophers began to flourish and assert their place in the Mexican intellectual landscape, including Monelissa Lina Pérez Marchand, Victoria Junco Posadas, Olga Victoria Quiroz Martínez, Vera Yamuni, María del Carmen Rovira Gaspar, and Elsa Cecilia Frost.[20] Perhaps due to Gaos's influence, most of these women went on to write on themes and issues in the philosophy of culture, feminism, or the philosophy of history, and often did so in ways that challenged the normativity of the *mestizo* male perspective.

Portilla's silence on issues related to gender and the oppression of women is thus not justified by "the times," and it is certainly not justified from a theoretical perspective. Portilla sought to understand the disintegration of community, and while his work sheds valuable insight on a wide range of factors contributing to communal disintegration—including diverse value inversions, mythologies, communal moods, relations of power, and ideologies—by ignoring the paternalistic and patriarchal tendencies that prevailed in the social order of his day, the rampant oppression of women and the female perspective in all things political, and the marginalization of women in philosophy and other sites of cultural production, his work ignores structures that clearly contribute to communal disintegration. If this is correct, then Portilla's own silence contributed to the marginalization of women and so to the disintegration of community, thus exacerbating and obfuscating the very phenomena he sought to analyze.

We offer these assessments in the spirit of an invitation. Krauze, Castellanos, Frost, and Zambrano are giants in the history of Mexican philosophy, and as we move ahead in normalizing this tradition in the English-speaking philosophical academy, their contributions should not be overlooked. Portilla's philosophy did not develop in a vacuum; it was influenced by the history of philosophy and the writings of his peers, formed in a life of conversations, agreements and disagreement. As Krauze recalls, "with him, everything was a conversation. He spoke always with contagious enthusiasm. He didn't need an entourage; he didn't pick his interlocutor. . . . His life was wasted in talking . . . we would've gained so much if [he would have written things down], if his disposition would have been different."[21]

3. The Plan of this Book

The appendix of this book contains our translations of three of Portilla's previously untranslated essays. We have selected these texts because we believe they collectively present the essential elements of Portilla's social and political philosophy, so that English-speaking readers may develop their own interpretations of this intrepid Mexican philosopher. In order to provide readers with some guidance as they make their way into the texts—as well as offer some provocations to stimulate future discussions— the first six chapters of this book present complementary perspectives on Portilla's three essays.

In chapter 1, "The Terrorism of the Social," Sánchez provides an interpretation of the critique of nationalism and political Manichaeism in Portilla's 1955 essay "Critique of Criticism." Sánchez discusses the historical context of Portilla's urgent concern with an ideological and exclusionary form of cultural criticism that adopts an aggressively puritanical approach to political correctness. Sánchez reflects on the relevance of this text for our own times, and he draws out the ethical ideals that underlie Portilla's concerns and can oppose the Manichaean attitudes that he warns about.

In chapter 2, "Portilla's Conceptual Framework: Phenomenological Nationalism," Gallegos argues that "Critique of Criticism" exhibits Portilla's commitment to the view that nationality functions as a phenomenological horizon of intelligibility, and in particular, that many nations are in the grip of a mood or "affective attunement" that profoundly shapes the way individuals in these nations experience themselves, others, and the situations they encounter. Gallegos locates this idea of "phenomenological nationalism" at the intersection of phenomenological tradition's ambivalent fascination with human sociality and Latin American philosophy's guiding concern with liberation from the legacies of colonization.

In chapter 3, "The Politics of Innocence," Sánchez turns to Portilla's 1952 essay "The Spiritual Crisis of the United States," thinking through, with, and beyond Portilla about US American culture and its grounding myths. Drawing on the perspectives of philosophers including Hegel and Emerson, Sánchez reflects on what Portilla means when he insists that US Americans are "innocent" and willfully naive concerning the dark sides of human life. Sánchez then invites us to think *with* Portilla about how the myth of innocence is deployed in contemporary US American social and cultural arrangements, such as in policies that reflect a belief in "American exceptionalism" and a fear of immigrants.

In chapter 4, "Portilla's Method: A Phenomenological Social Theory," Gallegos examines the methodology that Portilla employs in his analysis of the US American way of being. Gallegos extracts from Portilla's essay the general methodological principles that guide Portilla's innovative use of a mood-oriented approach to the phenomenology of nationality as a means of explaining widespread patterns of behaviors and attitudes that are found in a given nation. Gallegos raises a few concerns regarding Portilla's empirical claims about life in the US, suggesting that Portilla's analysis would have been strengthened if he had acknowledged the diversity of the US and explicitly focused his critique on the sense of innocence found within the White mainstream of US society.

In chapter 5, "From Irrationalism to Complacency for the Death of the Other," Sánchez examines the topics of nihilism, death, and violence through the lens of Portilla's 1962 essay, "Thomas Mann and German Irrationalism," where Portilla examines what he calls the "the intellectual and affective climate" that gave rise to Nazism. Sánchez explores connections between Portilla's views and those of fellow Mexican philosophers and others, including Immanuel Levinas. Thinking *beyond* Portilla, Sánchez concludes by considering his remarks in light of the epidemic of violence and death in twenty-first-century Mexico.

Finally, in chapter 6, "Portilla's Hope: Phenomenological Flourishing and Affective Liberation," Gallegos argues that in Portilla's critique of Mann, we can discern Portilla's positive political vision. This vision is grounded in Portilla's conception of "phenomenological flourishing," a kind of wellbeing grounded in the development of our capacities to disclose the meaning of our experience. On the basis of this quasi-ethical ideal, Portilla's work calls for us to do what is necessary to dissolve the rigid and problematic moods that grip our nations, while warning us about some of the most difficult challenges we are likely to face as we work to realize this ideal of "affective liberation."

We hope and expect that we will not have the last word on Portilla's social and political thought, and we look forward to a new generation having the opportunity to think with one of Mexico's greatest philosophers.

Notes

1. As Portilla explains, the term *relajo* refers here to the breakdown of a group activity that is intentionally brought about by individuals who refuse to take the activity "seriously"—typically by joking around incessantly. In this essay, Portilla argues that *relajo* is pervasive in Mexico and is detrimental to Mexican society. But *relajo* is also philosophically illuminating, he says, because these breakdowns in normal social cooperation reveal important features of our experience that philosophers have taken for granted and overlooked, such as the way that an individual's experience of values depends on the cooperation of others.

2. Jorge Portilla, *La fenomenología del relajo y otros ensayos* (Mexico City: Fondo de Cultura Económica, 1984). Originally published in 1966 by the Mexico City publisher ERA.

3. Carlos Sánchez, *The Suspension of Seriousness: On the Phenomenology of Jorge Portilla* (Albany: State University of New York Press, 2012).

4. Published discussions of Portilla's work in English include Sánchez, *The Suspension of Seriousness*; Carlos Alberto Sánchez, *Contingency and Commitment: Mexican Existentialism and the Place of Philosophy* (Albany: State University of New York Press, 2016); Carlos Alberto Sánchez, "Serious Subjects: On Values, Time, and Death," *Spaziofilosofico* 18 (2017): 463–473; Shoni Rancher, "The Political Relevance of Kierkegaardian Humor in Jorge Portilla's *Fenomenología del relajo*,"

APA Newsletter on Hispanic/Latino Issues in Philosophy 18, no. 1 (2018): 12–16; Francisco Gallegos, "Seriousness, Irony, and Cultural Politics: A defense of Jorge Portilla," *APA Newsletter on Hispanic/Latino Issues in Philosophy* 13, no. 1 (2013): 11–18; Francisco Gallegos, "Surviving Social Disintegration: Jorge Portilla on the Phenomenology of Zozobra," *APA Newsletter on Hispanic/Latino Issues in Philosophy* 17, no. 2 (2018): 3–6; Andrea Pitts, "Carlos Alberto Sánchez: *Contingency and Commitment: Mexican Existentialism and the Place of Philosophy*," *Human Studies* 39, no. 4 (2016): 645–652.

5. *La fenomenología del relajo y otros ensayos*, the anthology of Portilla's collected works, contains a total of eight chapters. Besides "Phenomenology of Relajo" and the three chapters that are translated in this book, the remaining chapters include "Comunidad, grandeza, y miseria del mexicano" (a translation of which is included in *Mexican Philosophy in the 20th Century: Essential Readings*, ed. Carlos Alberto Sánchez & Robert Eli Sanchez (New York: Oxford University Press, 2017); "La nausea y el humanismo" and "Dostoievski y Santo Tomas" (discussed in Sánchez, *Contingency and Commitment*); and " 'Quinta Columna' y 'Cuaderno de Notas' " (discussed later in this introduction).

6. The Grupo Hiperión was an influential circle of intellectuals—including Portilla, Uranga, Zea, and Villoro, among others—who worked closely together in Mexico City between 1948 and the early 1950s, most famously addressing the question of *mexicanidad*.

7. See Christopher Domínguez Michael, *Octavio Paz en su siglo* (Mexico City: Aguilar, 2015). See especially Chapter 7, "Mexicanosofía," where Domínguez provides an excellent summary of the Grupo Hiperión and its relationship with Octavio Paz. It is here, also, where Domínguez mentions Portilla's suicide. Domínguez's claim that Portilla committed suicide in 1963 is unconfirmed and unsupported by the obituaries of the day or the eulogies. In any case, if true, it is an end that would cohere with other accounts of this great thinker's reckless behavior. Most references do not mention his manner of death, only that he was a heavy drinker and somewhat reckless with his health. See, especially, Rosa Krauze, "Sobre la *Fenomenología del relajo*," *Revista de la Universidad de México* 20, no. 8 (1966): 9–14.

8. Juan José Reyes, *El péndulo y el pozo* (Mexico City: Consejo para la cultura nacional, 2004), 66. In a similar fashion, Antonio Ibargüengoitia recalls Portilla's "tormented yet agile thinking." Antonio Ibargüengoitia, *Filosofía mexicana: en sus hombres y en sus textos* (Mexico City: Porrúa, 1967), 254.

9. Reyes, *El péndulo y el pozo*, 66.

10. Ibid., 69.

11. Ibid., 67.

12. Portilla, "Phenomenology of Relajo," in *The Suspension of Seriousness* by Carlos Alberto Sanchez (Albany: State University of New York Press, 2012), 126.

13. Reyes, *El péndulo y el pozo*, 68.

14. See Reyes, *El péndulo y el pozo* & Krauze, "Sobre la *Fenomenología del relajo*."

15. Portilla, *La fenomenología del relajo y otros ensayos*. We will cite these pieces by date and page number in square brackets within the text to make quick reference to the newspaper columns where these appear.

16. Portilla, "Phenomenology of Relajo," 132ff.

17. That is, those who were in the business of philosophy—teaching, writing, advocating, or promoting philosophy.

18. Krauze, "Sobre la *Fenomenología del relajo*."

19. See Rosario Castellanos, "On Feminine Culture," trans. Carlos Alberto Sánchez, in *Mexican Philosophy in the 20th Century: Essential Readings* (Oxford: Oxford University Press, 2017), 206–215.

20. See Francesca Gargallo, *Las ideas femenistas latinoamericanas* (Mexico City: UACM, 2006).

21. Krauze, "Sobre la *Fenomenología del relajo*," 9.

PART I

ON "CRITIQUE OF CRITICISM"

Chapter 1

Terrorism of the Social

CARLOS ALBERTO SÁNCHEZ

La filosofía de lo mexicano, a philosophical movement that has come to define the most controversial yet innovative moment in the history of twentieth-century Mexican philosophy, sought to identify, diagnose, and treat the *being* of the Mexican, or Mexicanness, namely, those "essential," identifying, characteristics that lent Mexicans a distinctive cultural and historical difference. The philosophical project, which had begun in earnest some years before the start of the Mexican Revolution (1910–1920),[1] had officially run its course by 1952, stalling before certain unavoidable contradictions.[2] Afterward, philosophers once dedicated to *la filosofía de lo mexicano* found themselves preoccupied with a different task, that of restoring the status of philosophy as universal, objective, and unbiased—a status once given over to the post-Revolutionary furor of nation-building, ideological construction, and identity formation. But if philosophers had given up on the task of highlighting the Mexicanness of Mexicans with the recognition of the project's logical inconsistencies (for instance, the circularity of presupposing an essence they sought to find), the project continued in other humanistic areas, such as theater, drama, poetry, art, and politics, as the political establishment insisted on the power of a unified, which is to say institutionalized, sense of Mexican identity.

Portilla was a central figure in the philosophy of *lo mexicano* between 1947 and 1952, capturing in his brilliant "Phenomenology of Relajo" what he considered an essential feature of the Mexican will to nothingness, namely, a kind of value nihilism that he called *relajo*. In that

17

work, published posthumously in 1966, the source of Mexico's ills, and particularly the obstacle to social and personal flourishing in Mexico, is a culturally accepted and previously undiagnosed attitude to values, and its corresponding behaviors that seek to bring about value inversion, value suspension, and value destruction. This attitude and its behaviors is *relajo*, which he characterizes generally as "the suspension of seriousness." In a broader sense, *relajo* is cultural illness that in inverting, suspending, and destroying values destroys also the possibilities of meaning, cultural wellbeing, and community; as it spreads it implicates all Mexicans in a nihilistic project of value inversion where what is valued is not community or projects conducive to individual human flourishing, but disintegration, distraction, negation, resistance, and dislocation. The antidote to *relajo* is seriousness, irony, rationality, and an open and tolerant spirit. But arriving at this antidote requires a cultural critique that exposes its underlying causes, which, for Portilla, include irrationalism, the fear of otherness, and those cultural and political ideologies that motivate them, that encourage closed-mindedness, xenophobia, and intolerance to difference.

In "Critique of Criticism," the focus of the present chapter, Portilla explicitly rejects the exclusionary gesture of those projects that seek to find, or are rooted in, a Mexican "essence." While his "Phenomenology of Relajo" presupposed the truth of an essential Mexican difference (namely, that Mexicans, in essence, suffered from *relajo*), here he highlights the dangers *in practice* of the myopia that blinds one to openness, difference, and authentic community.[3] Portilla's target in "Critique of Criticism" is the literary critic, specifically the literary critic who roots himself in the national ideology so as to critique any artistic achievement that does not celebrate a purported national difference. Said differently, Portilla aims to expose the limitations of a cultural obsession (in the arts and humanities) with Mexicanness, previously a central tenet of the philosophy of *lo mexicano*, but a tenet now embodied in the professed exceptionalism of a nationalist identity politics actively promoted by what Marxists like György Lukács and Louis Althusser called "the Ideological State Apparatus."[4] In keeping with Portilla's political philosophy, which, as we have stated in the introduction, is grounded in a normative ideal of community as structured by reason, love, and openness, an ideal that necessarily transcends the immediacy of culture and the prejudices of the times, we see in what follows Portilla's disdain for that kind of nationalism and Manicheanism that closes off the possibilities of experience in sometimes subtle, other times explicit and "terrifying," rejections of otherness and difference.

My aim is to highlight, with Portilla, the dangers of an ideological, exclusionary criticism that ends by reflecting what he calls "the terrorism of the social." I begin, in section 1, with what I see as Portilla's main political worry; in section 2, I consider Portilla's critique of the nationalist critic, who represents the embodiment of that worry; next, in section 3, I take up three areas highlighted by Portilla as motivating the critic's exclusionary politics, namely, a nationalist ideology, a nationalist concept of race, and the influence of social pressure (i.e., "terror"); in the last section, section 4, I think with Portilla about human agency in conditions of "the terrorism of the social"; particularly, and in keeping with previous characterological analyses undertaken elsewhere by Portilla, I think about the *type of person* constituted by exclusionary politics and insular ideologies. In the conclusion I suggest what could be Portilla's ethical solution to his main political worry.

1. The Political Worry

Let us begin at the end of "Critique of Criticism," where Portilla points to that which is at the root of that false consciousness and lazy thinking that justifies all sorts of nationalisms and politics of division and exclusion, *Manichaeism*:

> This is the key to everything. At bottom it is all about Manichaeism, that sad ally of stupidity and insufficiency, which allows some to become respectable and righteous; a Manichaeism that allows "hatred of evil" to turn into "love of the good," for which it has to invent both the good and the evil. That is, it he has to lie. For Manichaeism everything is clear as long as we renounce our need for clarity; for this reason, it is the weapon of the mediocre and the father of bad faith. But it is also everywhere the true enemy that is capable of crushing those rare individuals who today, as always, represent the only hope of peace in the world: men of goodwill. [167][5]

We ask, how is this the "key to everything"? To begin with, understanding the origins of this "kind" of Manichaeism helps us understand the political philosophy purportedly at work in mid-twentieth-century Mexico. I say "purportedly" because it seems to be a political philosophy artificially read back into the Mexican circumstance in order to justify a needed national enthusiasm in the post-Revolutionary era.[6]

Those of us familiar with Carl Schmitt's *The Concept of the Political* recognize the Manichaeism that Portilla diagnoses in the "Critique." For Schmitt, the true foundations of a political arrangement lie in the identification of enemies, and consequently, in the identification of those that are not enemies, namely, friends.[7] The boundaries of the body politic are drawn so as to exclude the enemy and include the friend. Because such politics *require* enemies, the suggestion is, if there are no identifiable enemies, they must be *invented*. Thus, as Portilla writes, "hatred of evil," i.e., hatred of those that stand against me, turns into "love of the good," i.e., love of those that stand with me, and if neither exists, they must be created.

In this way, Mexican nationalist politics, Portilla suggests, depends on the creation of enemies. And the first enemy, or the most locatable enemy, is the person who does not recognize the self-contained value of *la patria* (that is, the nation), or who does not dedicate her intellectual energies to showing this to be the case. Portilla calls her "the writer," and the one who locates her as enemy, "the critic."

The idea that Mexican politics is grounded on the friend–enemy distinction (an idea we find in someone like Schmitt), and that this ultimately explains the closed-mindedness and xenophobia of critics who considered non–Mexico-specific cultural productions as threatening to the nation, is not new to Portilla. In fact, the idea was commonly deployed to refer in a critical and negative way to Mexican politics as a whole. In 1951, Emilio Uranga (friend and contemporary of Portilla) referred to what he saw as the current political "constellations of power" that made the "world appear . . . primarily [as the distinction] between friends and enemies." Uranga writes:

> There exists, for the Mexican, the possibility, which is always open, that the world gives itself as "friend" or "enemy," as a danger or salvation, as threat or ally. These categories are especially valued in what is known as the political attitude. . . . And it should not be surprising that the Mexican should be interested in the constellations of power, since the world appears to him primarily in the background of the distinctions between friends and enemies, as with political Manichaeism.[8]

Here we notice a difference between Portilla and Uranga, one that captures a difference in their political attitudes. For Portilla, the Manichaeism that motivates Mexican politics of his day is an invention; for Uranga, it is a phenomenological fact. Thus, for Uranga, the enemy "gives itself" in the Mexican lived experience in the same way that "danger" or "threat" give themselves. According to Portilla, on the other hand, the phenomenological fact is more the "need" to invent the enemy and the "need" to protect the invention. The phenomenological fact, that is, is not an *a priori* distinction of threats and allies, but an *a posteriori* division of a Mexican particularity and that which is other to it, and this for the sake of justifying nationalism and exclusion. I call this difference Portilla's political worry.

The artificiality of this political construction shows up more vividly in the work of the Mexican literary critic—which is the main protagonist of Portilla's "Critique."

2. Mexican Literary Criticism

What can the accusation (not critical judgment) of "foreigner" mean to a Mexican writer? Obviously, it means that this foreign writer has no right to address Mexicans. Put another way: It means that this foreign writer is not, properly speaking, a Mexican writer, for the simple reason that he writes in the manner of the French, English, Spanish, or American writers.

This presupposes the previous acceptance that Mexico is not a nation, that it is not a participant of the universal community, but a sealed and separate repository of human culture. That is, that we have nothing in common with men of other nationalities. This assumes that Mexico *is* or *possesses* a specific good that is put in danger by the communicative action of the foreign writer; that, furthermore, Mexicans possess an excellence that can be contaminated when it is put in contact with the foreigner. [160]

Portilla's strictly political writings are scant and restricted to newspaper columns collected and published after his death (see the introduction). But in those columns, we get a sense of his Marxist sympathies, his disdain for industrial capitalism, and his struggles to bring philosophy to bear on the problems of the day. He regrets the influence of the "petite bourgeoisie" and wishes his countrymen would better understand the realities of the class struggle; he rails against the public intellectual and the conceit of high culture. However, he emphasizes *rational* critique, both social and personal, as a means for personal and social liberation—liberation from ideology, history, and those cultural "moods"[9] that restricted and constricted the possibilities of authentic community. Portilla's critical gaze thus challenges not only the social and political ideologies of Mexican society prevalent in his day, but also those ideologies that promise absolute solutions to contingent problems. His suspicion extends to any theory, ideology, philosophy, worldview, or prejudice that fails to question its own legitimizing principles or fails to account for the complexities, nuances, and limits of apparently absolute positions on politics, identity, or the good life.

Portilla's critical spirit is evident in the "Critique." As the title suggests, the essay is a *critique of criticism*, or more specifically, it is a critical confrontation with a specific kind of criticism popular among critics of his day that judged all literary and cultural production through a Manichaean evaluative logic (i.e., an exclusionary logic) that called products good or bad depending on their fit with and within the national ideology.

According to Portilla, the critic relied on an overly simplistic division of literary production that fell into two categories: either from-Mexicans-and-for-Mexico, on the one hand, or for-Mexicans-and-from-Elsewhere, on the other. According to this Manichaean evaluative logic, the former was intrinsically valuable to the Mexican people and the latter was harmful, a kind of colonialism or imperialism in disguise. Portilla's specific target in "Critique of Criticism" is the critic who traffics in this Manichaean logic, the one for whom literary productions that are for-Mexicans-and-from-Elsewhere are anti-Mexican and deleterious to the national soul and to the spirit of a hard-won Revolutionary ethos.[10]

At the time of the publication of Portilla's essay, Mexican politics continued its Sisyphean attempt to fulfill the promises of the Revolution, and by the mid-1950s it was fully in a process of another transition in the arts, literature, philosophy, and politics begun on the inauguration of President Miguel Alemán in 1946.[11] The obsession with *lo mexicano*, with the philosophical quest to find and articulate the meaning of what it meant to be Mexican, was also in the process of being replaced with a more cosmopolitan (or "global") urge to be "contemporaries of all mankind," as Octavio Paz famously puts it in his *The Labyrinth of Solitude* (1951).[12] However, this cosmopolitan urge[13] did not call for Mexican writers and artists to give up their quest to find the essence of Mexicanness (of *lo mexicano*); rather, it assumed that being on the quest already meant that

Mexicans were contemporaries with all non-Mexicans—that the difference implied in that sought-for essence was a difference that could contribute something to the rest of humankind. In true cosmopolitan fashion, it would seem, then, that the exclusionary Manichaeism that worried Portilla and that was promoted by the nationalist critic was overcome by the turn toward an inclusive cosmopolitanism. The nationalist critic, however, saw in the quest for a Mexican particularity an affirmation of the sought-for difference, which meant that (in a triumph of circular logic) the Mexican difference did, in fact, exist and it needed to be preserved in advance and in spite of those cosmopolitan intentions.

That contemporaneity that Octavio Paz hoped for was doomed from the start. At the root of Mexican nationalism, Portilla tells us, is a "naive individualism" [158], one in which what matters is the immediate emotional and material fulfillment of the individual and the individual's needs and wants; this means that the material and emotional needs and wants of the community are secondary. In a technical sense, naive individualism is defined as "acting solely according to one's own wishes and commands—as if cut off from [the] social order."[14] According to Portilla, practices of literary critics in Mexico reflect this sort of naive individualism, one in which they find fault with any type of literary work that does not speak for, about, or from Mexico; Mexico and that which is Mexican are taken to be the limits and horizon of value and significance, an attitude that Portilla finds offensive to the essential worldliness or cosmopolitanism of literature (and thought) itself. To write from this enclosed and narcissistic perspective is to write for no one but oneself, an act which should be impossible, since writing is always an act of communication, and communication can only happen between a self and an other.

For Portilla, the critic shows that a certain Manichaeism, i.e., an exclusionary logic, is operative in the call for cosmopolitanism itself, since the *raison d'etre* of this call in Mexico, as Deborah Cohn suggests, meant "to legitimate a cosmopolitan definition of Mexican culture."[15] In other words, the strategy was to speak cosmopolitanism into existence. This means that the call for cosmopolitanism was a call in bad faith, a way to insert Mexican culture into a global community of cultural producers without denying the sense of its own privilege and priority over all others. Cultural products, in this sense, would be judged according to their order in the orbit of Mexican uniqueness. This false cosmopolitanism plays itself out in cultural and literary criticism as an overt preference for nation over world, a tendency to divide cultural products into the familiar and the strange, and cultural producers as friends or enemies. Critics thus employ readily available criteria to judge good and bad literature, art, and philosophy—criteria which are justified by their coherence in a largely exclusive "cosmopolitan" discourse that privileges the national or regional over the truly global. Again, this is an inauthentic cosmopolitanism. Whether false, inauthentic, or genuine, however, the critic assumes her role to be one in which she must enforce the evaluative criteria, which means promoting the value of that which is authentically Mexican, or re-framing that which is not as non-Mexican, imperialistic, or anti-Revolutionary.

The critic who protects the integrity of a Mexican vision of cosmopolitanism is not the target of Portilla's criticism. His target is the critic who protects the value and uniqueness of a purely (or essentially) Mexican literature by criticizing as anti-Mexican whatever does affirm the uniqueness or essence. The question is why, if arts and literature are moving toward internationalization, does Portilla feel the need to criticize what is most certainly a minority among the critics (those who promote the ideology of *lo mexicano*)? I suggest that the answer has to do with Portilla's critical sensibilities themselves. That is, he finds internal to the Mexican cosmopolitan urge a politics of exception that he indirectly aims to confront through a critique of the figure of the nationalist critic (this is a theme that we also find in his "Spiritual Crisis of the United States," as we point out below in my "The Politics of Innocence," included in this volume).

To illustrate Portilla's point, take, for instance, Mexican drama critics of the 1950s. The mid-twentieth century is a period of modernization in Mexican history, a time of social progress and economic growth, especially among the middle class.[16] At this time, post-Revolutionary Mexican consciousness continues on the search for its unique cultural and historical identity.[17] The aim in the arts, according to the nationalist ideology, is to resist the reproduction of European and Western theater and produce "Mexican" drama written by "Mexican" playwrights that reflect Mexican reality. The role of the critic is thus to promote that which is Mexican as opposed to that which is not. They believe theirs to be more than an intellectual exercise: It is a political and social act; theirs is an "educative" function, one, however, not meant to educate the populace about the state of Mexican theater, but to educate playwrights (and poets, essayists, etc.) about their responsibility, and shortcomings, in producing it.[18]

Portilla criticizes this particular critic, ironically, for their lack of a truly critical sensibility. I read Portilla here as suggesting that criticism for the sake of a political agenda, or for the sake of popular opinion, is criticism in bad faith—that is, it seems to be an intellectual deconstruction for an interest external to the literary work, itself undertaken under external pressures (what he will call below "the terrorism of the social"). As Cohn notes, regarding criticism in Portilla's time, it was a criticism whose criteria were created by "an elite whose notion of 'the literary' and 'the national' were based on exclusive assumptions that reflected their own interests and ultimately reproduced their privileged place in the cultural hierarchy."[19] So, even while insisting for a cosmopolitan turn in matters cultural, critics demanded allegiance to a Mexican particularity, to *lo mexicano*, while failing to respect otherness as true cosmopolitanism would have demanded.

Critics held positions of power in the Mexican cultural landscape, and they sought to enforce it by prescribing the criteria for acceptable intellectual products. A group of them, led by notable figures such as Octavio Paz, was known as "la mafia" and their task was to uphold a nationalist agenda that promoted a Mexico-centric art, philosophy, and literature *under the guise* of internationalism, or the more philosophical view that inclusion in the international conversation required the promotion of the national difference. As Cohn describes it: "While monopolizing periodicals, publishing houses, and the media in general, this group advocated internationalism, set the standards for literary canonization, and, in effect, determined the course of Mexican culture by deciding who and what was 'in' or 'out.'"[20] "La mafia," or any critic who saw his role as that of determining the course of Mexican culture, was then at the same time a mouthpiece for the ideological establishment; or, we could also say, the critic was the guardian of the means for the production of the national identity and, as such, of nationalism.[21]

Thus Paz, whose *El laberinto de la soledad* affirms the contemporaneity of Mexicans with all mankind, "put forth a vision of *lo mexicano* that embraced the nation's autochthonous heritage and Western influences alike."[22] That is, Paz retains in his cosmopolitan urge a political commitment to the uniquely Mexican, and hence, reflects those "exclusive assumptions" that reflect privileged interests. If Portilla's suggestion is right and criticism on behalf of a national interest is criticism in bad faith, then even Paz's cosmopolitanism rests on a politics of bad faith.

The nationalist ideology promoted the notion of Mexico as an exceptional space for the creation of meaning and identity, a space wherein meaning could be created even in isolation. The cosmopolitanism of Paz and his followers challenged this view and pretended to promote a synthesis of the regional with the worldly, the particular with the universal. Portilla, like Paz, recognized the value of openness and cooperation for the creation of authentic community. Critics who resisted openness and otherness, Portilla called "naive individualist" and stressed that meaning could not be created in a cultural or historical vacuum; that meaning is an intersubjective construction and, thus, that there is no such thing as a "Mexican" literature that is purely a Mexican invention. To push the issue is to push a false and unrealizable ideal. Just like the project that sought to bring about a "Mexican" philosophy, the project of Mexican literature must seek to transcend its enclosures and engage itself with the *human* community.[23]

Portilla writes:

> Clearly no one writes for himself. It is evident that the act of writing, even if one keeps the writing in a safe, is a plan for communication, it is the plan for a possible dialog whose interlocutor, or at least, concrete witness is, in the end, the critic. [159]

So, if writing is essentially a transcendental act, then the critic, in criticizing that which does not refer back to, or remain within, the particularity of nation or culture, is operating with evaluative criteria which is subjective, limited, and thus naive. The point is that the literary critic has suddenly empowered himself to set the rules for criticism, which is a futile task, since the only evaluative criteria for a transcendental act like writing must be objective and not subjective, cultural, or national.

3. Nation, Race, and Terror

Three influences converge on the critic, making his task unreasonable yet necessary. Necessary because the choice to be authentically open to difference and otherness is not available due to these influences, and unreasonable because the critic's task conforms to opinion rather than truth. These influences are the influence of nation, race, and social pressure, or what we call with Portilla "social terror."

3.1. NATION

> In either case, the critic is supposed to be a representative of the society in whose name he condemns. But this assumption introduces an element that diverts criticism from its original meaning. Things take on the aspect of a nationalist McCarthy-

ism, since the reasons put forward are not properly aesthetic, but rather reasons of cultural politics. On one side are the good and his representative: the critic; and on the other are the bad guys and their spokesperson: the writer. [160]

The brutality of the Mexican Revolution of 1910 awoke in the Mexican intellectual consciousness a desire to figure out, once and for all, *that which made them* all "Mexicanos." What was that uniquely Mexican essence that made Mexicans special, different, and *one people*? The Revolution had been a highly intimate affair, one having to do with an internal struggle about who mattered and why, a struggle historically grounded in the Conquest and the colony. The end of the Revolution meant that something had been won, if not materially, at the very least, a sense of pride in the willingness of the nation to self-destruct. This also meant that what had been won had to be protected and kept in its pure form—a task that also meant purging that which was *not* Mexican from Mexico, such as people of Chinese descent or the Roman Catholic Church.[24] The xenophobia was thus partly driven by a fear of repeating the Revolutionary death-struggle, a struggle which was always in danger of having been in vain if that Revolutionary identity was not kept pure or (culturally or ideologically) un-*contaminated*.

Portilla recognized then—as we recognize today in our post-phenomenological postmodern historical milieu—that the sort of purity demanded by the post-Revolutionary ideology is unrealizable and its desire morally and politically problematic. More than that, Portilla sees that the denial of otherness implied in the fear of *contamination* is self-defeating: It defeats both our self-fulfillment (what matters about our particularity) and our very humanity (that which connects us to the universal). He speaks of this in the most abstract terms as a paradox of denying the universality implicit in all nationalism. He writes:

The negation of universality, masked behind the negation of particularity, cannot transform itself into something positive, and hence the notorious infertility of all nationalisms—of *all* nationalisms, including the Mexican. Because, in the best of cases, if we convert the negation of universality into the affirmation of particularity, we would affirm as excellent a Mexican particularity. But which one? This particularity cannot be geographical, since, in human affairs, geography cannot be decisive as a source of value. It would have to be a cultural

> particularity. But culture is nothing but the concrete expression
> of the *universal*. [161]

That is, nationalism, like all exclusionary or Manichean politics, is infertile—it gives birth to nothing and nothing springs from it. In Mexico, a Mexican "essence" was thought to become visible from drawing a boundary around the nation, one that closed it off to the outside. But this essence, Portilla points out, would have to be *culture*, which turns out to be "nothing but the concrete expression of the universal." Hence, nothing is gained from nationalism since, at its most harmless, it turns out to be but a redundancy that ends by affirming what it tried to deny—i.e., universality.

The larger philosophical point that Portilla is making here is that a politics grounded on exclusion and denials is a politics doomed to repetition—a repetition of sameness and negation. As he puts it, a politics of exclusion is a politics that "cannot transform itself into something positive." This point is one that makes sense at the level of intersubjective experience, where denying the other for the sake of remaining subjectively pure is an empty (yet ultimately destructive) gesture.

Portilla resists the totalizations of popular morality and politics. There is no uniquely "Mexican" character, style of life, or culture, just as there is no purely universal character that in its abstractness refers to anything or anyone in particular. Neither is there a perfect synthesis of the particular with the universal, for instance, of the Mexican with the Western. The fear of the other (of the strange, the alien, or the different) that motivates the exclusionary politics of mid-century Mexico (and, in our contemporary milieu, the insular politics of post-9/11 America) justifies itself on the basis of such totalizations or perfect syntheses. When it totalizes the Mexican, it does so by affirming that which makes it distinct and *exceptional*. In this narrative, the strange, the different, or the *other* is paradoxically "the rule," while the same, the self, the "I," is the exception. That which is thought to be preserved in this narrative is the integrity of what there already is, a self-sameness assumed to be unique yet corruptible by all-pervasive otherness that as a "rule" demands conformity and equality to itself.

3.2. Race

The impossibility of totalization (of preserving sameness at all costs) is illustrated by Portilla with the idea of race. In Mexico, race (as a natural, biological difference) is thought to be a complex and sensitive negotiation of the Spanish and Indigenous inheritance; in affirming one's *mestizaje,* one affirms both; in affirming either, one excludes one; and in excluding either, one suppresses what is essential to Mexican identity. Mexicans themselves would prefer to suppress their Spanish inheritance in favor of the Indigenous, but when they do, it is but an affirmation of a desire for a non-existent purity. A dangerous desire, indeed. Portilla writes:

> Our search for the particular would have to take us to that which could particularize culture, give it local color. The source of this peculiar color would have to be race.
>
> Race is the only thing that can offer sufficient guarantees of peculiarity. From the racial point of view, the most active and fruitful aspect of our history, the mestizo aspect, offers a danger, since to affirm it is to imply the affirmation of a "piece" of the Spanish; however, we all agree that what race has of value comes from our indigenous "blood." What are the excellences of the indigenous people? The answer is: that they are indigenous. But this is exactly what Hitler said about the Germans. The Germans were excellent because they were Germans. If we appeal to the indigenous cultural past, then we are doing what Mussolini did when he appealed to the imperial past of Rome to prove Italian "superiority," and when Hitler appealed to "Germanness," polluted by Rome and Christianity, to arouse Germany's homicidal and anti-universalist enthusiasm. When a group of people begins to consider itself wonderful because of what it has of its "own" and what makes it "different," it is already preparing the destruction of other peoples. But this is no longer "culture"; this is war. [161–162]

Of course, this particular concept of race has been sufficiently discredited, and it is now commonly thought that race is, at the very least, a social construct.[25] Nevertheless, Portilla's point is that the totalizing desire for particularity, the desire to preserve uniqueness and purity, will naturally force us to adopt such a "racial point of view." If the goal is to *keep difference out,* then the reason is that something about us is threatened by that difference, namely, our "blood." However, the racial point of view, Portilla continues, is circular. When Mexicans affirm their *mestizaje,* they do so because an aspect of that *mestizaje* is the "indigenous blood," and they find value in that inheritance. But when asked what about the indigenous they value, the answer is that the indigenous is valued because it is indigenous. This circular racial reasoning is the same employed by Hitler and Mussolini and it ultimately represents, Portilla concludes, a preparation for "the destruction of other peoples."

Portilla's critique of Mexican literary criticism is thus also a diagnosis of a much deeper cultural crisis. The nationalism of the Mexican critic is tied to a view of racial purity that, although misconstrued from the start (since Mexican *mestizaje* is already a *mixture* of bloods), forces a closed politics and a narrow conception of human community. And this is a lesson that transcends Mexican politics itself: A politics based on a narrative of national exceptionalism will soon run out of things to promote as exceptional and will have to revert to primitive conceptions of difference, such as race or blood. This primitive rationality is necessarily divisive, yet, as primitive, appealing and easy to adopt. Once it enters the social realm, nothing can be said against it and if something is, it represents that which is other to the exception—it is difference, threat, danger, and death.

3.3. SOCIAL TERROR

The racial point of view adopted by a community that thinks of itself as exceptional justifies exclusions and denials that serve no other end than to perpetuate the self-narrative of exception and purity. The racial point of view is self-referential, turned inward toward the legitimization of a community's privilege and uniqueness and closed off onto itself. As such, it is a narrow consciousness of sameness that finds that which is different to be a threat to a fragile narcissism.

As with the attitude of *relajo*, i.e., what elsewhere Portilla called "the suspension of seriousness,"[26] the ideology of nationalism spreads through the social realm as an infectious urge to affirm one's particularity at the expense of some abstract humanity; this ideological infection roots itself in notions of a unified communal self as exceptional, leading to the casting of clear divisions between those who subscribe to the exception ("friends," associates, "Mexicanos") and those who do not ("enemies," others, foreigners). According to Portilla, the Mexican critic preaches the ideology of exceptionalism as the national gospel; far from being "good news," however, this ideology insists on an insular and narcissistic perspective that reveals a propensity to deny those excellences that the preacher (i.e., the critic) does not recognize in himself. The constant repetition of this exclusionary rhetoric through various normalizing practices such as criticism is what Portilla refers to as "the terrorism of the social":

> The critic deploys the terrorism of the social, as in another time, and in another respect, other critics exercised the terrorism of science or that of freedom. In fact, this criticism is simple and overwhelming. He criticizes the writer for what he does not do, and not for what he does. Against this charge there is no possible defense. The writer finds in it a monstrous negative image of himself in which he does not recognize himself. It shows him, or rather, it hits him over the head with what he is not, without appreciating the value of what he is. His guilt is infinite and without appeal. The critic, on the other hand, is a mass of positivity and innocence; he is what the writer should strive to be. [163–164]

Before considering this passage a bit more carefully, we can pause here and consider the nature of the terror for which the social may be responsible. Terror results from facing a "threat of violent death" that leads to fear, panic, and the impulse to flee.[27] In an act of "terror," persons are subjected to a spectacle that threatens their very being and they seek to flee for safety, or away from the threat. Terrorism is the extension of this act in time, a state where the threat of violent death is always present and where fear and panic become constant states of everyday being. While the terrorism of the social to which Portilla alludes is not one grounded on the "threat of violent death," it suggests this threat when it becomes criticism of one's identity, when the critique is a critique of one's belonging to the culture, or a meritless accusation of one's guilt. As history has shown, the threat of death is not far behind such criticisms.

Criticism turns to terrorism when criticizing is deployed for the sake of intimidation, when it is used as a means to frighten members of the community into flight or paralysis (either leave the place to which your allegiances are suspect or remain silent). The social terrorizes when it assumes the truth of the critique and stands by it, enforcing it in social sanctions, gossip, implied threats of violence, death, and expulsion, etc., thereby inducing fear and trembling; it terrorizes, that is, when it simultaneously causes flight and freezes one in place, a process which turns thought into self-worry (panic), into a concern over one's self-preservation;

in other words, the social terrorizes when it coerces one into a corner where there is only one way out, one thing to do, namely, to think what it wants one to think. The intimidation of the social is carried out by the imposition of a duty that anyone who seeks to remain faithful to the national narrative must obey. The critic carries out the terror through admonishments and dismissals, seeking to paralyze the writer, artist, thinker, etc., keeping them in place and demanding obedience to ideological principles, to hegemony and sameness meant to protect a presumed purity or authenticity. The terror of modern-day populism, for instance, manifests itself in the denial of the value of immigrant life, LGBT rights, or universal health care. The social here being "the Average American," "the People," "the Middle Class," whose vision of the good life *ought to be* fulfilled at any cost. Portilla's example in the quote above is of the critic who deploys the terrorism of the social against writers who do not toe the popular line, who do not attend to what *ought to be* but seek to express their own, ultimately corrupting (as opposed to innocent), reality; that is, social terrorism is deployed against artist *for what they do not do*, a terrifying idea in its own right, since what we *do not do* is always infinitely greater than what we actually do. Of course, the terrorism of the social is another name for what Alexis de Tocqueville had already labeled the *tyranny of the majority*.

What is this corrupting reality that the writer—the creator of worlds—imposes against the dictates of "the social"? According to the critic, the writer corrupts by presenting an anti-reality, a narrative that by not reflecting class struggle, oppression, or the popular ideology is deemed anti-national and anti-Revolutionary. The writer is thus an "enemy" of "the people"—or what's the same, an enemy of the majority, the social, or the nation.

> [According to the critic,] the writer has not trumpeted his anti-imperialist views, he does not recount the struggle of the people or the proletariat for the sake of man's freedom, *therefore* he is the enemy of the people, of the proletariat, and of man. He is a traitor sold for Yankee gold and, for that reason, also a bad writer. [164]

By refusing to be a propagandist for the national interest, the writer becomes the "enemy." This is another consequence of the underlying Manichaean logic: the creation of enemies; it is a necessary moment in the ideological process motivating a narrow nationalism, or the politics of social terrorists. And this, because the nationalist needs enemies. Portilla continues:

> His accuser [the critic] must be a hero of the resistance and serving the cause; *after all*, he exposes the villainous writer and is, perhaps, an excellent writer himself, as evidenced by the fact that he does literary criticism. The result of the criticism is twofold: it creates an enemy of the proletariat, which it exposes and annihilates in the very act of creating it, and also creates a proletarian defender who continues to exist afterwards, with the clear conscience of a just man. [164]

For the cause to be good—for ideology to be good—the enemy of the people must be named. For the nationalist critic, this enemy will be the one who does not defend, contribute to, or in their work legitimate, the narrative of national uniqueness and exceptionalism that "heroes" protect.

4. Human Agency and the Terrorism of the Social

We can take these three ideological forces that converge on the critic as formative or impactful on human agency. That is, cultural ideologies of nation, considerations of race, and a felt sense of duty to social demands construct the critic's very own sense of personal identity.

Indeed, we can see in Portilla's critique of the *critic* a recognition that the critic is unable to see past her own ideological "prison," as Fredric Jameson would say about our inability to see past our linguistic habits, which leads the imprisoned critic to condemn the writer for forgetting the reality of the social situation.[28] Portilla's defense of the *writer* is simply that his (apparently negligent) amnesia is not an intentional blindness to the reality of class struggle or the threat of imperialism; to see and address struggle or imperialism is just not the writer's task. The writer's task and his intention is to create and offer a new vision of the world if not a new world altogether. The critic fails to see this, however, because his formative ideology does not allow or encourage a broadening of his vision.

In defense of the *writer*, Portilla argues that, while imperialism and class struggle are facts—destructive facts about social reality that must be addressed—it is not the writer's responsibility to make these explicit. However, the nationalist ideology, and the exclusionary Manichaean logic operating as background, seeks to make an enemy out of difference (i.e., of the writer) or, in more a more subtle move, seeks to glorify the terrorism of the social (i.e., seeks to validate the work of the critic). "Undoubtedly," he writes, "imperialism is a reality, as is economic oppression and the struggle against it throughout the world" [165]. But the fact of imperialism or economic oppression does not imply an obligation to respond to it, or to address it, or to change it; this is, however, an obligation that the critic seems to want to impose on the writer as an existential duty to Mexico and the Mexican people.

This concern with what should be the writer's obligation is a limit to human agency. That is, Portilla worries that although it is true that imperialism and economic oppression are realities of our modern world, it is also true that those realities can be, and are in fact, appropriated for imperialistic or oppressive means. The anti-imperialist warrior (the "hero" critic) is an example of such appropriation, deploying those realities in the construction of category division (implicit in the motivating ideology) between those who are oppressed and those who fight against oppression, and that ends by manifesting itself as an intellectual conceit about the value of *the very same people* that fight against oppression. The anti-imperialist warrior, that is, as a naive individualist, will internalize her importance, leading her to privilege herself over those *for whom she speaks*—in other words, those who suffer from imperialism are secondary to the narrative that inscribes or describes them. In contemporary postcolonial thought, this is perfectly summarized by Gayatri Spivak, who writes, "Elite 'post colonialism' seems to be as much a strategy of differentiating oneself from the racial underclass as it is to speak its name."[29] In other words, in the decision to *be* the person who raises the flag in support of nation, a particular people, or a specific cause, lies the risk of losing oneself in the narrative or ideology of nation, people, or cause and forgetting for whom or why raising the flag matters. Thus, one can fight against imperialism and oppression, but one can also allow one's fight against those conditions to fully define one's identity, in which case the fight is no longer for the sake of those affected by imperialism or oppression nor against imperialism and oppression itself, but against anyone who might challenge one's fight, who might question one's motives, or anyone who may *not* promote and enjoin one's fight or one's cause.

According to Portilla, the critic is such a flag-raiser and his cause fully embodies him; in the case of the Mexican critic, she has become her ideological commitment—she embodies it and it has embodied her:

> But one can also take advantage of the world's movement toward
> justice so as to serve oneself [*darse cuerpo a si mismo*]. In this
> way one finds a thousand ways to justify oneself. When declaring
> oneself a defender of justice it may *seem* that one is really doing
> something to bring it about, and in this way one can come to
> believe oneself to be a righteous man. It is evident, however,
> that it is not enough to declare that one is something in order
> to become that thing in reality; but the declaration also offers
> an easy path to self-justification. There is a very easy way to
> give substance to one's own self-righteousness: Denounce that
> which is evil—in this case, the imperialist. [166]

Portilla analyzes this phenomenon more carefully in his "Phenomenology
of Relajo." There, he discusses the type of individual he terms (following
Mexican cultural norms of the time) the *apretado*, who, like the self-justified defender of justice, is also formed and informed by her ideological
commitments.

Let's briefly consider the *apretado*, who elsewhere I've translated as
"snob" or the "snobbish-type."[30] In our contemporary political discourse,
the "cultural conservative" type would closely resemble what Portilla means
by "apretado." Like its modern incarnation, the "apretado," Portilla tells us,
"considers himself valuable" in such a way that he *embodies* the values that
he values.[31] In this embodiment of values, moreover, values "are properties
that he possesses with the calm certainty with which a rock possesses
hardness."[32] The *apretado* in Mexican culture is thus that individual who
has committed him or herself to *being* what they *value,* to becoming the
unity between being and value. This is shown in the way they act, the way
they dress, and the seriousness with which they play the roles that they've
assumed. "In a certain sense," Portilla continues, " 'apretado' individuals
are also their car, their house, their plots of land, their elegant furniture,
their works of art. It couldn't be any other way."[33] Thus, in their everyday
life they appear "stuck up," conceited, and overly intolerant of anyone or
anything that clashes with who they are, that is, with what they value, with
what they possess, including their cars or their beliefs. And the other, i.e.,
the cultural heretic or the enemy of the people, is anyone who resists con-
forming to or affirming those values chosen in advance as values worthy
of affirming or worthy of internalizing as constitutive of identity.

Returning to Portilla's "Critique," the fervent and committed warrior
for anti-imperialism, the defender of national and cultural sovereignty, will

stake his life—and more importantly, his identity—on *being* a warrior and a defender. As an "apretado,"[34] Portilla says in "The Phenomenology of Relajo," he will "need witnesses, without which his supposed value-filled being would disappear into silence and into unreality."[35] This desire for witnesses, for those who will testify and thus vindicate his own reality, makes of those who dare not testify on his behalf the enemy. The Manichaean political logic of friend/enemy is, in this way, *foundational* to the terrorism of the social. This is why Portilla suggests that when looked at it from a purely phenomenological standpoint, the anti-imperialist nationalist critic suffers from a "lack of foundations." He writes:

> The true anti-imperialist is irresistibly compelled to be the watchdog [*a la vocación de gendarme*]. Just like his well-known counter-figure: the anti-communist. The two are destined to frantically wave their flag, whether or not it is necessary. The lack of real foundations for their own talents compels them to uncover evil everywhere, since what makes us good is to defeat the bad guys. If one cannot find the evil one needs so as to be good, then one invents it. It is not difficult to do so, since for any lack of positive reasons, negative ones will always be at hand. The field of the "*not*" is infinite. [166]

Where there is a "lack of foundations," that is, there will always be an attempt to "invent" them. The "invention" that will be easiest to pass off as genuine will be the one that's easier to sell, and this will be the one that's easier to think, i.e., one coded in the binary and exclusive logic of the negative.

Portilla's concern with human agency and its entrapments is a common thread in his work. As well as the critic, the writer, the anti-imperialists, and the anti-communists he considers in his "Critique," we have the innocent-types in his critique of US culture, and the many individual types in his "Phenomenology of Relajo," including the *relajiento* and *apretado*, as well as the humorist and the ironists; in his more political journalistic pieces, he talks about the *mocho*.[36] What these characterological accounts reveal is the fragility of human agency, the ease in which individuals can fall into their commitments, give their identities away in the process, and become what they value—who give themselves over to values at the expense of truth, open-mindedness, or freedom. Such blind commitment is not a positive commitment, it is a negative commitment:

As these individual types lose themselves (that is, their identity and their *being*) in and for what they value, they become the value at the expense of their freedom to become.

Thus, lost in the terrorism of the social, the subject becomes herself a terrorist—someone who paralyzes movement, closes openings, corners the writer into an exclusionary possibility. Commitment to the national identity project, to a particular view of race, or to the social sanctions believed to protect cultural integrity, constitutes one's existential project. Portilla's claim is that this is a project of bad faith—a project of closure, exclusion, and unwillingness. According to Jean-Paul Sartre, whose account of bad faith is the standard account, individuals in bad faith have decided in advance that it will not take much to persuade them of what they want desperately to believe; they are comfortable in their faith with the evidence that they have, and this because that which they believe need not prove itself with any justified standards of truth. Sartre writes: "Thus bad faith in its primitive project and in its coming into the world decides on the exact nature of its requirements. It stands forth in the firm resolution *not to demand too much*, to count itself satisfied when it is barely persuaded, to force itself in decisions and adhere to uncertain truths."[37] Thus, the critic, as an *apretado*, or a snobbish-type (or, today, the staunch conservative), has committed himself to see the world in one way rather than another; he is convinced in his decision and counter-factual evidence will not change his mind.

In the "Phenomenology of Relajo" Portilla, like Sartre, attributes the *apretado*'s bad faith to something like a getting-lost-in-the-frenzy, a forgetfulness of self, resulting from an absorption into a not-I, i.e., into a value that he has deemed righteous in advance. In a similar way, the nationalist critics, naive individualists, and anti-imperialists that he describes in "Critique of Criticism" have traded a critical consciousness for the popular political perspective, one through which everything is judged as good or bad depending on its coherence with a nationalist ideology or political agenda.

5. Conclusion: Openness and Respect

The terrorism of the social is founded on absolutisms, themselves arrived at through a logic of exclusion that frames human experience on the binary of friend–enemy, good–bad, Mexican–non-Mexican. The either/or of the

Mexican nationalist critic who insists that cultural products must either be a genuine reflection of Mexican culture or not count themselves as Mexican, the either/or of the cosmopolitan critic who insists that the work must either reflect a synthesis of the local and the global or not count itself as valuable—this either/or ultimately reflects a Manichaean politics of exception that closes up the possibilities for a heterogeneity of possible cultural constructions, in art, literature, or politics, that would benefit the Mexican people. Portilla is a postmodern in this sense: Absolutisms have no place in criticism or art do not exist, even if the regulative, formative, force of a politics of exception, of absolutes, does.

To deny that the role of the Mexican writer, poet, or philosopher is only to write about, think about, or philosophize about Mexico doesn't mean that the Mexican philosopher or poet will not speak of a Mexican reality; the reality of the Mexican experience will be part of what the writer writes even if he doesn't explicitly write about Mexico. This is a circumstantialist truth that seems obvious for Portilla. He writes, "Society is a permanent field, a dimension of existence that can be evaded by no one, and even less by the writer who has left an objective testimony of his being in his work" [159]. The writer, like the philosopher or the poet, is part of the community and his work makes community in turn: "They cannot be expelled from our cultural community, not even by executing them all so as to remove them from the world of the living, because their work, whether good or bad, is *constituent* of that cultural community" [159]. What this means, ultimately, is that the critic's resistance to non-Mexican work done by Mexican writers is unfounded. As Leopoldo Zea would come to say about Latin American philosophy, "we should do philosophy, and what is Latin American will arise by itself."[38] Similarly, Portilla thinks that that which is Mexican will reside in whatever the writer writes, whether or not it takes Mexico as theme.

The real danger in all of this is, ultimately and importantly, political Manichaeism, a term used by Portilla to refer to an attitude of closed-mindedness in which the moral universe is clearly compartmentalized, divided into good and evil, right and wrong, friend and enemy, or love and hate.[39] Manichaeism is a refusal to see beyond good and evil, a refusal grounded on an unjustified allegiance to a pre-established conceptual scheme or ideological framework that identifies evil, wrong, and hate with otherness, with the strange, or the foreign.

But Portilla's reference to the political and moral attitudes of the time as Manichaean points to something more significant, namely, Portilla's view that Mexican nationalism lost its grasp of the possible and committed itself strictly to a moral binary in which no options, or gradations of Mexicanness, goodness, or rightness, were possible. Politics, in this sense, had committed itself to an us-versus-them rhetoric that mirrored the *apretado*'s worldview and closed itself off from the possibilities inherent in any cosmopolitan, dialogical, or open relationship to the non-Mexican.

The solution is an ethics of openness and respect. The notion that the world or the other always already shows up as threat or ally is one that already presupposes the truth of the Manichaean vision of the world. If anything, the world and other show up as mysteries to behold and not as threats of my possible destruction. Portilla suggests this view by proposing its obstacle: "The dirty game is obvious. What we have here is criticism in a void. A man is judged for what he does not do" [164]. Cleaning up the game requires an openness to difference and an avoidance of those presuppositions that categorize and objectify in advance—it requires love and humility, the enemies of terror and bad faith.

Portilla's critical gesture asks us to consider the entrapments of our nationalisms, of our insulations, and transcend ourselves in the name of justice and fraternity—a human fraternity more symbolic than real, but more loving.

Notes

1. See Carlos Alberto Sánchez and Robert Eli Sanchez, "Introduction" to *Mexican Philosophy in the 20th Century: Essential Readings* (New York: Oxford University Press, 2017).

2. See Abelardo Villegas, *La filosofía de lo mexicano*. Mexico City: Universidad Autonoma de México, 1979.

3. The "ideology of lo mexicano" is understood as a set of beliefs or doctrines in the service of the Mexican state that aim to define and affirm the characteristics of what it means to be "Mexican," a task firmly dictated by the ideological state apparatus and the power elite; the "philosophy of *lo mexicano*," on the other hand, seeks to find those transcendental characteristics of the Mexican *being* and promote them as differences that may and should contribute to a deeper understanding of humanity as a whole. For more on this distinction, see Carlos Alberto Sánchez, "On Emilio Uranga's *Análisis del ser del mexicano*: Decolonizing Pretensions, Recolonizing Critiques," *Southern Journal of Philosophy*, 57, no. S1 (2019): 63–89.

4. See Louis Althusser, *Lenin and Philosophy and Other Essays*, translated by Ben Brewster (New York: Monthly Review Press, 1971).

5. Page numbers in brackets refer to the pagination of the essays translated in the appendix as they appear in the 1984 edition of *Fenomenología del relajo y otros ensayos*.

6. The armed conflict of the Mexican Revolution (or Civil War) lasted from 1910 until 1920. The period immediately after is referred to as the post-Revolutionary era and is characterized as a period of social, political, economic, and cultural upheaval; this time saw the rise of post-Revolutionary ideologies that sought to unify Mexicans under a national identity and a national culture.

7. See Carl Schmitt, *The Concept of the Political*, translated by George Schwab (Chicago: University of Chicago Press, 2007).

8. Emilio Uranga, "Essay on the Ontology of the Mexican (1951)," translated by Carlos Alberto Sánchez, in *Mexican Philosophy in the 20th Century: Essential Readings* (New York: Oxford University Press, 2017), 1173.

9. See chapter 2 of this book.

10. One of the presumed victories of the Mexican Revolution of 1910 was the expulsion, by the late 1920s, of all corrupting foreign influences from Mexico. Thus, oil was nationalized, the Catholic church was expelled, and a constitution was established that promised land reform for the benefit of the Mexican rural poor. The expectation was that the national spirit would be created through these actions, lending value and significance to the death and destruction of the Revolution itself. See Alan Knight, "Mexican Revolution: Interpretations," in *Encyclopedia of Mexico*, vol. 2 (Chicago: Fitzroy Dearborn, 1997), 873.

11. See Stephen R. Niblo, *Mexico in the 1940s: Modernity, Politics, and Corruption* (Washington, DC: Scholarly Resources Inc., 1991), especially chapter 4ff.

12. Octavio Paz, *The Labyrinth of Solitude and Other Writings*, translated by Lysander Kemp (New York: Grove Press, 1985), 194.

13. "Cosmopolitanism" is here taken straightforwardly as the ideology that all peoples should belong to a unified human community and that differences, whatever they may be, should be respected and valued. In the Mexican case, cosmopolitanism says that Mexico has arrived at a historical moment where it has something to offer that human community. In Immanuel Kant, we also get the cosmopolitan idea that a truly cosmopolitan people has achieved a state of historical maturity, where its own selfish interests are no longer its driving force. These two senses seem to be contained in the use of "cosmopolitanism" here. See Kant, *Universal History from a Cosmopolitan Point of View*.

14. Tracie Matysik, *Reforming the Moral Subject: Ethics and Sexuality in Central Europe 1890–1930* (Ithaca: Cornell University Press, 2008), 52.

15. Deborah Cohn, "The Mexican Intelligentsia, 1950–1968: Cosmopolitanism, National Identity, and the State," *Mexican Studies/Estudios Mexicanos* 21, no. 1 (2005): 142.

16. See Nora Jaffary, Edward Osowski, and Susie Porter, eds., *Mexican History: A Primary Source Reader* (Philadelphia: Westview Press, 2010), esp. 361–373.

17. Cohn, "The Mexican Intelligentsia," 148.

18. See Eleanore Maxwell Dial, "Drama Critics in Search of an Identity in Mexico in the 1950s," *Latin American Literary Review* 2, no. 4 (1974): 113–125, cf. 117ff.

19. Cohn, "The Mexican Intelligentsia," 144n5.

20. Cohn, "The Mexican Intelligentsia," 143.

21. The power of guardianship also gave the critics the power to make or break careers. When Portilla refers to the "terrorism of the social" he means also this: the critic who, through fear and intimidation, will promote the nationalist agenda. See below.

22. Cohn, "The Mexican Intelligentsia," 151.

23. See Carlos Alberto Sánchez, "The Gift of Mexican Historicism," *Continental Philosophy Review* 51, no. 3 (2018): 439–457.

24. For an account of Chinese racism, Chinese expulsion, and anti-Chinese violence in Mexico, see Robert Chao Romero, *The Chinese in Mexico, 1882–1940* (Tucson: University of Arizona Press, 2010); for an account of efforts to expel the Roman Catholic Church, or the Cristero wars of the late 1920s, see Jean A. Meyer, *The Cristero Rebellion: The Mexican People Between Church and State, 1926–1929* (Cambridge: Cambridge University Press, 1976).

25. See, for instance, Paul Gilroy, *"There Ain't No Black in the Union, Jack": The Cultural Politics of Race and Nation* (Chicago: University of Chicago Press, 1991).

26. See Sánchez, *The Suspension of Seriousness*.

27. See Adriana Cavarero, *Horrorism: Naming Contemporary Violence*, trans. William McCuaig (New York: Columbia University Press, 2009), 4–5.

28. See Fredric Jameson, *The Prison House of Language: A Critical Account of Structuralism and Russian Formalism* (Princeton, NJ: Princeton University Press, 1972).

29. Quoted in Ofelia Schutte, "Continental Philosophy and Postcolonial Subjects," in *Latin American Philosophy: Currents, Issues, Debate*, edited by Eduardo Mendieta (Bloomington: Indiana University Press, 2003): 160.

30. Sánchez, *The Suspension of Seriousness*.

31. Portilla, "Phenomenology of Relajo," 191.

32. Ibid.

33. Ibid., 192.

34. In saying that the anti-imperialist critic is an *"apretado,"* whose defensive strategy is one of denial, I differ from the interpretation offered by Gallegos, who thinks of the critic as employing a defensive strategy of what he calls "problematization." The critic for Gallegos is not an *apretado* in this sense. See chapter 2.

35. Portilla, "Phenomenology of Relajo," 193.

36. See the introduction to this volume.

37. Jean-Paul Sartre, *Being and Nothingness*, trans. Hazel Barnes (New York: Washington Square Press, 1956), 113.

38. Leopoldo Zea, *Filosofía latinoamericana como filosofía sin mas* (Mexico City: Siglo XXI, 1969).

39. This is how Glenn Greenwald has described this attitude: "to the Manichean believer, the battle between Good and Evil is paramount. It subordinates all other considerations and never gives way to any conflicting or inconsistent goals. Measures intended to promote Good or undermine Evil are, by definition, necessary and just. They cannot be abandoned for pragmatic or prudential reasons, or because of growing opposition, or in response to evidence of failure. Insufficient progress when attacking Evil never justifies re-examination of the wisdom of the action, but instead compels a redoubling of one's determination to succeed. In sum, complexities, pragmatic considerations, the restraints of reality are trumped by the imperative of the moral crusade" (48). See Glenn Greenwald, *A Tragic Legacy: How a Good vs. Evil Mentality Destroyed the Bush Presidency* (New York: Three Rivers Press, 2007).

Chapter 2

Portilla's Conceptual Framework

Phenomenological Nationalism

Francisco Gallegos

In the previous chapter, the philosophical significance of Portilla's essay "Critique of Criticism" began to come into focus. In this essay, Portilla offers valuable insights into the psychological dynamics underlying political nationalism. The target of Portilla's critique is the tendency toward nationalism among literary critics in mid-twentieth-century Mexico. These critics—sometimes referred to as "la mafia" for the way they wielded power over the arts scene—regularly accused writers of being "xenophiles" and evaluated works of art in terms of the artist's perceived loyalty to Mexico. Portilla diagnoses the critics' nationalistic fervor as a strategy for coping with *zozobra,* an anxious sense of lacking an identity, being insufficient or even unreal—a type of anxiety that he and many of his contemporaries saw as being widespread in Mexican society. Thus, what animates the critics' nationalistic fervor, according to Portilla, is a repressed fear that Mexico lacks a coherent identity, and that there is ultimately nothing that makes the Mexican nation distinctively valuable in contrast to other nations. However, the critics' way of coping with this *zozobra* is ineffective (as well as dangerous), because their nationalistic fervor ironically creates a stifling atmosphere that inhibits artistic production and diminishes the vibrancy of Mexican culture. Portilla's essay thus teaches that political nationalism is self undermining. Although nationalism seeks to forge a stronger sense of national identity, it drives behaviors that are ultimately harmful to the nation, weakening the social bonds that are its foundation.

In this chapter, I argue that we can deepen our appreciation of the philosophical significance of "Critique of Criticism" by understanding how it advances Portilla's broader philosophical program—a program that, with the translation of the three essays included in the appendix of this book, can finally be appreciated by English-speaking philosophers. In my view, the central idea of Portilla's philosophical program can be articulated as follows: *It is possible for nations to fall into the grip of certain powerful and stubborn moods that undermine the capacity for individuals in the nation to flourish; but by bringing such national moods and their manifestations into people's awareness, philosophy can help to loosen the grip of these moods, and thereby help to bring about the "affective liberation" of our nations.* This idea will be clarified over the course of this book. In this chapter, I argue that when we examine "Critique of Criticism" in the context of this larger philosophical program, we can see that the essay helps to establish a concept that motivates and guides Portilla's entire project, a concept I call "phenomenological nationalism."

I define *phenomenological nationalism* as the view that individuals' sense-making capacities are mediated and structured by their belonging to a nation. In other words, according to my interpretation of his work, Portilla holds that our nationality functions as an interpretive framework, always already shaping the way we experience ourselves, others, and the situations we encounter. For Portilla, then, our experience is intrinsically marked by our *nationality*, in much the same way that, for Heidegger, the way the world "shows up" in our experience is always already marked by our *mortality*, so that at each moment, even when we are not thinking about it, we are "being-towards-death." In short, Portilla holds that *nationality* should be thought of as an "existential category," just as *mortality* is for Heidegger, *gender* is for Beauvoir, and *the body* is for Merleau-Ponty.[1]

It should be emphasized from the start that what I call "phenomenological nationalism" does *not* involve the use of phenomenology for nationalistic purposes. Portilla has no interest in trying to articulate and preserve that which makes Mexico (or any other nation) distinctively valuable in contrast to other nations. Indeed, while he does express affection for Mexico and a sincere hope that his nation may flourish, his assessments of Mexico as a nation are almost entirely critical in nature, as are his assessments of the other nations he examines, including the United States and Germany (analyzed in "The Spiritual Crisis of the

United States" and "Thomas Mann and German Irrationalism," respectively). Moreover, Portilla displays nothing but contempt for those who speak in self-aggrandizing ways about their own nation. Thus, if Portilla is a phenomenological nationalist, as I claim he is, then it is only in the sense that he believes that—for better or worse, and *oftentimes for the worse*—our sense-making activity is shaped at a deep, existential level by our nationality. Of course, if this claim is true, it implies that the fates of individuals are tied up with the destinies of the nations to which they belong, and so there may be good reason for us to create the conditions in which our nations may thrive.[2] Nevertheless, as we will see, Portilla's work suggests that our nations are served not by childish outbursts of nationalistic fervor, but by the cultivation of the emotional maturity required to face up to our circumstances in all of their complexity.

In what follows, I unpack the idea of phenomenological nationalism in more detail and discuss its relationship to "Critique of Criticism." In section 1, I contextualize the idea of phenomenological nationalism by examining how it engages with some of the central concerns of two philosophical traditions, phenomenology (and its concern with *community*) and Latin American philosophy (and its concern with *liberation*). In section 2, I highlight the role played by phenomenological nationalism in Portilla's analysis of the peculiar case of Mexico, a nation that, on his view, is ironically distinguished by Mexicans' widely shared worry that the nation has no distinctive identity. In section 3, I extract from Portilla's analysis of Mexico some general principles regarding how nationality mediates and structures human sense-making. These principles, if correct, promise to shed new light on a wide variety of social and political issues that we face today.

1. The Phenomenology of Community and National Liberation

Portilla's thought can be located at the intersection of phenomenology and Latin American philosophy. With this in mind, we may wonder: How does Portilla's perspective as a Latin American influence his thinking in ways that are distinctive within the tradition of phenomenology? And, conversely, how does Portilla's affiliation with phenomenology influence his thinking in ways that are distinctive within the tradition of Latin American philosophy? A satisfying answer to these questions, in my view, must address Portilla's phenomenological nationalism, where, as we will see, we find an approach to the phenomenological analysis of community that reflects the particular social and political challenges facing Latin America in the postcolonial period.

1.1. The Phenomenology of Community

A hallmark of the standard phenomenological analysis of community is the view that the human being is fundamentally and inescapably *relational*. As Heidegger puts the idea, Dasein is essentially *Mitsein*; in other words, the human way of being is essentially being-with-others.[3] Heidegger's view challenges the commonsense notion that communities are formed when individuals come together for some purpose, such as to perform a particular activity or to live out their lives in a cooperative way. From a Heideggerian perspective, this commonsense view is misleading. It is a mistake to suppose that human beings *first* exist and *then* join communities, because this assumes that a human being is basically an isolatable entity, like a rock, whose defining features can be described without reference to anything that lies beyond the outer boundary of its physical form. In contrast, Heidegger argues that there are no human beings whose natures can be properly understood when examined in isolation from the communities to which they already belong. This is because human beings (in contrast to rocks) are essentially *sense-making entities*, defined by their interpretive activity, their distinctive way of interpreting themselves and the meaning of the things they encounter—and belonging to a community is a condition of the possibility of engaging in this interpretive activity that is definitive of the human way of existing.

Communities are necessary for our interpretive activity in at least two ways. First, all of our interpretations and self-interpretations are made possible by the historical traditions into which we have been socialized.[4] These historical traditions establish a shared interpretive background, a taken-for-granted understanding regarding what exists and what is appropriate, and this shared interpretive background enables us to make sense of what we encounter and thereby shapes our experience in advance. As Heidegger puts it,

> The everyday way in which things have been interpreted is one into which Dasein has grown in the first instance, with never a possibility of extrication. In it, out of it, and against it,

> all genuine understanding, interpreting, and communicating,
> all re-discovering and appropriating anew, are performed. In
> no case is a Dasein, untouched and unseduced by this way in
> which things have been interpreted, set before the open country
> of a 'world-in-itself,' so that it just beholds what it encounters.[5]

Thus, our historical traditions generate the *common sense* that serves as the ground on which we stand whenever we engage in interpretive activity, even as we project ourselves (and our traditions) forward into the future in new ways.

Portilla agrees with this assessment. As he puts it, "a structure of the community is . . . a constituent feature or . . . a ground of all human action and thought" [158].[6] In another essay Portilla says that *community* is best understood not as a mere collection of people, but as a "horizon" of intelligibility, a relatively stable, background context of meaning that provides the orientation necessary for making sense of whatever we encounter.[7] He describes this horizon of community as both a kind of *container* holding the space within which we articulate and understand the meaning of human actions, and a *boundary* that resists and supports us as we construct our interpretations of the world.[8] In "Critique of Criticism," Portilla points out that insofar as the community is a condition for the possibility of our sense-making activities, "the community is the atmosphere" that we "breathe" [159]; like air, it is utterly necessary for our lives, but it remains largely transparent to us—until there is a breakdown of community, a disintegration of common sense, that brings it and its importance to our attention.

The second way that community serves as the condition for the possibility of our interpretive activity has to do with the way that the items of our experience make up a "referential totality."[9] In a carpenter's workshop, for instance, each object "refers to"—and is unintelligible without—the existence of other objects, in the way that a hammer refers to nails, wood, houses, and so on. Each of these objects, in turn, refers to people who have certain concerns, commitments, and identities, just as hammers and nails are what they are, in part, because of their relationship to the carpenter's concerns and commitments. And finally, the concerns, commitments, and identities of any particular individual will refer to the concerns, commitments, and identities of other people. The role of being a carpenter, for instance, refers to people who occupy other roles, such as the role of customer, salesman, builder, homeowner, and so on.

In this way, each of our interpretations and self-interpretations implicitly refers to a vast network of other individuals whose interpretations and self-interpretations give meaning to our own.

Again, Portilla agrees with this standard phenomenological analysis of the nature of community. He articulates this line of thought nicely in a passage about the writer's *a priori,* conceptual, or—more precisely—*existential* dependence upon the reader and the critic.

> Clearly no one writes for himself. It is evident that the act of writing, even if one keeps the writing in a safe, is an outline for communication; it is the outline for a possible dialog where the interlocutor, or at least the concrete witness, is, in the end, the critic. And it is equally true that the writer, even if he does not address himself or intends not to address himself to a community, even if he merely proposes to display to others the marvels of his interiority, remains "situated" in that community, constrained first of all by the language in which he writes, and establishes himself, whether he wants it or not, within a certain attitude and in a certain place within it. Society is a permanent field, a dimension of existence that can be evaded by no one, and even less by the writer who has left an objective testimony of his being in his work. [159]

Just as being a writer necessarily involves being a part of a referential totality that prominently includes the reader and the critic, so, too, all of our identities gain their significance in relation to the identities of others within the vast and inescapable network of inherently reciprocal relationships we call "community."

1.2. The Politics of National Liberation

What are the political implications of this phenomenological analysis of community? One obvious implication, it seems, is that we ought to be suspicious of the very notion of a "social contract." Contractualist accounts of social and political relationships often begin by asking why individuals are motivated to seek out relationships with others, join communities, and ultimately create governments. In many cases, however, this kind of inquiry assumes that human beings are essentially isolated entities, and as we have seen, this assumption is rejected by the phenomenological tradition. For this reason, phenomenologists tend to be skeptical toward contractualism. But beyond this point of agreement, the standard phenomenological analysis of community has been developed in a variety of ways. By comparing some of these lines of development, we can better appreciate how Portilla's distinctive standpoint as a Latin American may have influenced his thinking about the nature of community.

For many European phenomenologists, there is something disturbing and even alarming in the notion that community is a condition for the possibility of human sense-making. Indeed, one of the crucial questions for European phenomenologists has been not how or why communities are created but, rather, whether and how it may be possible for individuals to transcend the limits of their communities and avoid the tendency to conform to communal common sense. This concern with conformism and personal authenticity among European phenomenologists may reflect their historical circumstances.[10] It seems, for example, that European phenomenologists became more focused on the issue of conformism at the same time that Europe was becoming more industrialized and developed, a trend that prompted many city-dwellers to indulge in nostalgia about the virtues of older ways of living, where life in small rural communities was governed by natural rhythms rather than routinized schedules. Later, in the post-war period, as multinational cooperation began to diminish the power and importance of individual nations within Europe and elsewhere, it is perhaps no coincidence that European phenomenologists began to focus their critiques of conformism on the dangers posed by the globalization of culture, commerce, and technology.

Portilla does not seem to share these European concerns regarding conformism, globalization, and technology. This difference should not be surprising, however, considering that the situation in Latin America was, and remains, quite different from that of Europe. For example, as Portilla looked out upon the world from his vantage point in Mexico, it is likely that the dangers of excessive industrialization were not as salient to him as the dangers associated with widespread poverty and lack of development. Likewise, while Europeans may plausibly think of themselves as having left behind the "era of the nation," in some parts of Latin America the establishment of a minimally stable and effective government remains a challenge. Thus, individuals in Latin America may be more likely to see their own ability to live a free and meaningful life as very much depending on the strength and even unity of their nations.

Indeed, when we look at the writing of Latin American philosophers in this era, we find that the central concern is the possibility of *collective,* rather than *individual*, authenticity, and especially the possibility of genuine national self-determination in the context of the legacies of colonization.[11] In particular, we find a widely shared worry that Latin America remains dominated by ways of thinking that were imposed by European colonizers, so that even when Latin Americans are formally in charge of their own governance, the results do not reflect the unique life-experiences, concerns, styles, and perspectives of the people of Latin America. As the scholar Ofelia Schutte puts it, when we look at the work of many of the most prominent Latin Americans writers who address social and political issues, we see

> variations on the theme of how to free oneself from the heritage of inequality and exploitation originating with the Conquest and colonialism. Despite almost five hundred years of assimilation into Western European tradition, many Latin Americans still feel the conflict provoked by the conquistadores' subjugation and extermination of millions of Indians who dwelt in the region. The Indians have come to symbolize the ancient, exploited, maternal heritage of the Americas, in contradistinction to the technologically advanced, civilized, foreign conqueror. How to resolve this tension in an unalienated and authentic manner is one of the challenges of Latin American philosophy today.[12]

In this postcolonial context, when indigenous communities were decimated long ago, and every social and political institution of Latin America has been deeply influenced by colonial ways of thinking, national liberation requires more than simply evicting European colonizers and establishing territorial sovereignty. In addition to this formal, political freedom, Latin Americans yearn for "freedom of the mind," so to speak, so that they may conduct their affairs in ways that reflect what is distinctive about the Latin American spirit and circumstances.

Portilla's work, in my view, fits squarely within this tradition of Latin American thought. As mentioned in the introduction, and as we will discuss in more detail in chapters 5 and 6, Portilla sees the ultimate purpose of his own work as helping Mexico to achieve a genuine national liberation.[13]

> [Philosophy] has the function of promoting reason in a specific society, of clearly putting before the collective consciousness the ultimate base of its thinking, of its feeling, and of its acting.

> Philosophy, to the extent that it is a "logos" on humankind, performs an educating and a liberating function. . . . In Mexico, nothing is more necessary than this liberating action of "logos."[14]

Thus, Portilla's work is meant to be therapeutic in nature; indeed, his analysis of Mexican society can be understood as an effort to help Mexico along in its task of "freeing the mind" from the legacies of colonization.

Admittedly, Portilla does not directly address the topic of the Conquest in his work. The closest he comes is in passages that make reference to the two main elements of the Conquest—economic exploitation and racism—references that signal his appreciation of the importance of the ongoing "struggle between capital and labor or between imperial powers and colonial peoples" and his general solidarity with the oppressed.[15] Thus, even if we grant that Portilla should be placed within the tradition of Latin American writers calling for collective authenticity and liberation from the legacies of colonization, as I have suggested, it is undeniable that Portilla's voice is somewhat peculiar within this tradition. How, then, should we describe Portilla's place within the tradition of Latin American philosophy?

To understand Portilla's somewhat unusual approach to the typical themes in Latin American philosophy, we must recall his affiliation with the tradition of phenomenology. As noted above, Portilla agrees with the standard phenomenological view that community functions as a horizon of intelligibility and is an essential part of the referential totality within which people and things are experienced as they are. Thus, for Portilla, community operates at a deep, existential level; the community is already there whenever we think a thought, and it is ontologically inextricable from the people and things we encounter in the world. If this is correct, then national liberation will be an *existential*, rather than a merely *psychological* or *cultural*, task. From a phenomenological perspective, national liberation will require more than changing people's attitudes *about* the world and the ways that people *respond to* the things that "show up" in their experience. Instead, genuine national liberation will require a transformation at a deep, "pre-intentional" level—a change in *how the world shows up in the first place*, before we take up attitudes about it or respond to it in one way or another.[16]

It is this emphasis on the existential dimension of liberation that motivates Portilla to focus his analysis on the deep, underlying structures that give rise to the particular characters and cultural practices that he encounters on the streets of Mexico City—structures that, as we will see in the following section, he identifies as various kinds of affective dispositions. In order to better understand how Portilla's work brings an analysis of existentially deep affective structures to bear upon the concrete challenges of achieving national liberation in a postcolonial context, let us examine his phenomenological analysis of Mexico, the nation closest to his heart.

2. National Affective Attunement in Mexico

Phenomenological nationalism, as stated above, is the view that individuals' sense-making capacities are mediated and structured by their nationality. Formulated in this way, the basic idea of phenomenological nationalism leaves open a number of questions regarding *how* nationality is supposed to shape our sense-making. For example, by what means or mechanisms does nationality exert such a profound influence on our interpretive activity? And what, exactly, are the effects or outcomes of the existential influence that is supposedly exerted by our nationality? In this section, I begin to address these questions by examining Portilla's analysis of the nation of Mexico.

Throughout Portilla's work, we find a consistent emphasis on the role of the *affective* dimension of life—such as moods, emotions, and emotional dispositions. It is unsurprising, then, that his analysis of nationality focuses on what he sees as the distinctive emotional dynamics that pervade everyday life in a given nation. In each of the nations that he examines, Portilla finds a distinctive emotional atmosphere, and he argues that this emotional atmosphere exerts a profound influence on the individuals who live there. Thus, in Portilla's view, nationality shapes our sense-making capacities by way of the "affective attunement" of the nation to which we belong. In Mexico, this national affective attunement is one of *zozobra*.

2.1. Zozobra in Mexico and in Mexicans

Zozobra can be defined as a deep fear that a person may have—a worry that sometimes manifests itself explicitly, but mostly remains an inchoate, background feeling—that he or she is not substantial, not sufficient, not real, and so perpetually at risk of disintegrating and being annihilated. In contrast to a person like Martin Luther whose convictions and identity are fused so strongly that they can say, "Here I stand; *I can do no other!*," people suffering from *zozobra* are plagued by doubt and insecurity about who they are and what they stand for.

Portilla agrees with Emilio Uranga that Mexicans generally experience a high degree of *zozobra*—so much so that this *zozobra* is actually the most distinguishing feature of the Mexican way of being.[17] Here is how Portilla articulates the idea in the essay, "Community, Greatness, and Misery in Mexican Life":

> To be fragile, to be affected or transfixed by nothingness, or to be accidental—there lies the cornerstone on the basis of which an ontological description of the Mexican ought to be attempted. . . . On a concrete plane we construct our being from non-being; we construct our being out of a creation of possibilities whose foundations sink into the uncertainty of a future. . . . It is not strange, then, that human life, all human life, finds itself affected by an incurable nihilism, accidentality, or insubstantiality. However, it is a fact that this particular specification for being human, so proximal and yet so confusing for us Mexicans, is intertwined in a special way by the lived experience of fragility and *zozobra* that Uranga has highlighted.[18]

Thus, in Portilla's view, Mexicans tend to be afflicted by a deep identity-related anxiety, and without a strong, stable, and coherent sense of identity, they do not feel able to assert themselves with level-headed confidence and determination, and thereby to take effective action in the face of life's challenges. In this way, Portilla links a deep sense of *zozobra* to a number of unfortunate tendencies he observes among Mexicans, including tendencies toward inaction, procrastination, cynicism, nostalgia, sentimentalism, and apocalyptic thinking.[19]

After observing this pattern of emotional responses among individuals in Mexico, Portilla wonders how we ought to explain what he has observed. In accordance with phenomenological nationalism—the idea that people's sense-making capacities and activities are structured by their nationality—Portilla argues that the *zozobra* that is prevalent among individuals in Mexico is a direct result of a *zozobra* that operates at a national level. Despite the fact that the Mexican government sponsored intensive efforts to construct a substantive and coherent sense of Mexican identity after the bloody Revolution of 1910, Portilla perceived a lack of any widely shared understanding of what Mexico is and what it stands for.[20] Instead, what he saw was a widespread sense among Mexicans that Mexico as a nation is itself insubstantial, insufficient, unreal, and perpetually at risk of disintegrating or being annihilated, as well as the absence of the kind of solidarity among citizens that would be necessary to form a genuine national community, rather than merely being a motley collection of individuals and social groups who just happen to find themselves living in the same territory.

One sign of this lack of national solidarity, in Portilla's view, is the fact that bribery—"that specter that carries with it all the fault of our national misfortunes"—is commonplace in Mexico:

> the functionary does not act as a representative of that communal transcendence that we call the State, but rather as a representative of his own personal interests. Here we have a failure of that sentiment of solidarity that should have integrated this functionary to the total person of the State. . . . His community-State horizon disappears and the only thing that remains is the sufficient means for his particular relations to easily turn into personal relationships in which only personal interests are at play.[21]

Such corruption, Portilla says, is not so much an issue of "individual morality" but, rather, "an alteration or weakness of the moral foundation which is the community."[22] In other words, the source of the problem is not *psychological* but *phenomenological*: Because the community of nationality does not function effectively as a horizon of intelligibility that shapes individuals' sense-making practices, actions that would sacrifice self-interest for the sake of the national community simply do not show up as making sense to people in a compelling way.

In this way, Portilla's phenomenological conception of community offers a way to explain many of the tendencies he observers among Mexicans. If community is a necessary horizon of intelligibility that *enables* human sense-making, then a weak sense of community will partially *disable* the interpretive activity of the members of that community and bestow upon their sense-making practices a deep sense of insecurity and ambiguity. As he puts it, the "state of the sub-integration of Mexican society" is "a species of social malnutrition that forms a thin yet suffocating spiritual atmosphere for whomever must form their personality within it."[23] Thus, it makes sense that individuals in this communal context would develop a tendency toward quietism, inaction, and procrastination:

> In effect, if the community's reception or response in regard to our action cannot be determined with a certain amount of clarity, it is likely that we will indefinitely postpone the demanded action until the horizon clears up and, if this does not happen, we will carry it out only when the circumstances themselves turn it into a demand that cannot be postponed, and then it will probably carry within itself the mark of improvisation. Nothing slows down the impetus toward action more than uncertainty in regard to the manner in which the work to be done will be received.[24]

From Portilla's perspective, then, because the communal horizon of intelligibility in Mexico is not substantive, clear, and stable, there is a deep insecurity that pervades the whole of everyday life in Mexico, and this leads some individuals to indefinitely postpone actions that they might otherwise take.

In a similar way, Portilla points to the lack of a strong sense of national identity as the explanation for what he sees as the tendency toward cynicism among Mexicans.

> Thus, in a disarticulated community such as ours, the man of action, and even the intellectual, will find himself affected by a certain cynicism which is nothing more than a defensive maneuver or a movement of self-affirmation, which can be described with the analogy of whistling or humming in the dark so as to forget one's fears.[25]

Cynicism, like the other tendencies Portilla describes, is thus explained as a psychological manifestation at the individual level of the deep identity-related insecurity that affects Mexico at the national level.

In this essay, as in others, we thus find Portilla seeking to explain the attitudes and behaviors of individuals by pointing to the affective attunement of the nation to which those individuals belong. But on closer inspection, when we compare Portilla's account of Mexican cynicism to his account of Mexican quietism, we find an important difference in how he describes the psychological mechanisms linking the affective attunement of the nation to the emotional dispositions of individuals. In particular, the tendency toward quietism appears to be a *direct reflection* of the sense of insecurity that characterizes the national community, but the tendency toward cynicism is something that individuals resort to in order to *defend themselves* against this widespread sense of insecurity. How should we understand this notion of defensiveness, and what role does it play in Portilla's analysis of Mexican nationality?

2.2. Defensiveness, National Trauma, and Character

The notion of a "defense mechanism" has its conceptual home in the tradition of depth psychology. As Anna Freud explains, human beings routinely employ a wide variety of defense mechanisms (including repression, projection, introjection, and sublimation) in order to protect the ego from being overwhelmed by the influence of intense emotions, particularly when the ego is especially vulnerable, such as during life crises or in the aftermath of a traumatic event.[26] Defense mechanisms usually operate unconsciously, and unlike the operations of the id, they are usually experienced as a native and unproblematic part of one's personality; for this reason, despite the myriad ways that defense mechanisms can be problematic in a person's life, it is common for an analysand to resist an analyst's attempt to explore or challenge the defense mechanisms she has adopted.[27]

From this perspective, it would not be difficult to understand the psychological impulse to defend oneself against the experience of *zozobra* as Portilla has described it. After all, a breakdown in one's sense of identity can be one of the most disorienting and even life-disrupting things to befall a human being. However, this affective experience may be especially threatening in the context of Mexico, a nation that seems to have experienced some trauma in the process of developing a national identity. As many commentators have suggested, Mexico never quite came to terms with its violent birth in Conquest, and it remains unsettled with regard to its relationship to its Spanish and indigenous progenitors.[28] These wounds were reopened in dramatic fashion during the Revolution of 1910, which exposed deep divisions in the society. After the Revolution was "institutionalized," the nation embarked on an energetic (and perhaps desperate) attempt to stitch together a coherent identity, but by the late 1940s and early 1950s, when Portilla was taking up the topic of nationality in his work, it was clear that the task of creating a strong and stable national identity in Mexico was going to be more challenging than its early champions might have expected.

In this context, the experience of *zozobra* would be particularly threatening to Mexicans, and the compulsion to defend against *zozobra* would be even stronger. Indeed, as Portilla puts it, "We have no choice but to defend that fragile being that upon its own emergence appears vulnerable, threatened; we have no choice but to safeguard what we have already accomplished, to stabilize our situation, to conform ourselves with what we already have."[29] As Portilla emphasizes here, defensiveness surrounding issues of identity compels individuals to adopt an inherently conservative, inhibited, and rigid posture, and once this affective orientation is established, it can be difficult to escape or alter. Indeed, this is why Portilla so concerned about it—because defensiveness can diminish the capacity of a person or society to be open to the future and to cope flexibly, realistically, and creatively with the complex demands of the present situation.

In line with Anna Freud's account, Portilla's analysis shows that the felt need to defend against *zozobra* in Mexico manifests itself in a wide variety of ways and, for many individuals, these defensive strategies are taken up as central elements of their personalities. In this way, defensiveness not only generates a variety of character traits that are common among Mexicans, but also gives rise to various *character types* that Portilla identifies as being common in Mexican life. Portilla offers a detailed examination three particular types of characters that he encounters on the streets of Mexico City—the *apretado*, the *relajiento*, and the *literary critic*. Each of these types of characters exhibits a distinctive and holistic style of relating to the world that can be understood as a different way of defending oneself against identity-related anxiety.

Consider that, in general, defensiveness is a strategy for avoiding the discomfort that arises when we simultaneously acknowledge that (a) a certain concern is important to us, and (b) we are failing to address this concern. For example, if we feel that it is important to have a substantive, coherent, and stable identity, then it will make us feel uncomfortable to think that we do not have such an identity. In some cases, this discomfort may be unbearable, especially if the concern we are failing to address is associated with some sort of trauma we have experienced. With this in mind, we can identify three straightforward ways of defending ourselves against this kind of discomfort.

- *The strategy of denial*: deny that we are failing to address the concern.

- *The strategy of dismissal*: dismiss the concern as not being important.

- *The strategy of problematization*: insist that our failure to address the concern is the result of a specifiable "problem" that can (in theory) be "solved."

The first two strategies (the strategies of *denial* and *dismissal*) resolve the relevant tension between (a) and (b) by simply removing one of these possibilities from our consideration. The third strategy (the strategy of *problematization*) does not resolve the tension directly, but it does offer reassurance that the tension will be resolved as soon as certain steps are taken. The strategy of problematization helps us to cope with the relevant anxiety by shoring up our sense of knowledge and control, without which we might be left feeling disoriented and powerless in the face of the possibility that we may fail to address an important concern.

Returning, then, to Portilla's analysis of Mexico, we can see that the strategy of denial is adopted by the type of character he calls the "apretado"—a term that literally means "tight" or "pinched," and which, as noted in the previous chapter, refers in this case to an uptight and snobbish person. This type of character clings firmly to his qualities, roles, routines, institutional affiliations, and status symbols in order to prove to himself and others that there is, in fact, no possibility that he lacks a substantive, coherent, and stable identity.

> "Apretado" individuals are compact masses of value; they live on the inside like a dense volume of value-filled "being," like a bundle of valuable "properties," conceived according to the model of the properties of a thing. . . . No matter what they do, they are an intelligent, effective official, full of qualities. If an "apretado" individual says something stupid, if he or she makes a mistake, that doesn't prove anything, since it will be a stupid thing said by a very intelligent person; it will be the mistake of a very effective official. When an "apretado" goes for a walk, an official goes for a walk; when an "apretado" eats, an official eats. An intelligent and efficient person sleeps; a person with good taste walks along the street; a person of

> talent calmly enjoys breakfast. . . . In a certain sense, "apre-
> tado" individuals are also their car, their house, their plots of
> land, their elegant furniture, their works of art. It couldn't be
> any other way. Since these individuals have begun to conceive
> their own being according to the model of things, and since
> property has started out by being the way in which they relate
> to themselves, it seems inevitable that property become also
> their way of referencing the world.[30]

The *apretado* thus defends himself against identity-related anxiety by denying the possibility that his identity could ever seriously be threatened, given the security with which he possesses the qualities and items that define him. And when the *apretado* is a government official, his identity gets bound together with the identity of his nation, so that his own firm possession of his qualities serves to shore up the qualities of the nation itself.

In contrast, the type of character Portilla calls the "*relajiento*" adopts the strategy of dismissal, rejecting the notion that it is important to have a substantive, coherent, and stable identity. Instead, the *relajiento* passes the time by constantly joking around and making fun of anyone who tries to take themselves seriously.

> A "relajiento" . . . refuses to take anything seriously, to commit
> to anything; that is to say, a "relajiento" refuses to guarantee
> any of his or her own behavior in the future. The "relajiento"
> assumes no responsibility for anything; he or she doesn't risk
> doing anything; he or she is simply a good-humored witness
> of the banality of life. . . . The relajiento does not bring about
> preoccupation but rather unoccupation. He or she is an unoccu-
> pied person perpetually bent on the task of being unoccupied,
> of emptying one's consciousness of all seriousness and of all
> commitment. . . . A jovial and bitter person, the relajiento can
> be understood as having a life which is a series of accidents
> that coagulate together to endow him or her with a friendly
> and amorphous personality.[31]

While others might be filled with anxiety by the thought of failing to construct any substantive, coherent, and stable identity, the *relajiento* evades this anxiety by simply giving up on the pursuit of identity in advance. As Portilla puts it, "the relajiento is not totally a failure since he or she does not believe in victory."[32] After all, if identity is not actually important, then there is no meaningful sense in which one can be said to be have "failed" to attain it.

The final strategy, the strategy of problematization, is the strategy adopted by the literary critic. In order to diminish the anxiety of *zozobra*, the literary critic looks for someone to *blame* for the nation's lack of a substantive, coherent, and stable identity—and by extension, to blame for the critic's own insecure sense of identity. By throwing himself into the task of attacking those writers he sees as "xenophiles" who have abdicated their responsibility to the nation, the literary critic can sustain the absurd fantasy that, by his heroic actions, he might soon solve the problem of national and personal identity once and for all. The critic's immense simplification of the situation offers a way to avoid the discomfort of not having knowledge and control with respect to a matter of great importance.

In this way, we can see that the critic's behavior is reminiscent of a child who, lacking cognitive or emotional maturity, feels overwhelmed and disoriented by complexity of the world, and compensates by constructing simple narratives in which the challenges of life are problems that are caused by "bad guys" and that will be resolved when the "good guys" fight back. In this way, Portilla says, the critic invents and exaggerates the writer's misdeeds in order to stabilize the critic's own simplistic and self-serving interpretation of the situation: "If one cannot find the evil one needs so as to be good, then one invents it. . . . At bottom it is all about Manichaeism, that sad ally of stupidity and insufficiency, which allows some to become respectable and righteous" [166–167]. Likewise, just as a child might pretend that he has magical powers in order to compensate for the frustration of not yet having developed the skills and abilities to effect his will in the world, so, too, the critic pretends that his pronouncements against a writer, or against imperialism, were a "magical act of expulsion" [160] that makes a real difference in the world. In this way, the critic pretends that there is a relatively straightforward solution that will enable him to address the concern of national identity and take effective action on behalf of global justice. As Portilla points out, however, the critic's pretense is a farce. "When declaring oneself a defender of justice it may *seem* that one is really doing something to bring it about, and in this way one can come to believe oneself to be a righteous man. It is evident, however, that it is not enough to declare that one is something in order to become that thing in reality" [166].

To summarize, Portilla's analysis of Mexican society demonstrates the central features of his phenomenological nationalism. On his view, the affective attunement of the Mexican nation is defined by *zozobra*. This affective attunement mediates and structures the sense-making activities of individual Mexicans, who "must form their personality within" this anxiety-laden "spiritual atmosphere." There are two basic ways that this national affective attunement influences the members of the nation. In some cases, the influence is direct, in the sense that the affective attunement of the nation molds the emotional dispositions of individuals in the image of the nation itself, as when individual Mexicans exhibit traits associated with insecurity and anxiety, such as a tendency toward quietism, inaction, and procrastination. In other cases, the influence is indirect, in the sense that individual Mexicans exhibit character traits—such as the overly confident aggressiveness of the literary critic—that function as defenses against the identity-related anxiety that afflicts the nation. Such traits are problematic, in Portilla's view, because as defense mechanisms, they tend to manifest themselves in inflexible and compulsive attitudes and behaviors, and therefore they diminish individuals' capacity to cope with reality in effective and creative ways.

We are now in a position to step back from the details of Portilla's analysis and to consider whether we can extract any general principles regarding the influence of nationality upon our most basic ways of being in the world.

3. Nationality as a Horizon of Intelligibility

From what we can tell, Portilla never attempted to articulate the foundational principles of his social and political philosophy in a systematic way, nor to explain and defend the philosophical program that underlies his works. Perhaps he would have done so if he had lived longer, but as it is, all that interpreters have at their disposal is a handful of essays and columns, each of which offers a brilliant and original intervention into a particular issue, but contains few clues about how his various philosophical interventions might hang together as parts of a coherent whole. Thus, it is up to scholars to compare his works and look for common underlying concerns, assumptions, methods, and views, as well as to "read between the lines," so to speak, in order to discern why Portilla may have approached his topics in the ways he did, rather than taking other paths that he might have chosen or that were taken by his contemporaries.

Fortunately, it is possible, in my view, to piece together some general principles that guide and motivate Portilla's philosophy. Consider the essays translated in this volume, for example. These three essays examine Mexico, the US, and Germany, respectively. Each of these essays focuses on the emotional dynamics that structure and pervade everyday life in these nations. In each case, moreover, Portilla is especially concerned to show how the particular emotional dynamics of the nation give rise to problematic and dangerous tendencies among individuals and in the society as a whole—thereby revealing the existential and national origin of what we would otherwise assume to be psychological or cultural idiosyncrasies.

With this in mind, we can begin to identify some broadly applicable ideas that appear to underlie Portilla's thought. The first such idea is this: *At least in some nations, it is possible to identify a particular affective attunement that strongly influences everyday life in a relatively stable, enduring, and pervasive manner.* For example, as we have seen, Portilla suggests that Mexico is dominated by the affective attunement of *zozobra*; in the chapters that follow we will examine his claim that life in the US is marked by the affective attunement of "innocence" and moral self-righteousness, and that Germany has struggled for many years with a profound sense of meaninglessness. Generalizing, then, Portilla holds that some—and perhaps many—nations exhibit a certain affective attunement that shapes everyday life within the nation over long periods of time in ways that distinguish the nation from others.

The basic thrust of this view will likely strike the reader as being fairly intuitive and plausible. After all, it is not uncommon to identify and discuss characteristic differences between people of various nations with regard to their affective style. For example, those who travel to Brazil or Japan will almost certainly notice a certain distinctive mood and emotional atmosphere that pervades everyday life in these nations and influences the people who live there. On further reflection, however, it seems equally clear that such observations rely on stereotypes that overlook the diversity of the nations in question. Indeed, critics have long raised concerns about the stated goal of the Grupo Hiperión to pursue a philosophy of *lo mexicano*.[33] From this perspective, the very idea that there is such a thing as *lo mexicano*—a singular essence of Mexicanness—is likely to strike some readers as being patently absurd, given the size and diversity of Mexico.

When we follow this critical line of thought, however, it is not clear whether we should be satisfied with where it leads. Shall we discard stereotypes about nations altogether, or refuse to generalize about them? Perhaps—but on the other hand, it may not be so easy to escape the nagging suspicion that, at least with regard to stereotypes about the mood or emotional character of various nations, these generalizations do, in fact, capture something true and important. When we compare Mexico, the US, and Germany, for example, we do seem to find *something* distinctive about the emotional atmosphere in these places, even if it is difficult to say exactly what it is. Thus, neither of these two opposing intuitions— nations are emotionally unified, and nations are emotionally diverse—is so easily dismissed.[34]

This, in my view, is where Portilla's sophisticated analysis of nationality is particularly helpful. Portilla's account aims to articulate the unity beneath the diversity, identifying the deep structures that generate and explain the myriad and diverse concrete manifestations we may encounter among individuals in the nation. In this way, Portilla's analysis can help us to articulate the logic underlying the various expressions of a given nationality, revealing these disparate expressions as parts of relatively coherent whole.

It is thus important to emphasize that Portilla makes explicit and concerted efforts to acknowledge the diversity of the nations that he analyzes. For example, in his analysis of the affective attunement of the US, Portilla does not fall into the trap of arguing that US Americans share a certain perspective or way of living. In Portilla's view, there is an affective attunement that is distinctive of the US, but it operates at a deep, existential level, below the level of beliefs or cultural practices. As such, Portilla is happy to acknowledge that there are "*innumerable* forms and interpretations of life and man that characterize US American culture" [142].[35] Likewise, in his analysis of Mexico, Portilla does not rely on any single figure to illustrate the Mexican way of being. Instead, he identifies a whole *cast of characters* that a person might encounter on the streets of Mexico City, suggesting that it is only when these characters are considered collectively that we can discern the emotional orientation that is distinctively Mexican.

Indeed, the three Mexican character types examined above are quite different from one another: The literary critic is a radical, left-wing member of the intelligentsia who is passionate about art and philosophy; the *apretado* is a conservative government official who is wealthy and values order and efficiency; and the *relajiento* is an apolitical and hard-drinking individual who lives on the margins of society, passing the time by constantly joking around. Of course, anyone who investigates a large group of people will be open to criticism for ignoring some members of the group in their research, and Portilla is no exception. His analysis certainly would have been more rich, interesting, and persuasive if he had focused his gaze on women or indigenous communities, for example. Nevertheless, given the diversity of the characters that Portilla *does* analyze in depth, it would not be fair to dismiss his efforts simply on the grounds that he ignores societal diversity.

The question that arises from Portilla's work is this: What, if anything, do these three types of characters have in common? What is the emotional logic that explains why some Mexicans in the mid-twentieth century might find themselves taking up one of these three ways of relating to the world? As we have seen, each of these three types of people can be understood as employing a defensive strategy for avoiding *zozobra*, an anxiety about identity that, in the case of Mexico, may have its roots in the violent and disorienting processes that originated in the nation's founding and exploded anew in the recent past. Generalizing from this case, then, we come to another broadly applicable idea that appears to underlie Portilla's thought: *In some cases, at least, a nation's affective attunement centers around a particular concern to which members have become especially sensitized as a result of traumatic events in the nation's past, and which generates and structures a variety of ways of relating to the world among the individuals in the nation.* Thus, to say that a nation exhibits a distinctive affective attunement does not imply that everyone in the nation has a particular mood or emotional disposition. Instead, a national affective attunement is better thought of as a "field of play," a dynamic but structured affective space within which individuals can take up a wide variety of postures and strategies, each of which may be quite different from the next, but which will be best understood as a way of dealing with the particular concern that organizes the emotional life of the nation.

Taking this line of thought a step further, Portilla's analysis of Mexico reveals a number of specific ways that individuals within a nation might relate to the nation's organizing concern. Articulating his analysis in general terms, then, we can make the following predictions. First: *Many members of a nation will directly reflect the nation's affective attunement in their character traits.* For example, in Mexico, many individuals will reflect the national identity-related anxiety in character traits that exhibit insecurity, hesitation to act, and so on. But, second: *Some of the more notable types of characters in a nation will have personalities that reflect one of the three defensive strategies described above—the strategy of denial, the strategy of dismissal, or the strategy of problematization—in order to defend themselves against the possibility of failing to address the concern that is central to the nation's affective attunement.* Because these types of characters seek to avoid the discomfort associated with the possibility of failing to address an important concern, these types of characters are prone to unrealistic and inflexible attitudes. As such, the influence of these character types upon the nation will be particularly problematic and even dangerous. In the case of Mexico, for example, each of these defensive strategies—taken up by the *apretado,* the *relajiento,* and the literary critic, respectively—constitutes a rigid and self-destructive way of relating to the world that presents a significant obstacle to the goal of "freeing the mind" from the legacies of colonization. In a similar way, all nations have reason to beware of the influence of such individuals if they hope to cultivate the emotional maturity that is necessary for genuine freedom.

This warning about the importance of the emotional maturity of nations, drawn from Portilla's work, becomes especially urgent as we now turn our attention to the US, a nation whose immense power casts a shadow upon the entire globe.

Notes

1. See Martin Heidegger, *Being and Time,* trans. John Macquarrie and Edward Robinson (1927; repr., New York: Harper & Row, 1962); Simone de Beauvoir, *The Second Sex,* trans. Constance Borde and Sheila Malovany-Chevallier (1949; repr., New York: Vintage Books, 2011); Maurice Merleau-Ponty, *Phenomenology of Perception*, trans. Donald Landes (1945; repr., New York: Routledge, 2012).

2. On the other hand, I find nothing in Portilla's work that would necessarily oppose the view that nations as such should be abolished. Phenomenological nationalism—the view that nations structure our sense-making practices—is a claim about not an *essential* feature of human beings, but merely a *contingent* feature of human beings who happen to belong to a nation. With this in mind, it would be fascinating to put Portilla's phenomenology of nationality into dialogue with a phenomenological analysis of the refugee or stateless person. (Thanks to Lori Gallegos de Castillo for this suggestion.)

3. For more on the concept of *Mitsein,* see Heidegger, *Being and Time,* §§26–27. "Dasein" is Heidegger's word for the kind of entity that we (humans)

are, defined by our specific kind of awareness of and responsiveness to the meaning of the world we inhabit—viz., Dasein is an entity for whom being in general, and its own being in particular, is "an issue" for it. Heidegger argues that Dasein's essential activity of *making sense of the meaning of being* always already depends upon, makes reference to, and is influenced by the sense-making activity of other Dasein.

4. As Heidegger puts it: "Whatever the way of being it may have at the time, and thus with whatever understanding of Being it may possess, Dasein has grown up both *into* and *in* a traditional way of interpreting itself: in terms of this it understands itself proximally and, within a certain range, constantly. By this understanding, the possibilities of its Being are disclosed and regulated. Its own past—and this always means the past of it 'generation'—is not something which *follows along after* Dasein, but something which already goes ahead of it." Heidegger, *Being and Time*, 41.

5. Heidegger, *Being and Time*, 213.

6. Jorge Portilla, "Critique of Criticism." Translation included in the appendix. Page numbers in brackets refer to the 1984 Spanish edition of this work included in *Fenomenología del relajo y otros ensayos*.

7. As he puts it, "community [is] . . . a horizon in which actions are articulated . . . the horizon for the comprehension of certain acts, and some would say for the majority of our human actions." Portilla, "Community, Greatness, and Misery in Mexican Life," 183.

8. Speaking of community as a horizon of intelligibility, Portilla writes that "one of its primary functions is that of serving as walls against which bounce the echoes that carry the meaning of our actions." He notes that although we typically take this horizon for granted, we suddenly appreciate its importance in moments of breakdown, when, perhaps because we are traveling or because our own community has undergone a historical change, the echo that bounces back to us "makes it evident that our [action] did not have the exact meaning that we were giving to it." Portilla, "Community, Greatness, and Misery in Mexican Life," 184.

9. See Heidegger, *Being and Time*, §16.

10. For a detailed examination of this view, see Julian Young, *German Philosophy in the 20th Century: Weber to Heidegger* (London: Routledge, 2018).

11. For introductions to the central themes of Latin American philosophy, see Jorge J. E. Gracia, ed., *Latin American Philosophy in the Twentieth Century* (Buffalo, NY: Prometheus, 1986); Ofelia Schutte, *Cultural Identity and Social Liberation in Latin American Thought* (Albany: State University of New York Press, 1993); Eduardo Mendieta, "Is There Latin American Philosophy?" *Philosophy Today*, 43 (Supplement, 1999): 50–61; Susana Nuccetelli, *Latin American Thought: Philosophical Problems and Arguments* (Boulder, CO: Westview Press, 2001); Eduardo Mendieta, ed., *Latin American Philosophy: Currents, Issues, and Debates* (Bloomington: Indiana University Press, 2003); Susana Nuccetelli and

Gary Seay, eds., *Latin American Philosophy: An Introduction with Readings* (Upper Saddle River, NJ: Prentice Hall, 2003); Arlene Salles and Elizabeth Millán, eds., *The Role of History in Latin American Philosophy: Contemporary Perspectives* (Albany: State University of New York Press, 2005); María Luisa Femenías and Amy Oliver, *Feminist Philosophy in Latin America and Spain* (New York: Rodopi, 2007); Jorge J. E. Gracia, "What Is Latin American Philosophy?" in *Philosophy in Multiple Voices*, ed. George Yancey (New York: Rowman & Littlefield, 2007); Susana Nuccetelli, Ofelia Schutte, and Otávio Bueno, eds., *A Companion to Latin American Philosophy* (Malden, MA: Wiley-Blackwell, 2010); Stephanie Rivera Berruz and Leah Kalmanson, eds., *Comparative Studies in Asian and Latin American Philosophies: Cross-Cultural Theories and Methodologies* (New York: Bloomsbury, 2018); and Robert Eli Sanchez, Jr., ed., *Latin American and Latinx Philosophy: An Introduction* (London: Routledge, 2019).

12. Ofelia Schutte, "Toward an Understanding of Latin American Philosophy," *Philosophy Today* 31, no. 1 (1987): 27.

13. Note that Portilla is not claiming (in a manner that would be similar to the literary critics he condemns) that all philosophers, or all Mexican philosophers, should dedicate their efforts to the betterment of their nation. Instead, this is simply the mission that he has set for his own work, based on his view of the power of philosophy to contribute to personal and collective liberation.

14. Portilla, "The Phenomenology of Relajo," 126f.

15. Ibid., 124.

16. For a detailed discussion of the distinction between changes that occur at a *phenomenological* or "pre-intentional" level and those occurring at a merely *psychological* level, see Matthew Ratcliffe, *Feelings of Being: Phenomenology, Psychiatry, and the Sense of Reality* (Oxford: Oxford University Press, 2008).

17. Uranga, "Essay on the Ontology of the Mexican (1951)," 173. For a discussion of Uranga's view, see chapter 1 of this text, as well as Sánchez, *Contingency and Commitment*.

18. Portilla, "Community, Greatness, and Misery in Mexican Life," p. 186.

19. Ibid., 186ff.

20. For a discussion of the construction of Mexican national identity after the revolution, see Rick López, *Crafting Mexico: Intellectuals, Artisans, and the State after the Revolution* (Durham, NC: Duke University Press, 2010).

21. Portilla, "Community, Greatness, and Misery in Mexican Life," 185.

22. Ibid.

23. Ibid., 189.

24. Ibid., 188.

25. Ibid., 191.

26. Anna Freud, *The Ego and the Mechanisms of Defense* (1936; repr., London: Routledge, 1992).

27. Ibid., 29.

28. See, for instance, López, *Crafting Mexico*; Knight, "Mexican Revolution: Interpretations"; and Jaffary et al., *Mexican History*.

29. Portilla, "Community, Greatness, and Misery in Mexican Life," 190.

30. Portilla, "The Phenomenology of Relajo," 191f. I have altered the translation here and in the following passages by changing the references to "he or she" to "he," because I believe this better reflects the original meaning of the text. It seems that Portilla thought of all of the characters he describes as being men, and issues of gender equity were not prominent in his thinking.

31. Ibid., 147f.

32. Ibid., 148.

33. See, for example, Andrea Pitts, "Carlos Alberto Sánchez: *Contingency and Commitment.*"

34. This line of thought builds upon Manuel Vargas, "Lessons from the Philosophy of Race in Mexico," *Philosophy Today* 44 (*SPEP Supplement* 26, 2000): 18–29.

35. Portilla, "The Spiritual Crisis of the United States," emphasis mine.

PART II

ON "THE SPIRITUAL CRISIS OF THE UNITED STATES"

Chapter 3

The Politics of Innocence

Carlos Alberto Sánchez

It is never untimely to ask, What myths sustain our politics? Reflecting on what he considers "the spiritual crisis of the United States," Jorge Portilla proposes that that which sustains and underlies US politics is *innocence*, or the *myth* of *its own* innocence, and that only by properly understanding what this is and how this is so can the different cultural crises affecting US culture in the twentieth century (and beyond) be properly understood and addressed. In the US, it turns out, the myth of innocence is at the root of all evil.

But what is "innocence"? Portilla appears to understand the concept of "innocence" in three different ways (although he employs it interchangeably) in the essay we are presently considering, "The Spiritual Crisis of the United States."

> When I say that innocence, that is, the *absolute unfamiliarity* of evil, is the *foundation* of the *American Way of Life*, I mean that the idea of innocence *serves* to make sense of almost every particular nuance of that way of life. [141; italics mine][1]

Innocence is understood, first, in its experiential aspect, namely, as the experience of an "absolute unfamiliarity of evil." The term Portilla uses here is *extrañeza*, which means unfamiliarity, but also strangeness, estrangement, alienation, and surprise. The idea is that Americans (collectively and individually), and by this Portilla means White US Americans,[2] *think of themselves as* "absolutely" or completely estranged or alienated from evil, finding it strange and thus shocking or surprising on encountering it. Innocence is understood, second, metaphysically, as that which *founds* a way of life. At its foundation, i.e., at its ground, the "American Way of Life" *is* the estrangement of evil, it is purity; the American way of life is uncontaminated. And, third, innocence turns out to be an interpretive category, or, he says, "a capital category for the interpretation of the US American way of life" [141].

These three senses of innocence—what we can call the experiential, the metaphysical, and the interpretive—coalesce into one interpretive framework through which the US is understood from the *Mexican point of view* as absolutely resistant to whatever is not already internal to its own self-understanding. In other words, the "American Way of Life," so much desired, admired, and mythologized in our contemporary world, is seen from the external perspective as reflecting an ignorance, alienation, and estrangement from evil, an ignorance or estrangement that seems to permeate "almost every aspect" of that way of life. Xenophobia, anti-immigrant sentiment, anti-black racism, homophobia, religious intolerance, etc., are all cultural or social attempts (conscious or unconscious) to protect innocence in its metaphysical, and social, manifestations—to protect purity from contamination.

Of course, it is a generalization to say that a people is "absolutely unfamiliar" with evil; after all, random massacres, rampant poverty, exploitation of children, and other grotesque social ills are as familiar in American life as in any other "way of life." The point here, however, is that in their social and political attitudes, or those attitudes familiar to Portilla, the American way of life operates *as if* evil is a radical otherness that does not—and ultimately, should not—affect it. Contemporary post-9/11 anti-immigrant social policies assume that foreigners—and, eventually, all non-White Americans in general—introduce a heretofore unknown evil whenever and wherever they introduce their own cultural, political, religious, or philosophical perspective. The consequence of this stranger-bias is that in order to "Make America Great Again" these strange others must be expelled from the body politic. Thus, while it may seem like an overly hasty generalization on Portilla's part, it pays to consider it a bit further if only to make sense of Mexico's attitude toward the United States, not only in Portilla's time, but in our own.

The aim of this chapter is thus twofold: one, to reflect on what Portilla means when he insists that Americans (again, White US Americans) are absolutely unfamiliar with evil and the extent to which this is an accurate portrayal of the American way of life; and two, to think *with* Portilla, from a broadly theoretical standpoint, on the manner in which the myth of innocence is deployed in contemporary American social and cultural arrangements, i.e., in its politics and broader social policy.

1. The Spiritual Crisis of America

There is a sense in which innocence is the virtue that best describes the American character. A sense in which everything—culture, politics, art, and philosophy—flows out of the virtue of innocence. This sense is related to the founding of America, to its landscape, to its people, both to those who, fleeing persecution, found refuge in a "New World" and to those who were already here; it is related to its promise as a place of renewal, rebirth, or reinvention; it is related to the Western idea that everything found from its shores to its interior was pure, untainted by thousands of years of war, greed, and culture in the "Old World"; untainted, that is, by European history and its politics of sin. It is related to the notion, articulated at its founding, of America as a "redeemer nation" that in its purity showed itself to have been "touched by God."[3]

Jorge Portilla's reflections on the "American Way of Life" take as their point of departure America's self-understanding as this is communicated in mass media—in TV, radio, and magazines. Portilla was writing in the 1950s after a brief visit to the United States on a Rockefeller Grant,[4] and as a Mexican and from a Mexican point of view; one can't help but wonder to what extent his ruminations are based on stereotypes and misinformation, on preconceptions and hearsay that are sure to bias his "philosophical" interventions. However, despite these shortcomings—shortcomings that one can't truly overcome due to the limits and prejudices of our own reason, even as information becomes more readily available and immediate thanks to the advent of social media technologies such as Twitter and Facebook—Portilla is able to attune himself to what is being communicated, thereby capturing an essential aspect of that which America believes about itself, of its political and cultural identity.

Before embarking on his analysis, Portilla tells us *why* this embarking is important. It is, he suggests, a matter of understanding a "radical otherness" (I quote here at length):

> all Mexicans are presented with the need at one time or another, and by the nature of things themselves, to take a position that is as clear as possible regarding the historical facts of our

northern neighbor. The need to take such a position is based, it seems to me, on the fact that the United States always appears to us in the form of a radical "otherness." . . . The ultimate foundations of US American civilization are almost absolutely strange to us. [139]

The effort to understand the peculiar American way of being is thus imposed on us as a first step toward adopting a lucid and well-defined attitude toward American culture, and it is on the basis of this radical feeling of strangeness and as a result of that will to understand that we can see the fact and breadth of the American crisis.

> Succinctly put, we believe that what is in crisis is precisely the very foundation of US American life as such—the foundation of what in the US they have come to call *The American Way of Life*. [139–140]

A full understanding of that which is radically other, or absolutely strange, is, of course, not possible. It is to understand that which does not fully give itself and stands beyond the subjective horizons of intelligibility. Nevertheless, one can approximate understanding, one can approach the radically other and the absolutely strange. This approximation, or approach, is what the radical other demands in its very essence. So the goal, Portilla says, is to adopt a "lucid and well-defined attitude toward US American culture," one that will likewise allow Mexicans—for whom the strangeness and otherness of *el norte* appears as promise and possibility, a mystery that beckons Mexicans northward now as it did then—to also see the "breath of the American crisis," of its *spiritual* crisis.

Portilla's prelude to the analysis also gives us a sense into the intimidating shadow cast by the United States in the geopolitical arena, a shadow that is darker and heavier to those standing right underneath, namely, its southern neighbors—Mexico and Central America. Inevitably, anyone living under this shadow must address himself or herself to it, affirm its presence, and respond to its strange power, to that otherness that looms as threat or opportunity. Inevitably, if one is Mexican, Portilla suggests, one must try to *understand* it. Understanding it thus becomes, for Mexicans, something of a moral and political responsibility, since the historical fate of Mexicans is necessarily tied—literally and figuratively—to the US, whereby its triumphs and its crises become issues *for* Mexicans, whether they want them to be or not.

Motivated to understand by that radical otherness, Portilla's reflective gaze turns north. He notices that within America's strangeness, along with its mystery, there is something obvious and explicit that it itself announces. This "something" is reflected in American politics, its foreign policy and domestic agenda; the something is the illusory *self-conception* that America is *innocent*. This illusory self-understanding constitutes for Portilla a foundational crisis since on this illusion lays what we've come to know as the "American Way of Life."

The crisis can be articulated in the following terms: The Puritan ideal of innocence that lies in the foundations of the "American Way of Life" does not lend itself to the reality of a global world, to the necessity for openness or a politics of interconnection and intercommunication, a phenomenon that undermines the positive aspects of that "way of life" or what that way of life means to represent. Because the ideal, or we can say the myth or ideology, of innocence ultimately grounds that which makes the American way of life "American," a crisis of ideology is thus a crisis of cultural and political identity. As Portilla sees it, however, this is an inevitable crisis since any self-conception that relies on the categories of innocence, or what's the same, uniqueness, purity, and exception, will regard anything foreign or other to itself as a threat to this uniqueness, purity, or exception.

From the Mexican point of view, however, the ideology of innocence has fully interpellated American consciousness. In the Althusserian sense, interpellation describes the manner in which human subjectivity is constituted by ideological forces, the manner in which one's identity is "hailed" and thus affirmed by ideology itself.[5] In this way, the ideology of purity, innocence, or estrangement from evil has constituted US American identity. Portilla illustrates this by relating the strange case of an American funeral director who, traveling the world in search of a painting of Christ, insists that it reflect a "happy" and "smiling" (or innocent) Christ. The funeral director goes as far as holding an competition where he intends to choose the statue of Christ that best represents Christ as he understand him and *wants him to be*. In the end, he is unable to find a suitable representation of a "happy" Christ, protesting that "all these paintings, even the smiling ones, look sad and definitely European. What I need is a radiant Christ who looks upward with an inner light of joy and hope, I want a Christ with an American face" [140]. For the funeral director, echoing the ideology of innocence that constitutes his own viewpoint, "joy" and "hope" mark the "American face." An American face, that is, will not reflect the troubles and tribulations of other faces, such as the European face, which, even when smiling, looks sad. The suggestion here, is, of course, that suffering is a symptom of evil and not of innocence and purity, or radiance and the "inner light of joy."

With this example, Portilla wonders about the extent to which Americans will hold on to the myth of innocence *in spite* of history or common sense. As he puts it, the funeral director's insistence that Christ be a smiling Christ "radically ignores the difficult nuances of the relationship between the historical Jesus and the humanity of the men who followed him and those who killed him. It erases the *sense* of Christ's appearance in history, the sense of His life and His death" [141].

Ultimately, the crisis to which Portilla refers has to do with a disconnect between what is *the case* and what Americans desire the true to be the case, with the lack of correspondence between truth and belief, idea and reality. The reality of Christ, in the person of the Bible or as a historical figure, is one of persecution, passion, and rebirth, acts that in themselves are violent and not deserving of smiles or happy "close ups." Similarly, the claim to innocence in social life clashes with a reality of America's historical experience. Americans resist the truth, Portilla suggests, because it itself is not innocent. (In our contemporary milieu we talk about living in the "post-truth" era, one where truth is not as important as *what feels to be true*. As Portilla illustrates, however, this is not a *new* era at all; historically, Americans would rather live in something *more* than true, in a more radical conception of what is true, in a conception of life that is pure, that feels right and good; post-truth is foundational to the very identity of America itself.) Ultimately, the cultural desire *to be* innocent and to remain so clashes with the reality that innocent is not something one can be or maintain without shutting out or expelling all external, strange, or alien influences.

2. On American Innocence

2.1. THE DEGRADATIONS OF EVIL

The case of the "smiling Christ" seems to accurately represent the manner in which Americans assume the ideology or myth of their own innocence;

it reflects the way in which Americans are interpellated by that ideology. It is an interpellation that manifests itself in professions of uniqueness and exemption, where what is an ordinary fact for the rest of the world does not apply here. In the geopolitical arena, this is known as "American exceptionalism," the idea that the United States is different from every other nation on earth and thus deserves special privileges and exemptions.[6] In Portilla's account, one of these exemptions is the exemption to evil, or, the privilege of absolute innocence. This is a radical exemption, since innocence as defined by Portilla is more of an ideal than a reality. He writes:

> he is innocent who is not defiled by evil in general or by sin in particular. An innocent world will thus be that world in which evil has not penetrated, where evil has not corrupted the root of life itself. [142]

Depending on how we understand evil or sin, rare would be "he" who is "innocent"; even as an "ideal" toward which to aspire, an entire people uncorrupted by evil (or sin) would be hard to come by. Even if we consider the most abstract definition of "evil," the idea would be that *innocent* describes a state of affairs or a person wherein all corrupting influence, all impurities, and all that is generally disruptive to pure living "has not penetrated" or "corrupted" that state of affairs or that person. It thus seems like an aspirational ideal, if nothing else, making it impossible to find an entire culture exempt from evil.

In spite of the funeral director's insistence that a smiling Christ would best represent American innocence, Portilla argues that the myth of innocence is not usually manifested in such declarations of purity, incorruptibleness, or perfection, but in something much more "American": It shows up in a belief in America's *quantifiable* superiority. This belief is expressed as a "tendency to identify the *most* with the *best*" [142], or with equating quantity with quality. Thus, having the most money, the highest buildings, the most advanced technology, is translated in the American consciousness as factual evidence of having the *best* "way of life." So, for example, if San Francisco has the most expensive housing market in the Northern Hemisphere, this is understood as a reflection of the quality of life there, which is then assumed to be the best (a simplistic generalization, to be sure).

Behind this tendency to equate quantity with quality is the myth of innocence and the accompanying belief—derived from America's Puritan roots and the Protestant ethic—that one's blessedness is reflected in one's material wealth, so that the more one has, the more one's life approximates what God has determined as the right and good life for us. In turn, the more one approximates God's will, the more innocent and pure one is, and vice versa. As Portilla puts it:

> Indeed, in a world where evil does not penetrate, any *increase* can only be an *increase of good*. Any affirmation of quantitative superiority is then the realization of *genuine* superiority. The mere consciousness of a great magnitude is bound, in this hypothesis, to the consciousness of a superior good. [143]

The myth of innocence can thus be broken down as the belief that "evil does not penetrate" the American way of life, evidenced by its economic, political, cultural, and technological superiority. We can see, then, how an ideology of innocence operates as the engine that drives ambition and, simultaneously, fear of the other and the foreign.

We can also see how these expressions of superiority play out in contemporary political attitudes: Nativist objections toward immigrants, segregationist social policies, exclusionary rhetoric, etc., all assume that foreign elements, if allowed to penetrate American culture, will pollute or degrade it, ruining its purity and demeaning its *quantifiable* superiority—others will make America poorer, less technological, more diverse, and less definable. Ultimately, evil is defined as that which penetrates from the outside and, once inside, changes, modifies, or erases; all otherness, the alien, the stranger, the foreign, is *evil* and, as such, must be kept at a distance—marginalized, abolished, suppressed, oppressed, or destroyed—if American superiority (that is, its innocence) is to be preserved.

In Portilla's time, American superiority (and its grounding myth, i.e., the myth of innocence) played out most prominently in popular culture, and in particular in certain characteristic themes in American films and literature. Portilla gives us two examples that are worth mentioning: the hero and the detective.

2.2. CASTING OUT THE DARKNESS: THE HERO

> The American hero always appears justified, he is the center that determines the sense of the world that surrounds him, and in determining this sense he becomes the lord of that world. The "others" cannot take a point of view on him that is not easily surpassed by the most elemental moral judgment and precisely by a moral judgment; the others are *evil*, they desire evil, the American hero wants the good, and it can be said that,

more than desiring it, he embodies it, this is his strength; his weakness is that he sits precisely in the "outer darkness" where evil has an important place and therefore can corner him and put him in difficulties so serious that can only be bettered with the providential arrival of steel angels, aerial fortresses, which at the end of the film appear as a glorious and roaring symbol of light and the good, cleanliness and order. [144]

The appearance of the hero in American cinema is emblematic of a culture already obsessed with its own superiority and its own purity (its innocence). The hero is the self-justified, world-constituting, "lord of the world" who, as morally perfect and morally blameless, offers himself as warrior against evil and darkness; those who threaten his life, his superiority and purity, are the enemy, they are "evil, they desire evil," and thus his battle is good and "glorious." The hero *is* American exceptionalism personified. His eventual victory over the forces of evil—over the *others*—is thus more than a victory of good vs. evil, it is the victory of purity and light over "outer darkness"—over the outside, over the not-I.

In the fictional world of "super" heroes, the outer darkness is the birthplace of villains and destroyers of worlds. In the modern world of alarmist propagandists on cable news and social media, the outer darkness is beyond the border of the nation, where darker skins reside, where accents and the poor thrive, where the light of innocence does not shine. This is likewise the birthplace of bad guys and corrupters, the unclean and the impure, of them who appear disguised as Mexican immigrants, Central American, African, and Middle-Eastern refugees, and other environmental and economic exiles. The hero's task is to cast these others out, to cast out the dark and maintain the privilege of light.

Ultimately, the fictional hero of American cinema embodies all that is essential in the symbolism of what is called the "American Way of Life": innocence (he is not evil), purity (he is clean, has a "feeling of purity [*incontaminación*]" [146]), and superiority (he is *better than* because he has *more than*).

2.3. CLEANLINESS AND ORDER

2.3.1. *The Detective*

While the hero in American cinema is an embodiment of an American consciousness that believes itself to be superior in *being* over all others, the detective in American crime novels is the embodiment of the culture's belief that it is superior in *knowledge* and *ability* over all others.

According to Portilla, the American crime novel treats crime, or what's the same, social "evil," not as a general condition of human coexistence or, more particularly, as a result of social inequities or personal psychoses, but as a technical issue, one that can be solved by technical means, i.e., in laboratories, through the meticulous examination of evidence, etc. With the proliferation of crime novels, and thus with the proliferation of the myth of evil as a technical matter to which an entire science (namely, forensics) is devoted, Americans hold on to the truth of their myth of innocence, believing that through technical means they can cleanse their social life of any corruption or contamination; in other words, through the procedures of forensics, the belief is affirmed via fictional detectives that evil can be reduced to a science and, because of this reduction, the purity of innocence can be maintained. Portilla writes:

> the detective novels remind one that there is a whole scientific world, with laboratories full of precision instruments and perfectly trained and capable men who keep crime on the periphery of the world. [148]

2.3.2. *Psychoanalysis*

Related to the detective novel, at least in what it represents in the American imaginary, psychoanalysis is another way in which Americans protect their innocence. If a foundational innocence is not threatened by a real other, alien and external to the self, then the threat may very well come from an imagined, or suppressed, other *internal* to the self. This threat comes in the form of neuroses, such as anxiety, depression, obsessive compulsion, and other emotional or psychological conflicts that contaminate one's unconscious life. Despite their immateriality, these neuroses have presence, and so their expulsion from the individual body becomes necessary to maintain the appearance of innocence in the body politic.

The procedure for removing this threat to one's inner purity is psychoanalysis. According to Coriat,

> [Psychoanalysis] is the study of man's unconscious motives and desires as shown in various nervous disturbances and in certain manifestations of every-day life in normal individuals . . . [which] influence the formation of character traits, but likewise are responsible for many forms of nervous illness.[7]

To a people obsessed with its own innocence, it is the unknown and strange (in this case, one's own "unconscious") that represents the greatest danger to one's integrity in the form of "disturbances" and "illness." Psychoanalysis promises to rid the individual of these *evils*.

Moreover, if innocence itself is the absence of guilt, and guilt is an unconscious expression of a more dangerous disturbance, then psychoanalysis, as the procedure whereby guilt is removed from the unconscious, allows Americans to stay innocent; it allows them the opportunity to renew their purity again and again in repeated acts of self-cleansing.

Both the detective novel and psychoanalysis represent the accomplishment of keeping evil on the periphery of the world. Both keep innocence intact, both keep American culture pure from contamination; both represent the work that goes into keeping American spirit *clean*. That is, Portilla conceives the American fascination with therapy (psychoanalysis) and crime solving as representing the cultural obsession with cleanliness.

> Psychoanalysis and the detective novel can therefore be interpreted as a technical dressage of evil, but such domestication can only occur when an innocent world has previously been postulated. Banishing evil to the periphery of being and controlling it with psychological and police techniques, all that remains is, literally, to wash our hands. [148]

This idea that to stay clean, and more importantly, to stay *spiritually* clean, all one has to do is engage in certain techniques of self-care or self-cleansing is an American idea rooted in the not-so-humble belief in an always already superior spiritual constitution. Thus, in American cinema, the hero himself, who is always already ontologically superior to his enemies, is revealed at the end of the film to be smart, insightful into the ways of good and evil, and handsome (and, thus, impeccably clean). (We need not look too hard for examples: Mel Gibson's character in the *Lethal Weapon* series comes to mind, "Dirty Harry," and even Ethan Hawke's character in *Traffic*. [Notice that all are male, White, and "all-American."])

3. The Limits of Innocence

The ideology (or, we can also say, myth) of innocence is thus reproduced in popular culture through the tropes of heroism, cleanliness, and order.

As these tropes are repeated and institutionalized into culture and tradition, so is the belief that the greatest enemy to the American way of life is whatever threatens that tradition; that the greatest threat is *whatever doesn't work* toward the maintenance and continual justification of that tradition; and that anything that threatens the tradition is, by definition, evil and, ultimately, un-American.

Ultimately, the ideology of innocence justifies a naive view about American life held by many who espouse the dangers of the threat of otherness, namely, that when unthreatened and undisturbed, this way of life "exists" as a homogenous and harmonious coherence of sameness. That is, that unhindered by external influences, by alien or surprising strangeness, Americans (again, White US Americans) *are* one people, with one culture, innocent and great in their ways, with a supreme morality, prudence, work ethic, and divine ability to solve problems and expose truth.

According to Portilla, this ideology and its corresponding beliefs can be found at the core of American philosophy itself—that is, in *pragmatism*. Portilla (correctly) understands pragmatism as the view that a belief will be true when it is verified by its results. However,

> [w]hat is implied in such a conception is a naive trust that everything will go well. To refer truth to its practical results is possible only on the assumption that the practical results will eventually reflect the Truth with a capital "T". That is, it is possible only on the naive belief that man will not lose his way. The truth depends on behavior, but the criterion of that behavior, not expressed philosophically but revealed in this conception itself, is the good diffused in a world where evil has no place.
>
> Pragmatism can only be sustained under the assumption that men will propose only morally valid ends. It is only within a community composed of substantially virtuous men that it is possible to postulate the action of men as a criterion of the good and of truth.
>
> Pragmatism is representative, on a more respectable level, of the same world in which we find the *Happy Ending* of US American filmmaking. Relatively speaking, both pragmatism and cinema respond to the most serious questions by saying that everything will work out. [150]

As Portilla understands it, at the core of pragmatism itself is that stubborn belief in the American will to goodness, moral uprightness, and innocence. The belief that truth will be verified by the consequences it brings about—by the work it does—speaks to the fundamental belief in the goodness of the truth and the righteousness of the work. If the belief, the truth, the proposition, the act—if these are good, then so will be the work that these do, a correlation that forgets that great evil can always be the result of good intentions. As Portilla interprets it, pragmatism is an essentially American philosophy with an essentially American flavor.

In spite of the success of pragmatism as an "American" philosophy, the grounding ideology of innocence is in crisis. To highlight the crisis, Portilla turns to the work of the Protestant theologian Reinhold Niebuhr.

According to Niebuhr's *The Irony of American History* (1952), in the chapter titled, "An Innocent Nation in an Innocent World,"[8] America is a nation founded on the belief that the "outside" world is corrupt and corrupting and that only here, in the US, can one find shelter from the corruption. However, as history advances, and social and economic globalization becomes more and more of a reality, the nation finds itself once again under attack by those old corrupting influences. This is America at a crossroad, *in crisis*, and Niebuhr seeks to locate "the origin of [the] fault, [the] fissure that explains the situation, that is, he undertakes a review of the spiritual foundations of America" [152]. He finds this "fault" in America's geopolitical situation, in the role that it plays in the modern world. America's politics is a politics of power, and a politics of power seems to run counter those values of innocence that are "constitutive of the nation," making it "impossible to maintain the atmosphere in which they flourished" [153]. Niebuhr's conclusion is that "the nation that at one point represented a new beginning in a corrupt world now seems to corrupt itself in the act of imposing on the world its most valued assets" [153]. American innocence, that is, is lost.

Holding on to a primordial innocence amid a complex and evolving historical reality is, of course, a fool's errand. Innocence will be lost at the first difficulty. This explains why innocence must be mythologized, institutionalized, and codified, so that it may survive the reality of its historical decay.

Of course, neither Portilla nor Niebuhr is the first to think critically about innocence. One of the first "American" thinkers to think about America through the trope of innocence was Ralph Waldo Emerson. But his was more of a warning than a description of the state of the American soul. In his *Journals* he tells us that "A man is not to aim at innocence, any more than he is to aim at hair; but he is to keep it."[9] That one should aim to "keep it" suggests that innocence is already marked on the character, like the possibility of hair when one is forming in the mother's womb. Thus, one should not strive to be innocent, as one already is; one should merely strive to hold on to whatever innocence one can, suggesting, of course, that innocence flees and disappears in time, like hair.

But is Emerson telling us that innocence is a virtue proper to Americans (or North Americans)? No. Neither is he telling us that Americans are innocent, only that one should, American or not, hold on to one's innocence. Why? Because in acting from innocence one is fearless, one is unhesitatingly brutal, and direct; that is, presupposing the purity of one's intentions, one also assumes that the consequences, whatever they may be, will likewise be pure—or correct, or *true*. Innocence, as I said above, is aspirational. In "Self-Reliance," Emerson writes,

> The nonchalance of boys who are sure of a dinner, and would disdain as much as a lord to do or say aught to conciliate one, is the healthy attitude of human nature. A boy is in the parlour what the pit is in the playhouse; independent, irresponsible, looking out from his corner on such people and facts as pass by, he tries and sentences them on their merits, in the swift, summary way of boys, as good, bad, interesting, silly, eloquent, troublesome. He cumbers himself never about consequences, about interests: he gives an independent, genuine verdict. You must court him: he does not court you.[10]

This, again, points to that feeling of being *beyond*, of being superior to both others and to nature itself. In the state of innocence of the boy, he is irresponsible precisely because he does not need to respond to or respect limits, which are evil and a constraint on his freedom. In this state, he thinks he is above the rules of causality, and the more he achieves (the more quantity he accumulates) in his irresponsibility, the more his confidence grows that those rules do not apply to him and, that, moreover, his truths are justified in their accomplishment.

However, Emerson does not condone such irresponsibility; he seeks to instill in his (American) readers precisely that missing sense of personal responsibility, respect for causality, and an appreciation of their own freedom. To act from the standpoint of innocence and irresponsibility is the role of the child, not the "man." He continues:

> the man is, as it were, clapped into jail by his consciousness. As soon as he has once acted or spoken with eclat, he is a committed person, watched by the sympathy or the hatred of hundreds, whose affections must now enter into his account. There is no Lethe for this. Ah, that he could pass again into his neutrality! Who can thus avoid all pledges, and having observed, observe again from the same unaffected, unbiased, unbribable . . . innocence, must always be formidable. He would utter opinions on all passing affairs, which being seen to be not private, but necessary, would sink like darts into the ear of men, and put them in fear.[11]

Here, Emerson highlights what happens when innocence is lost. One is taken for one's word; one is watched and judged; one is partisan and one is biased; one is no longer formidable. As such, innocence is lost at the first sign of man's maturity, when he learns to make promises, to keep them, and thus exposes his vulnerability to the world—he exposes his human weakness, i.e., the necessity to do evil and to have evil done to him.

Philosophically, then, the idea of innocence is only that—an idea. The mythology of this idea, or ideal—the ideology of innocence—is ultimately a form of religious sentimentality that has no ground in actual, concrete reality. Hegel, in his *Lectures on the Philosophy of Religion*, talks about the "original state of innocence"[12] that could be found only in Adam's Paradise, where purity without sin was conceived for the sake of maintaining the coherence of the story. The moment that Adam and Eve are expelled from Paradise, and freedom of the will enters the picture, so does *guilt*, which is opposite of innocence. Hegel writes:

> the state of innocence consists in the fact that nothing is good and nothing is evil for human beings; it is the state of the animal; paradise is in fact initially a zoological garden; it is the state where there is no accountability or capacity for guilt, and this is now the human state. "Guilt" means in general "holding to account."[13]

Hegel's description suggests that innocence and freedom are incompatible in practice: If America is innocent, then it cannot be free. This paradox is unaccounted for in America's conception of itself as innocent. In fact, freedom is thought to be our most cherished value, that which defines the American way of life itself.

But according to Hegel, innocence describes an immediacy with being that precludes the self-awareness required to *hold (someone) into account*—it precludes ethics itself. In the "original condition" where innocence operates, there is a "perfect . . . unity with nature" that describes a state of nature, without law, without self-consciousness, without separation.

> It is only when the two are separated, when I am for myself and things are outside of me, that things become enveloped in the bark of sense that separates me from them, and nature erects a screen before me.[14]

Separation, which is the actual condition of socialized being (i.e., in her alienation from nature), is thus the end of innocence and the beginning of ethical life. Thus, for Hegel, ethical life and innocence are ultimately incompatible (as are freedom and innocence). Hegel's suggestion is that

> this innocence is not genuinely human existence. Free ethical life is not the same as the ethical life of the child, and is at a higher level than this form of innocence; it is self-conscious volition, a willing that determines its purpose for itself by thoughtful insight. In the ethical realm this is the first genuine relationship. Just by being free will, human beings have passed beyond this state of innocence.[15]

Hegel's declaration that innocence does not represent "genuine" human life points to the fact that innocence is assumed as always as an ideal—something to strive for, something to seek to hold on to, as Emerson says, but something that is, essentially, not *real*. Ethics itself requires the loss of innocence. Thus, a nation that truly thinks itself innocent will not have the moral vision to reach outside of itself in acceptance or care of others—*it will lack an ethical will.* The American way of life as innocent and pure is, consequently, a closed life, one that must reject "genuine relationships," and as such, is not free.

4. Innocent Superiority

Why have I titled this chapter "The Politics of Innocence"? In short, because innocence, according to Portilla, grounds the manner in which America (or, more precisely, the United States) positions itself as a geopolitical entity. The ideology of innocence dictates the political stance America takes toward its neighbors, toward strangers and friends alike. Innocence is thus political. That is, as we reflect with Portilla on innocence and its various manifestations (heroism, cleanliness, exception, superiority, etc.), we see how the ideology of innocence can ground political positions as extreme as eugenics or White supremacy.

In recent years, the issue of superiority—specifically, the question of White superiority—has re-entered the national conversation in the US. We can locate the desire to *claim* racial superiority in the narrative of innocence that says that innocence is pure and that purity must reject otherness as corrosive and corrupting; it says that otherness is not innocent, but *guilty* of some evil, and so it must be blamed for whatever befalls the innocent. This motivates Portilla to think about race and race relations in the US: "We note, however, that the basis of racial discrimination is precisely that refusal of the White man to assume his guilt" [147]. This is an important insight, as it suggests that "the White man" truly does believe that he is free from any blame that might befall him in relation to his history of oppression and slavery and that, ultimately, he is blameless (i.e., innocent).

Pursuant to this insight we can make declarations like the following: An extreme manifestation of a *politics* of innocence is White supremacy. That is, the way that innocence is forced into the social imaginary is meant to uphold a view of racial superiority that benefits the "White man," understood as *any* individual who believes himself corruptible by otherness and difference because of a claim to an original purity.

Still, even if Americans are not *in fact* innocent, the next question is: What role does this belief play in the organization of our social and political life? More interestingly, what happens when such a contingent virtue is used as the basis for politics or for the political foundation of American culture itself?

What we get is American exceptionalism, or the belief that US culture is unlike any other, that its history is unlike any other, and that its "way of life" is unlike any other. While corruption, death, and the weakening of institution is the fate of all nations and all cultures, America thinks itself the exception. This exception extends to what it can and cannot get away with: imperialism, manifest destiny, empire—these are to be held not as moral stains on the American cultural spirit, but as rights of privilege.

American innocence and American exceptionalism are two sides of the same ideological coin. And they depend on each other. As a "real" American, one believes oneself to be exceptional, to be an exception, because of a fundamental innocence that can be traced back to the purity of the American spirit in relation to Europe and to native cultures; as a "real" American, one believes oneself to be innocent, free of guilt, *because* one is the exception—because everyone else is guilty, or corrupt, or unworthy.

Daniel Bell conceives American exceptionalism as an inability to recognize that maturity means being responsible and committed to the needs of others and not only to the needs of oneself. Exceptionalism is a selfishness, an irresponsible narcissism, that blinds itself to the realities of both history and the actual world. Bell writes, "America was the exemplary once-born nation, the land of sky-blue optimism in which the traditional ills of civilization were, as Emerson once said, merely the measles and whooping cough of growing up."[16] This idea of being a "once-born nation" is the one that justifies a belief in the original uniqueness of America, in its perpetual innocence. A nation must be "twice-born"—first through a founding and then through "reflection and commitment" born of struggle—in order to enter maturity. In other words, as Emerson tells us above in "Self-Reliance," the innocence of youth—of a once-born nation—must be lost in order to be born again, to be, Bell says, "humanized among the nations."[17] Without self-reflection and commitment (to others, to principles of inclusion and justice), America will continue to exempt itself from sin and so think itself *first*; as first, *best*; as best, *superior*; and as superior, *innocent*. And maturity, its humanization, will be a long ways away.

5. Conclusion: Innocence in the Twenty-First Century

In the twenty-first century, the ideology of innocence continues to function as a ground for US policy and public opinion. After the catastrophe of September 11, 2001, which some would say represented the interruption of the peaceful and serene progress of US history, while others would insist was an attack on American innocence itself,[18] anti-immigrant sentiment, which had been there for hundreds of years, became policy. A social narrative took hold that said that immigrants—those among us and those without—were intent on destroying our *way of life* and thus something had to be done. To sway public opinion, the media and lawmakers didn't have to do much, since all their work was ready to hand in the archives of America's (darker) history. Anti-immigrant myths abound, and most of these speak of what immigrants will do to the purity, innocence, and greatness of this "once-born nation." Immigrants, the myths go, *corrupt* what is otherwise pure and clean. What results is anti-immigrant legislation that harkens back to a fabled time of peace and flourishing among the people and creatures of an American Eden. Immigrants, as intruders, as uninvited guests to this (Impossible) Eden, are thus configured by the ideology as impure, inferior, parasitic, and threatening. Immigration, says the ideology, weakens America. A politics of innocence thus asks itself how America can become great (which is to say, innocent) again. And its answer is simple: rid itself of all corrupting influences—namely, immigrants.

The ideology and corresponding politics of innocence thus seek to protect an innocence inscribed in America as a "once-born," young and innocent, nation. The Southern Poverty Law Center (SPLC), which monitors hate groups all across the US, refers to those who profess this ideology as "nativists."[19] This moniker directly references an unjustifiable belief that White US Americans are somehow *original* or native to the nation-state. The nativists that the SPLC monitors are not, of course, the *Native Americans* of the Cherokee or Sioux Nations or the Acoma or Laguna Pueblos, who are historically "native" to the US; the nativists are usually US citizens who define their existential and social position *in opposition* to non-citizens, or immigrants. They are native in virtue of not (currently) being immigrants. It is a weak nativism that nonetheless finds in the immigrant other a threat to an imagined purity and innocence that is usually associated with the historical romanticized threat to purity and innocence that White Europeans posed to *true* Native American peoples.

Nativists usually espouse a litany of myths to legitimate their anti-immigrant ideology. Aviva Chomsky lays out 20 such myths, among them the myth that immigrants take American jobs (Myth 1), the myth that "illegal" immigrants have overrun the country (Myth 8), the myth that immigrants threaten the national culture (Myth 12), and the myth that immigrants want to take for themselves what Americans have (Myth 14).[20] In one way or another, these myths are grounded on the notion of America as superior and exceptional and thus possessing everything that is best and desirable (Myths 1 and 14) but also innocent and vulnerable (Myths 8 and 12). If immigrants are thought to threaten the "national culture," then this is because it is thought that they will contaminate this (presumably "original" and pure) culture with their own, alien, culture by introducing traditions, languages, and ways of being that are other, strange, and disrupting. Moreover, if "illegal" immigrants have "overrun" the country, as Myth 8 suggests, then not only is the national culture threatened, but so is the law that protects it, since what we have is an infestation of illegality, a pestilence of law-breakers running loose in our clean, pure, and innocent cities! Both of these myths, however, are grounded on a somewhat paradoxical assumption, namely, that America is the greatest country in the world and, simultaneously, that it is the most vulnerable country in the world. If the "national culture" or the laws that support it can so easily be threatened or broken, then this means that neither was strong nor fit to begin with.

Anti-immigrant sentiment in the US points to the *fear* that the "national culture" will lose the privilege of its innocence. And this fear, Portilla suggests, points to guilt—a guilt, prominently inscribed in history, related to not taking responsibility for its own behavior, for the lives of others outside its borders who should remain anonymous but who, on "illegally" crossing the border, lose their anonymity and become real, flesh-and-blood human beings *who must be faced*. The myths are meant to de-realize the immigrant, to objectify them, to mask their faces. But this guilt also points to the means whereby America can become responsible for itself and others. Portilla writes:

> There are good reasons therefore to assume that if US Americans now consider themselves vulnerable *as Americans*, this is certainly a sign that the assumption of innocence of the US American world, if not completely gone, at least is beginning to lose its efficacy. I do not mean to say, then, that the main tenet of US American life has ceased being innocence and has become guilt. This would not be a crisis but a conversion. [154]

Such a conversion would mean that America is now "humanized among the nations," as Bell puts it. But Portilla doubts that such a humanizing conversion can ever take place. Thus, he writes by way of conclusion:

> It remains alien to our purpose to point to solutions or ways out of the crisis.
>
> What we can say is that if the resolution of the crisis is understood in terms of America's participation in that guilt

common to all humanity, a guilt that would be fully accepted by that nation, then we can also say that such a solution involves a conversion capable of subverting the very foundations of that culture, and, of course, this seems highly unlikely. [156]

∼

The ideology of innocence that Portilla diagnoses is one that obscures truth and reality. The politics of innocence, the policies and behaviors that emerge from the ideology, are likewise blind to the realities of our modern world. If assuming a sense of guilt is the way out of this false self-conception, then this would mean that America (US White America) would have to assume responsibility for what it has done in the name of innocence: It would mean taking responsibility for those it has harmed on its way to achieving its self-proclaimed greatness. However, as Portilla points out, and as we can readily see today, this ideology and its politics is deeply ingrained in our social imaginary—purity, incorruptibility, heroism, strength, and greatness are still ways of describing the US American way of life and still provide reasons to protect it. This presumed innocence continues to operate and prevent the US from becoming humanized among nations.

Notes

1. Jorge Portilla, "The Spritual Crisis of the United States," translated by Carlos Alberto Sánchez and Francisco Gallegos. Translation included in the appendix. Page numbers in brackets refer to the 1984 Spanish edition of this work included in *Fenomenología del relajo y otros ensayos*.

2. That Portilla refers to "White US Americans" is not as obvious as I'm making it out to be. See chapter 4, below.

3. Deborah L. Madsen, *American Exceptionalism* (Jackson: University of Mississippi Press, 1998), 3. Madsen writes that the idea of an "untouched innocence" "permeates every period of American history . . . it is the single most powerful agent in a series of argument concerning the identity of America and Americans" (1).

4. See Ana Santos Ruiz, *Los hijos de los dioses: El "Grupo Filosófico Hiperión" y la filosofía de lo mexicano* (Mexico City: Bonilla Artigas Editores, 2016).

5. See Louis Althusser, *On Ideology*, trans. Ben Brewster (London: Verso, 2008).

6. Horold H. Koh, *On American Exceptionalism* (New Haven: Yale Law School Legal Repository, 2013), 1480–1526. The term "American exceptionalism" is credited to Alexis de Toqueville who, in 1831, defined it as "the perception that the US differs qualitatively from other developed nations because of its unique origins, national credo, historical evolution, and distinctive political and religious institutions" (1481n4).

7. Isador H. Coriat, *What is Psychoanalysis?* (Abingdon, UK: Routledge, Trench, Troubner & Co., 1919), 12.

8. See Reinhold Niebuhr, *The Irony of American History* (Chicago: University of Chicago Press, 1952), especially chapter 2.

9. Ralph Waldo Emerson, *The Journals and Miscellaneous Notebooks: Volume XIII, 1852–1855*, ed. Ralph H. Orth and Alfred Ferguson (Cambridge, MA: Harvard University Press, 1977), 444.

10. Ralph Waldo Emerson, "Self-Reliance," in *The Works of Ralph Waldo Emerson: Essays, Lectures, Poems, and Orations* (London: George Bell and Sons, 1883), 20.

11. Emerson, "Self-Reliance," 20.

12. G. W. F. Hegel, *Lectures on the Philosophy of Religion*, trans. P. G. Hodgson (Berkeley: University of California Press, 1988), 211.

13. Ibid., 214.

14. Ibid., 239–240.

15. Ibid., 244.

16. Daniel Bell, *The Winding Passage: Sociological Essays and Journeys* (New Brunswick, NJ: Transaction Publishers, 1991), p. 271.

17. Bell, *The Winding Passage*, 271.

18. As Frederick Allen wrote for *Forbes* in his appropriately titled editorial, "September 11 and American Innocence: What Really Happened to US?": "The other day at the Republican debate, Jon Huntsman said "I think we have had our innocence shattered" by what happened on September 11, 2001. On *Morning Joe* the journalist Tina Brown called the date "the last moment of American innocence," and Mike Barnicle described it as "the end of our metaphorical summer as a country." Frederick E. Allen, "September 11 and American Innocence: What Really Happened to US?" *Forbes*, September 9, 2011.

19. See Southern Poverty Law Center, "Anti-Immigrant," accessed January 23, 2020, www.splcenter.org/fighting-hate/extremist-files/ideology/anti-immigrant.

20. Aviva Chomsky, *"They Take Our Jobs!" And 20 Other Myths About Immigration* (Boston: Beacon Press, 2007).

Chapter 4

Portilla's Method

A Phenomenological Social Theory

Francisco Gallegos

In the 1952 essay "The Spiritual Crisis of the United States," Jorge Portilla offers a critical analysis of the U.S., based in part on what he observed when visiting the country earlier that year.[1] As we saw in the previous chapter, Portilla argues in this essay that everyday life in the US has historically been structured by a deep-seated "innocence," a certain kind of naivety in which "sin, evil, and death" are experienced as being fundamentally "foreign"—not *unknown*, exactly, but *un-owned*, treated as though such things were not natural or proper parts of the "American Way of Life." According to Portilla, however, there are signs that this innocence is beginning to disintegrate, and that the nation as a whole is confronting the possibility that it is, in fact, culpable and vulnerable in ways that it had previously dismissed. Portilla describes this change as a "spiritual crisis" that threatens to undermine the foundation of social and political life in the US, and he warns that this crisis may give rise to dangerous, defensive reactions by those who seek to cling to, preserve, and renew the innocence that now seems to be under threat.

This analysis of the US exemplifies Portilla's commitment to what I have called "phenomenological nationalism," the view (examined in detail in chapter 2) that individuals' sense-making capacities are mediated and structured by their nationality. In particular, Portilla argues that the way individual US Americans interpret and relate to the world is profoundly influenced by certain affective attunements—namely, innocence and, increasingly, *threatened innocence.* Portilla highlights several ways these affective attunements manifest themselves, and by thinking *with* Portilla, we can identify similar trends that have emerged since the essay's publication. In US politics today, for example, we can find threatened innocence on the Right in the form of defensive hostility toward those who criticize the nation. On the Left, threatened innocence animates a sanctimonious preoccupation with the nation's guilt and a puritanical tendency to blame and demonize those who appear to personify and defend the nation's worst qualities—as though "they" were the greatest obstacle preventing the nation from finally claiming the innocence that is proper to it. Portilla's analysis thus suggests that the fate of individual US Americans is tied to the fate of their nation, but that crude political nationalism, naive idealism, or an insistence on "American exceptionalism" is not what is needed. Rather, the crucial question is: Can the US, as a nation, develop the emotional maturity required to accept, and come to terms with, its participation in the sin, evil, and death common to all humankind?

In this chapter, I shift the focus from the content and conceptual framework of Portilla's analysis of the US to the *methodology* that he employs in this text. The topic of Portilla's methodology is likely to be a salient point of interest to many of his readers. His conclusions are bold and troubling, and so it behooves us to inquire about whether they are well grounded. When we do so, we see that many of his conclusions rest on empirically verifiable assertions, such as his assertions that certain attitudes and behaviors are widespread in the US but not present to the same degree in other nations. Yet Portilla was not trained as a sociologist, anthropologist, or ethnographer. With this in mind, we may wonder: On what grounds does he make assertions about the characteristic and distinctive features of US society and culture? To put the question provocatively, we might ask: What, if anything, distinguishes Portilla's analysis of the US (and other nations) from *amateur, armchair social science?* In less pointed and more general terms, how should we describe Portilla's approach to cultural analysis, and how should we evaluate the credibility and merit of his approach?

In section 1, I begin by sketching the methodological principles that appear to guide Portilla's analysis of the US. After clarifying some of the central elements of what I call Portilla's "phenomenological social theory," I turn in section 2 to an examination of Portilla's innovative use of phenomenology, highlighting several ways that his analysis, which focuses on phenomenological structures operating at a *national* level, compares and contrasts with a more traditional approach to the phenomenology, which typically focuses on the experience of individuals. Finally, in section 3, I raise a few concerns regarding Portilla's empirical claims about life in the US. In my view, Portilla's analysis would have been strengthened if he had acknowledged the diversity of the US and explicitly directed his focus toward the "innocence" of the *White mainstream* of US society. Moreover, I argue that his account overlooks some reasons to suspect that this social group has *always* experienced its innocence as being "in crisis." If this is correct, it suggests that Portilla was mistaken to conclude that in 1952 he was witnessing a historical shift in the existential foundations of the US American way of life.

Whatever we conclude about these potential oversights, however, I believe that Portilla's analysis offers a rich resource for those who seek a deeper understanding of the US. His analysis points directly to one of the deepest puzzles about this nation: How can it be that a nation that is founded on such grave injustices as the genocide of Native Americans, the enslavement and mistreatment of generations of African Americans, and the violent domination and exploitation of people around the world, can maintain—however tenuously, defensively, and neurotically—a conception of itself as innocent, and indeed, as an indispensable force for moral righteousness in the world? Although Portilla's essay leaves unanswered many of the questions it raises, they are, at least, the right questions to ask. As we will see, pursuing the conversation that Portilla has initiated promises to shed light on the underlying logic behind some of the contradictory attitudes about matters of justice that animate US Americans—and perhaps point the way toward a more authentic American redemption.

1. Portilla's Analytical Strategy

Because Portilla rarely reflected explicitly about his methods, interpreters must rely on their own inferences in order to extract the general principles that appear to guide his reasoning in particular cases. In this section, I begin by sketching my view of Portilla's analytical strategy, and then I offer a few observations about what I see as some of the most innovative, problematic, and fecund aspects of his approach.

1.1. Portilla's Argument by the Steps

Portilla's line of reasoning in "The Spiritual Crisis of the United States" can be divided into two stages. In the first stage, Portilla argues that for much of US history, life in the US has taken place within what he calls "an innocent world," and as such, it has been profoundly and pervasively influenced by a distinctive phenomenological structure that operates at a national level. In the second stage, Portilla argues that this innocent world is now "in crisis," i.e., that it is becoming destabilized and is possibly on the verge of collapsing.

Each of these two stages of Portilla's argument involves three steps, which we can call *observation, generalization,* and *transcendental speculation.* In the first stage of his argument, Portilla begins by making observations about particular, manifest behaviors and attitudes of US Americans, such as:

- A naive lack of appreciation for the reality of death [146], and a desire for narratives to have "happy endings" [150];

- An arrogant sense of entitlement to power over others [151];

- A valorization of quantification and the assumption that bigger is always better [142];

- A valorization of action, initiative, and enterprise, and an insistence on thinking about life's challenges as *problems* that can and should be *solved* [144].

The next stage of Portilla's argument, which I call "generalization," remains implicit in the text. Generalization refers to the claim that the behaviors and attitudes that have been observed are representative of general trends in the US, or as Portilla puts it at one point, that they belong to "the US American in general" [146]. Portilla never explicitly defends the idea that the tendencies he observes have, in fact, been characteristic and distinctive of the US throughout its history—i.e., widespread in this nation, but not widespread in other nations—but his argument depends on this assumption. After all, if the behaviors and attitudes he observed were merely idiosyncratic to the particular individuals involved, or perhaps were common to only a small section of the population, then Portilla would have no grounds for making any claims about life in the US as a whole.

Thus, even though Portilla often runs together the steps of observation and generalization, I distinguish these steps here in order to highlight, for the benefit of future readers and scholars, the importance of Portilla's implicit assumption that his observations generalize.[2] As we will see in section 3 of this chapter, I find this assumption to be particularly problematic.

The final step of this stage of Portilla's argument involves what is known as "transcendental" reasoning—that is, reasoning about *conditions of possibility*. In this case, Portilla attempts to identify, through *a priori* reflection, the conditions that make it possible for US Americans to exhibit the characteristic and distinctive tendencies that he has observed. He asks: What conditions would give rise to these tendencies? In answer to this question, Portilla draws on the phenomenological notion of a "world," arguing that the behaviors and attitudes he has observed could only be possible if everyday life in the US took place within a world that was innocent, organized around a "peculiar feeling of purity, of unfamiliarity with the somber facts of existence, facts which are supposed to be absent from US American life" [146]. This line of transcendental reasoning appears repeatedly in the text. For example, as we saw in the previous chapter, Portilla begins the essay by recounting the story of Dr. Eaton, a funeral director in California who commissions a portrait of Jesus smiling with joy, thereby revealing his obliviousness to the significance of Jesus as a religious symbol of martyrdom.[3] Portilla argues that the idea to commission such a painting was "very original, and it is almost certain that Dr. Eaton's strange pretense has not occurred to anyone outside the United States" [141]. Just as Dr. Eaton's line of reasoning would be unthinkable for those who do not share his innocence, so, too, Portilla says, the characteristically American assumption that *bigger is better* only makes sense within an innocent world.

> The condition of possibility for considering quantity as the criterion of value is precisely an innocent world. . . . In a world conscious of evil, magnitude does not say anything; it is axiologically mute and may even take on a sinister aspect. Consider, for example, the dimension of apocalyptic beasts in the Tower of Babel, or the somber aura of giants in Greek mythology or the world of Germanic sagas. [143]

Portilla makes the same kind of claim with regard to many other phenomena, saying that the existence of a world marked by innocence is the condition for the possibility of American pragmatism,[4] the doctrine of Manifest Destiny,[5] the cultural preoccupation with sex, psychoanalysis, crime, and detective novels,[6] and so on. Portilla thus concludes that there is a phenomenological structure—that is, a certain kind of world—operating at a national level, making it possible for individuals in the US to think, feel, and act in the ways he has observed. Thus, if Portilla's reasoning is correct, we can expect that "the idea of innocence *serves* to make sense of almost every particular nuance of that [US American] way of life" [142].

This completes the first stage of Portilla's argument. But Portilla is not yet finished, because he observes a second set of behaviors and attitudes among US Americans that appears to contradict the notion that everyday life in the US takes place within an innocent world. For example, he observes:

- The emergence of numerous academic and popular critiques of the US, its history, values, and actions [152ff];

- Defensive reactions to such critiques, including McCarthyist attempts to persecute individuals and ideas that are perceived as threats to the dominant values of the nation [154f];

- A shift in political discourse, in which the source of justification for the US American way of life is located in the past, instead of in the future [156].

Once again, Portilla implicitly assumes that these observations generalize—i.e., that these behaviors and attitudes represent a historically new and increasingly widespread set of tendencies within the US. And again, on this basis, Portilla employs transcendental reasoning, inquiring about what conditions would make these changes possible. He argues that these new tendencies could only arise if the innocence of the US was beginning to disintegrate, giving rise to a profound sense of anxiety surrounding the central concern of moral righteousness. For example, he describes a kind of Cold War–era "propaganda" that "pervades all advertising media, according to which we must defend the threatened US American way of life" [153]. Portilla argues that this attitude is only possible in a world in which the underlying assumption of innocence is beginning to disappear.

> Why defend the American way of life and not just speak rather of freedom or human rights?

> More than any other point this one appears to . . . [reveal] the crisis of US American consciousness. Indeed, only the vulnerable can be defended and, at the very same moment in which the necessity to defend a form of life appears, so does the insufficiency of that form of life. . . . Innocence is by definition invulnerable, and what is invulnerable does not require any defense whatsoever. . . . There are good reasons therefore to assume that if US Americans now consider themselves vulnerable as *Americans*, this is certainly a sign that the assumption of innocence of the US American world, if not completely gone, at least is beginning to lose its efficacy. [153–154]

Portilla thus concludes that a new historical process is undermining the phenomenological structure that has previously organized everyday life in the US.

With this sketch of Portilla's analytical strategy in place, we are now in a position to make some general observations about his methodology.

1.2. Portilla as Social Theorist

As we have seen, each stage of Portilla's argument combines two distinct styles of reasoning. The steps of *observation* and *generalization* are empirical in nature, while the step of *transcendental speculation* is phenomenological. Within the tradition of phenomenology, this particular combination of methodological approaches appears to offer both benefits and drawbacks. On the one hand, by beginning with an empirically informed cultural analysis, Portilla is able to articulate creative insights into a number of pressing issues that have not been explored by other phenomenologists. On the other hand, Portilla's reliance on empirical claims also represents a significant liability for his project. His entire line of thought depends on the accuracy of his observations and on whether he is correct that these observations represent trends that are characteristic and distinctive of the US. However, Portilla is not equipped to demonstrate the validity of these claims; he is in no position, for example, to perform controlled experiments, surveys, or data analysis to compare the behavior and attitudes of US and non-US nationals over time. Thus, the viability of his project ultimately depends on whether future research in the social sciences can demonstrate the validity of his observations and generalizations.

Insofar as Portilla is making claims that directly depend on validation from the social sciences, it is reasonable to wonder what distinguishes his work from mere armchair sociology. After all, it seems undeniable that Portilla does not have sufficient grounds to make conclusive assertions about trends in US culture and society; therefore, if we take Portilla's central aim to be *making conclusive assertions about trends in US culture and society*, then we cannot avoid coming to a negative assessment of the credibility of his approach. However, there is an alternative interpretation of Portilla's project that I find more plausible. According to this interpretation, Portilla's work ought to be understood as an example of what I call "phenomenological social theory"—an approach to theorizing about social and political issues that draws on the tradition of phenomenology in order *to generate concepts and hypotheses* that can guide future research within the social sciences.

There are two elements of this interpretation that may save Portilla from being prematurely rejected for lacking a scientifically adequate methodology. First, if we read Portilla's essay as a work of *social theory*, then its present lack of evidential support can be seen as a feature of its innovativeness, rather than a sign of its inadequacy. After all, social theory always involves some amount speculation in order to enter into the so-called "hermeneutic circle," because articulating the larger significance of a set of facts necessarily requires a leap beyond those facts themselves. Whenever a social theorist attempts to establish a new conceptual framework for interpreting and guiding research in the social sciences, it is inevitable that they will do so "on credit," so to speak, with the promise and hope that future research will demonstrate the fruitfulness of the theory they are proposing. This enables social theorists to avoid—temporarily—objections that they would otherwise have difficulty answering. For example, even if we are compelled by Portilla's examples of US American innocence, a reader might accuse him of simply "cherry-picking" examples that already fit with the theory that he is trying to construct. After all, there are innumerable events that could be observed about everyday life in the US, many of which are utterly insignificant. How, then, does Portilla know which events are significant for the purposes of his theory, unless he is already viewing the data in a motivated and biased way? But although this is a significant concern for any theorist, it is not itself a sufficient reason to reject a theory out of hand. While we might wish that Portilla had been clearer about the principles of selection that guided his acquisition of data points to be explained, nevertheless, he is entitled, *as a theorist*, to take interpretive risks in order to get his theoretical model off the ground.

Understood in this way, every claim that Portilla makes should be thought of as a mere *hypothesis* to be confirmed or disconfirmed by those with the scientific training necessary to reach conclusions about such things. Admittedly, this interpretation of Portilla's work goes against the grain of his writing style, insofar as his pronouncements about life in the US and other nations often have the surface grammar of factual assertions or conclusions. If my interpretation is correct, we should read each of these sentences as being preceded by an implicit qualification, such as *"It is my hypothesis that . . ."* Thus, rather than simply asserting that US Americans have this or that characteristic tendency, Portilla should be read as hypothesizing that future research will show that US Americans have the tendencies he describes. Interpreted in this way, his essay is implicitly voiced in a subjunctive tense, and its ultimate aim is to articulate elements of a theoretical paradigm that may prove to useful for understanding the contemporary world. Ideally it would inspire social scientists to design new controlled experiments, surveys, and data analyses, and to reevaluate the relevant sociological and anthropological literatures, in order to corroborate and refine Portilla's theoretical outlook.[7]

Although Portilla does not have training in the social sciences, such training is not necessarily required of those playing the distinctive role of social theorist. And as a theorist, Portilla certainly has training that ought to give him some initial credibility. His central qualifications are the skills and sensibilities that he has gained from a lifetime of study, reflection, and conversation with intelligent and well-educated interlocutors about the ways that individuals' experiences can be shaped by both existential structures and socio-historical forces. These interlocutors include, of course, the other members of the Grupo Hiperión, who devoted an extraordinary amount of intellectual effort to understanding the nature and effects of national cultures. Moreover, it is clear that Portilla applied his skills and sensibilities to a massive amount of data about cultural trends in US, collected from careful observations of, and personal interactions with, a wide variety of individuals, institutions, and cultural artifacts in the US. In addition, Portilla's writing demonstrates that he is conversant with the work of some of the most prominent historians and social theorists of the time, including Reinhold Niebuhr and R. H. Tawney.[8]

Besides its *theoretical* nature, a second aspect of Portilla's approach that distinguishes it from pseudoscience is its *phenomenological* nature. Indeed, in my view, Portilla's innovative use of phenomenology is the most fecund aspect of his theorizing. As we will see in the following section, phenomenology can be particularly helpful for understanding the holistic nature of human life. As with any holistic structure, the ways that human beings think, feel, and act can be difficult to understand in terms of the causal interactions of component parts. For example, when seeking to explain a certain social trend, a non-phenomenological explanation—what Portilla calls a "genetic explanation" [143]—will seek to identify the underlying causes or mechanisms that give rise to the trend:

Genetic cause(s) → Particular behaviors and attitudes

However, because human life is so complex, and each individual element of our experience and behaviors is multiply determined by the innumerable elements with which it is interconnected, a genetic explanation is often exceedingly difficult to provide. In contrast, a phenomenological explanation of the same social trend posits the existence of an intermediary structure between the mechanical causes of the trend and the various effects to be explained:

Genetic cause(s) → Phenomenological structure (e.g., a "world") → Particular behaviors and attitudes

Phenomenology, as a discipline, is not in a position to explain why any given genetic causes would give rise to a particular phenomenological structure. That part of the explanation is left to the sciences, with the expectation that we may never fully comprehend the mystery of such emergence. However, phenomenology *is* poised to offer illuminating insight into the underlying logic of the particular behaviors and attitudes in question.[9] Let us turn, then, to a brief examination of how Portilla employs phenomenological concepts and methods in order to illuminate some otherwise perplexing features of the various ways that US Americans tend to relate to matters of morality and justice.

2. A Phenomenology of the Nation

In order to see more clearly what makes Portilla's approach distinctive within the tradition of phenomenology, consider how a phenomenological analysis typically proceeds. Typically, a phenomenological analysis begins with a description of an individual's experience from the first-person point of view; from there, it moves to a transcendental argument about the ontological conditions for the possibility of this experience, often concluding with a characterization of the human condition. We see this pattern, for example, in Heidegger's analysis of the emotion of fear in his classic text, *Being and Time.* In this analysis, Heidegger begins by describing the way an individual *experiences* fear, putting aside considerations of how brain produces this experience or whether the experience is provoked by something that is "objectively real" or "merely imagined." Starting from this first-person perspective, Heidegger notes several interesting aspects of the experience, such as the fact that fear involves the experience of being *threatened.* He then deploys a transcendental argument, saying that any experience of fear must be made possible by a preexisting affective attunement to the concern for safety and security, because without the previous influence of this affective attunement, one would not be disposed to register and respond to things that pose a threat.[10] He concludes that this fact reveals something important about the human condition—namely, that for creatures like us, our experience is always already structured by an implicit awareness of our vulnerability. Thus, vulnerability is not merely something "ontic" (i.e., concrete or particular) that we occasionally confront; rather, vulnerability is an "ontological" structure that mediates and influences the way we experience every particular thing we encounter.

In contrast to this classic approach, Portilla's work does not begin with a description of his own experience; instead, he begins with a description of the experience of a quite large group of people, namely, a nation. From there, Portilla offers a transcendental argument, not about the ontological conditions common to human beings as such, but about the existential conditions common to this particular group. Thus, between the ontic level of an individual's particular experiences and the ontological level of the ground of experience for human beings as such, Portilla posits an intermediary phenomenological structure—the nation, or more precisely, the world that members of a nation inhabit—which modifies the characteristics and potentialities of the human condition in distinctive ways:

- *Surface level:* the particular experiences of individuals (ontic);

- *Intermediate level:* the nation/national world (ontic-ontological);

- *Ground level:* the human condition (ontological).

When we articulate Portilla's approach in this way, two questions come to the fore. First, as I noted above, Portilla's analysis begins with a description of the experience of a group, rather than an individual. With this in mind, we may wonder: Does Portilla operate on the (undoubtedly controversial) assumption that a nation can have experiences—i.e., that a nation constitutes some sort of collective or plural subjectivity that has a kind of "first-person point of view"? Second, how should we think about a phenomenological structure that supposedly operates at an intermediate, ontic-ontological level? In particular, how does Portilla conceptualize a national "world," and in what sense does he think that the existence of such a world makes certain behaviors and attitudes "possible"?

2.1. Nationality and Collective Subjectivity

Does Portilla view nations as collective subjects? This question gains some urgency when we consider that in his essay "Phenomenology of Relajo," Portilla appears to endorse the possibility that experiences can be shared by groups of people. In that essay, Portilla argues that when individuals are participating in a group activity—such as a ballet performance, fiesta, university lecture, ceremony, or conversation—these individuals can experience the situation in a genuinely collective manner, sharing the experience in such a way that, as one philosopher puts it, "the sharing is not a matter of type, or of qualitative identity (i.e., of having different things that are somehow similar), but a matter of token, or *numerical identity*."[11] Portilla suggests that this may happen, for example, when the people in the audience at a ballet performance find themselves moved by the gracefulness of the dance, or when party-goers get swept up in the joyousness of the celebration. In moments like this—when a group of people is swept up in shared mood, responding to an evaluative property (e.g., the *gracefulness* of the dance, or the *joyousness* of the celebration) whose emergence depends, in part, on their own activity—the individuals involved will experience themselves as united together in a profound type of experiential solidarity that Portilla calls "coexistence."[12] Indeed, as we will see in more detail in chapter 6, Portilla argues that such experiences of coexistence are of great importance, because they are the true "foundation of a community."[13]

Nevertheless, although Portilla accepts the possibility that experiences can be shared in some circumstances, he does not claim that entire nations can share an experience in this way. To the contrary, Portilla's analysis of shared experiences provides reason to doubt that a group so large and disparate as a nation could ever constitute a collective subjectivity. The reason is that, because coexistence involves "the continuous self-constitution of a group in reference to a value," coexistence is a fragile state that can easily be disrupted.[14] Indeed, for Portilla, the primary danger posed by certain types of characters, such as the *relajiento* and the *apretado,* lies in their tendency to disrupt the mood that is sustaining a moment of coexistence, thereby undermining the existential foundation of a community.[15] In Portilla's view, the achievement of genuine coexistence is always fragile and fleeting, even in relatively intimate settings, because it requires that the people involved in a group activity orchestrate and navigate a collective mood and thereby sustain a certain kind of emotional engagement over time.

With this in mind, it is difficult to imagine how an entire nation might genuinely share any experience, given how unlikely it is that so many diverse people could be emotionally responsive to anything in a sufficiently similar manner, not to mention participate in a shared activity across such great distances. It is possible, perhaps, that some examples may be found in historic events that galvanize a nation in an extraordinary way. For example, in the immediate aftermath of the terrorist attacks on September 11, 2001, the US may have experienced a genuinely shared mood of anxiety as the nation collectively engaged in the activity of figuring out what had happened and what the implications of the attack would be. Nevertheless, the remarkable depth of national solidarity that is experienced in such moments is rare and relatively short lived. In contrast, the kind of structures that Portilla describes in his analysis of nations—such as the *zozobra* of Mexico and the innocence of the US—are supposed to endure for decades at a time.

It is thus likely that when Portilla undertakes the phenomenological analysis of a nation, he does not think of a nation as constituting a collective subjectivity that has a shared point of view. A better way to understand Portilla's approach, in my view, is to think of it as a kind of speculation about the way that *individuals* within a nation experience themselves and the world. Thus, any assertions that Portilla makes about a "nation" should be interpreted as shorthand for equivalent assertions about "the individuals who are members of the nation." For example, when Portilla talks about the ideals that have "led this nation [the US] to optimism and an unwavering confidence" [150], we should interpret such passages as referring to widespread dispositions among individual US Americans to experience themselves and the world in a certain way—in this case, in an optimistic and confident manner. This interpretation has the virtue of being consistent with Portilla's views regarding shared experiences, as well as the virtue of generosity, insofar as it relieves Portilla of the need to carry the heavy metaphysical baggage associated with positing the existence of large-scale collective subjectivities.

But if a nation is not a collective subject, then what is the organizing force that makes it possible for millions of individuals members of a nation to exhibit the characteristic and distinctive qualities that Portilla has identified?

2.2. Nation, World, and Possibility

In order to clarify Portilla's innovative understanding of "world" and "possibility"—concepts that play a crucial role in his argument—it may be helpful to begin once again with a comparison to Heidegger. One prominent difference, as we will see, is that while Heidegger focuses on *the* world, or perhaps the *human* world, Portilla is interested in what might be called a "sub-world," that is, a world that is inhabited by a certain group of people at a certain historical moment. This difference will have important implications that Portilla's readers will have to work through.

In *Being and Time*, Heidegger defines the "world" as a *context of significance* in virtue of which, and in terms of which, things become *intelligible* and *make sense* in the ways that they do.[16] As one interpreter puts it:

> The world is a horizon of understanding, a space of possibilities, on the background of which we understand both paraphernalia [i.e., the objects that surround us in everyday life, such as tables and phones] and ourselves. . . . The world is a unitary horizon for making sense of both human life and the paraphernalia with which we surround ourselves.[17]

Thus, in Heidegger's view, the world, as a context of significance, makes it possible for things to show up as intelligible objects of our experience. For example, to return to Heidegger's analysis of fear, the human world is one in which our safety and security can be threatened; in other words, the "space of possibilities" that we inhabit includes the possibility of being harmed. This inescapable vulnerability is one element of the context of significance in terms of which we make sense of the things we encounter, and as such, this context of significance makes it possible for us to experience a certain class of objects—namely, *threats*. Imagine, for instance, that we were not already attuned to the concern for our security, perhaps because we had a psychiatric condition that prevented us from understanding why it would matter if things affected our safety and security. In this case, a threat, as such, could never be present in our experience. Even if we were locked in a room with a hungry tiger, the situation would not show up, or make sense to us, as a "threat." Of course, *other* people observing the situation might see us as being threatened, but threats could never show up in our *own* experience, because the possibility of being threatened would not even be intelligible to us. The point is that if something is truly unintelligible to us in this way, we will remain oblivious to it. Heidegger thus conceptualizes the world as our outermost horizon of understanding, which serves as the ultimate condition for the possibility of things showing up in our experience.[18]

However, this does not appear to be the way that Portilla conceptualizes the "innocent world" inhabited by US Americans. If we relied on Heidegger's conception of *world* to interpret Portilla, we would be forced to read Portilla as making the implausible claim that US Americans have been *literally* unable to make sense of the notion that they are subject to death, and that they partake in sin and evil—as though these things were simply unintelligible to US Americans, and so could not even show up in their experience. This idea calls to mind an absurd alternative reality in which US Americans literally do not understand what death is, and so are bizarrely unaffected by the sudden disappearance of their friends and loved ones. Along these lines, Portilla teasingly mentions the preacher Vincent Norman Peale's book *Not Death at All*, the title of which seems to give voice to the innocence of US American in a humorously exaggerated way [146].

A more plausible way to understand Portilla's view, I argue, is to interpret his notion of "possibility" as roughly equivalent to we sometimes call a "live option"—i.e., a possibility for thinking, feeling, or acting that shows up to a person as *reasonable, fitting,* or *viable,* based on the person's prior experiences, and given what appears to matter most in the situation at hand.[19] Put another way, a live option is a possibility that has a significant degree of what I call "normative grip." Normative grip is the sense of being called upon or required to uphold some standard or norm in the way we think or behave, or in the attitudes that we take toward things. When we experience a high degree of normative grip, for example, we might find ourselves so gripped by the importance of acting in a certain way that acting otherwise becomes completely unthinkable. In contrast, when we experience a low degree of normative grip, we might understand in a "merely intellectual" way that a particular action is required or fitting, but find that this thought fails to move us emotionally or to be conclusive in our deliberations about what to do. When we interpret Portilla in these terms, we can describe his view as holding that an innocent world is a context of significance in which certain kinds of attitudes and behaviors—particularly those related to the concern of moral righteousness—appear to be live options, while others appear *not* to be live options. In such a world, the possibility of being vulnerable to sin, evil, and death may be perfectly intelligible, *strictly speaking*, but this possibility nonetheless has little or no normative grip. Individuals who inhabit this world may understand in a "merely intellectual" way that they are collectively responsible for grave injustices, and that life is often tragic and unfair and always ends in death; but if they should consider these thoughts, they are likely to turn their attention elsewhere relatively quickly, without allowing the implications of these ideas to reverberate deeply in their thoughts and actions. In this way, such individuals are like reckless young people who are innocent, in the sense of lacking life experience, and so relatively unresponsive to the possibility of seriously harming other people and being harmed themselves.[20] In contrast, a non-innocent world (such as we might find in Mexico, perhaps) would be a context of significance within which individuals experience themselves as being called upon, with some urgency, to respond in appropriate ways to sin, evil, and death, which have already marked their lives and may appear again at any moment.

2.3. Three Basic Elements of the World of Innocence

Although this way of conceptualizing "world" and "possibility" is not found in Heidegger, we can nonetheless draw from his work in order to develop these concepts further. In *Being and Time*, Heidegger distinguishes three basic aspects of our ability to make sense of our experience: (1) our cognitive and linguistic capacities, (2) our emotional responsiveness, and (3) our practical skills and tools, together with the relevant aspects of our bodies, traditions, and institutions that enable our skills and tools to be effective.[21] In order to make sense of something, it is necessary to have a concept and a word for it, or at least to have a conceptual and linguistic context that is congruent with the development of such a concept and word. Likewise, in order to grasp the meaning of something, it necessary to be able to respond emotionally to the ways the object impinges on one's concerns and values. Lastly, in order for something to be intelligible, there must exist a practical context that enables the thing to function in its characteristic ways. Each of these capacities make it possible for us to have meaningful experiences, and as such, alterations in any of these capacities will alter the limit of what we can understand and experience as real.

One of the most dramatic illustrations of this line of thought is found in Jonathan Lear's discussion of the collapse of traditional way of life of the Crow, an indigenous tribe in North America, in the late nineteenth century.[22] As Lear reports, one important traditional practice for the Crow was the practice of planting a coup-stick, in which Crow warriors would drive a stick into the ground in a mortal vow not to retreat beyond the where the stick was planted. The possibility of performing this action depended on the existence of a context of significance in which this action had meaning. This context of significance is constituted by (1) a vast network of concepts and words, including the concepts and words for *coup-stick, warrior, retreat, death,* and so on, that enable the Crow and their interlocutors to think and talk in meaningful ways about the practice; (2) a widespread disposition to respond emotionally in certain ways to the act of planting a coup-stick and a range of related actions, such as displaying courage or cowardice on and off the battlefield; and (3) an immense assortment of items (including, most prominently, coup-sticks), skills, traditions, and institutions that surrounded and supported the practice of planting a coup-stick and allowed it to have the meaning that it had (including legitimate procedures for determining whether a coup-stick was properly planted and whether the concomitant vow was upheld). The collapse of the Crow traditional way of life meant the disappearance of these cognitive and linguistic capacities, emotional dispositions, skills, tools, traditions, and institutions. The central point, for our purposes, is that without this *context of significance,* it is no longer *possible* to plant a coup-stick. A person can drive a stick into the ground and make a vow not to retreat, but in the absence of this context, such an act will not constitute planting a coup-stick and will not be intelligible to anyone as such.

Lear's analysis is Heideggerian in its focus on the conditions under which something is intelligible or unintelligible, possible or impossible.

But as we have seen, Portilla does not appear to think about innocence in these terms. Indeed, it seems clear that US Americans generally have the cognitive, linguistic, and emotional capacities to make sense (strictly speaking) of their subjection to sin, evil, and death, and likewise, US society already contains the traditions and institutions that would be required for the nation to take accountability for its sins and to respond appropriately to the reality of evil and death.

How, then, might these three basic elements of our sense-making capacities enter into Portilla's analysis? In my view, by distinguishing these three constitutive elements of sense-making, we can see that each of these capacities can be relatively *developed* or *underdeveloped*. We can thus imagine a spectrum or range in a person's or society's capacity to make sense of something in each of these three different ways that sense-making occurs. From this perspective, we can interpret Portilla's view as follows: Everyday life in the US has historically taken place in a context of significance in which these three sense-making capacities are underdeveloped with regard to the task of coming to terms in a genuine, mature, and realistic way, with our inescapable subjection to sin, evil, and death.

On this view, individuals in US society may be able to think and talk about sin, evil, and death, but in general, they have not been able to do so *very well*, in the sense that the meaning of these difficult aspects of human life often fails to reverberate deeply enough to shape what appears as a normatively gripping, live option. It is possible that certain concepts and words have been lacking that would help individuals to track the relevant distinctions and connections. For example, with regard to the capacity to think and talk about injustice, Miranda Fricker has argued that when the term "sexual harassment" came into public use in the 1970s, this concept helped people identify and understand the meaning of a kind of injustice that they had witnessed or experienced but failed to comprehend fully.[23] Today, terms such as "privilege" and "microaggression" are gaining acceptance and contributing to the capacity of US Americans to think and talk about injustice, and surely other terms that could be invented in the future would help as well. In addition to the lack of particular words and concepts, US society may demonstrate a relative lack of diligence and skill with regard to pursuing conversations about these topics over time and across different sectors of society. As a result, US Americans do not normally have access to the cognitive-linguistic environment in which the relevant assertions, questions, requests, and imperatives are able to function in a way that enables individuals to think and talk about injustice very well. A similar set of arguments could be marshaled with regard to the capacity to think and talk about death.

Likewise, according to the interpretation of Portilla's view that I am proposing, while US Americans have access to the basic emotional or practical capacities required to understand sin, evil, and death in a merely intellectual way, they have not developed these capacities as fully as would be required in order for the meaning of these aspects of life to resonate more deeply. With regard to the capacity to respond emotionally to sin, evil, and death, US Americans have suffered from a lack of sufficient opportunities to practice, from a young age and throughout their lives, the emotional skills required for engaging with these themes in a sustained and vulnerable way. As a result, US Americans often lack the "psychosocial stamina" required to respond emotionally to these painful aspects of life without resorting to defensive maneuvers, such as the defensive strategies of dismissal, denial, and problematization discussed in chapter 2.[24] With regard to the capacity to deal with these topics in a practically competent way, US American society has traditions and institutions that can address sin, evil, and death, but these traditions and institutions have generally not been able to do so very well. In courts of law and public opinion, there has been a lack of the precedents, policies, and mechanisms that would be required for dealing with these issues in a practically effective manner.

To summarize, I suggest that what Portilla calls the "innocent world" of the US arises from a lack of development of three modes of making sense of the nation's participation in sin, evil, and death, creating a context of significance in which a range of thoughts, feelings, and behaviors are unable to show up as normatively gripping, live options. This interpretation would help Portilla explain the behaviors and attitudes he observes in the US. For example, Portilla describes the so-called "panty raids" that were apparently common on college campuses in the 1950s, "naive and playful assaults in which young college students seize the most intimate garments of their companions for no other purpose than to display them innocently in the light of day" [147].[25] Using the conceptual tools I have just sketched, we might say that at this time, the possibility of partaking in such a practice showed up to many young men with a high degree of normative grip; at the same time, while these young men might have been able to understand, in a merely intellectual way, why someone might find this practice objectionable, such considerations often failed to resonate deeply or to be conclusive in their deliberations. Thus, we can explain the "ontic" behaviors and attitudes of these young men as a result of the way things showed up to them as meaningful, and we can explain the patterns in their experience of meaning, in turn, with reference to the underdevelopment of certain cognitive, emotional, and practical capacities in US society.

The same type of explanation can be offered for the other behaviors and attitudes that Portilla describes. Concluding a narrative without a happy ending, or forgoing an opportunity to gain power and control, solve a problem, or make something bigger—these possibilities may be intelligible (strictly speaking) to a US American, but they are likely to show up as obtuse or unreasonable. In this way, what I have called Portilla's phenomenological social theory bridges the explanatory gap between the kinds of empirical or genetic causes described by the social sciences and the intimate structure of the experience of individual US Americans. It does so by positing the existence of a *national world* that operates as an intermediate-level phenomenological structure. This national world modifies what is intelligible and possible for human beings as such, shaping the meaning of what is intelligible and possible according to what shows up as a normatively gripping, live option for those individuals whose sense-making activities take place within the context of significance that has been constructed by the members of the nation over the course of its history.

3. The Future of Portilla's Inquiry

While I hope that the above discussion goes some way toward clarifying the methodology that Portilla implicitly relies on in his analysis of the US, there are many questions that remain unanswered—phenomenological questions, empirical questions, and questions about the relationship between the phenomenological the empirical. For example, one set of phenomenology-related questions centers around Portilla's claim that the innocence of the US is "in crisis." What is involved in such a crisis? Is Portilla suggesting that the innocent world that existed in the US for much of its history is simply disintegrating, leaving an unstructured and chaotic context of significance in its place? Or is he suggesting that this innocent world is simply being modified in some fundamental way, while still remaining a coherent context of significance? Alternatively, Portilla may be suggesting that this traditional world is being displaced by the rise of a new world, such as the world of *threatened* innocence. But if the crisis involves the displacement of one world by another, how should we think about the relationship between these two worlds? Do some US Americans occupy one context of significance, while other members occupy a different context of significance—or do some or all US Americans occupy both contexts simultaneously, to some degree?

There are also a number of questions concerning the interpretation of Portilla's conception of a "world" that I proposed above. These questions inquire into the relationship between empirical social practices and institutions, on the one hand, and the phenomenological structures they allegedly generate, on the other. For example, what, specifically, are the concepts, words, and cognitive-linguistic practices that play or could play an important role in supporting or undermining the innocence of US Americans? How, exactly, are US Americans "trained" as emotional agents, and how could they be trained, in order to support or undermine that innocence? And which skills, tools, traditions, and institutions, in particular, play or could play such an important role at the intersection of the ontic and ontological? Much more would need to be said about these issues before Portilla's phenomenological theory could hope to succeed as an explanatory account in the social sciences.

Lastly, many questions remain unanswered regarding the empirical claims on which Portilla's project rests. For example, is it true that the behaviors and attitudes that Portilla describes as being reflective of innocence have, in fact, been characteristic and distinctive of the US for much of its history? And is it true that in 1952 Portilla was witnessing a historical turning point, a crisis in the existential foundation of the US American way of life?

When we step back and reflect on the number and quality of the questions raised by Portilla's work, we can see just how much interpretive work is left to future scholars who seek engage with Portilla's political philosophy. Although some might take this as evidence that Portilla's thinking was not adequately systematic or thorough, I would suggest instead that we see these unanswered questions as a sign of the fascinating philosophical terrain to which Portilla's work will take us, if we accept the invitation to think with him about these pressing issues. In conclusion, then, I will offer a few provocations related to the empirical validity of Portilla's claims.

One glaring mistake in Portilla's analysis of the US, in my view, is his failure to appreciate the diversity of the nation, and in particular, his failure to notice the ways that racial and ethnic minorities in the country have historically resisted validating or partaking in the "innocence" of the dominant, White mainstream.[26] For example, those African Americans who have been subject to slavery and social annihilation never had the luxury of denying the reality of death.[27] Indeed, according to Cornel West, the history of African American culture, music, religion, philosophy, literature, and politics is, in many ways, a history of this community's attempt to come to terms with the tragic and complex nature of life on earth, an attempt to give one another the courage to resist the temptation to dismiss or deny the dark side of the human experience, or to treat it as a mere problem to be solved. For this reason, in contrast to the forms of Christianity that have variously been historically popular among Whites in the US, which tend to be either fundamentalist or naively reassuring, "the black church [places] . . . profound stress on the concrete and the particular—wrestling with limit situations, with death, dread, despair, disappointment, disease, and so on."[28] Indeed, he says, "black evangelical Christianity is primarily concerned with human fallenness" and recognizes that "no individual or society can fully conform to the requirements of the Christian gospel, hence the need for endless improvement and amelioration."[29] In a similar manner, we find in the blues and in funk music (a genre whose very name reminds us of the stench of death and the musk of the living body), as in the writings of Richard Wright, Ralph Ellison, James Baldwin, and Toni Morrison, "candid narratives and painful truths about our all-too-human complicity with evil and evasion of dark realities, which no country or social experiment can ignore without danger."[30]

Likewise, Latinx folks have never been allowed to rest in the comfort of innocence, simplicity, and purity. To the contrary, the most prominent theme of all forms of Latinx self-expression is perhaps *multiplicity*, the pain and beauty of being forced to perpetually cross borders and dwell in a permanent "in-between" place along every dimension of human existence.[31] Moreover, the Latinx community has inherited some of the non-innocence of Latin America, a non-innocence that emerges in ways that are both life-affirming—such as in *Día de los Muertos* celebrations, *rasquache* decor, and a form of Catholicism colored by indigenous animism and Marxism—as well as problematic—such as in the tendencies toward *zozobra*, cynicism, and pessimism so eloquently described by Portilla and his contemporaries.

All of this may lead us to suspect that things are not quite as simple as Portilla suggests, even among the White community. As an outsider looking in, it is perhaps inevitable that Portilla focuses on the images of White innocence that the nation projects most energetically—images from Hollywood films in which White protagonists are confident and capable, while foreigners are villains or buffoons with "big mustaches and exaggerated gestures" [145], or images of White politicians who appear to have no qualms about executing "a program of hegemony reinforced by unprecedented military might" [150]. But on closer examination, we may see that this appearance of White innocence is a facade that is in need of perpetual reinforcement and policing at the margins. As many philosophers of race have argued, Whiteness itself was socially constructed in an incredibly fraught social and political context and has been used as a central tool in the continual effort to maintain an unnatural and cruel economic and cultural system that often seems poised to collapse.[32] If this is true, it would not be surprising to find that White innocence has always been "in crisis" to some extent.[33] Indeed, as one scholar notes, behind the apparent naturalness and neutrality of Whiteness in the White experience is a perpetual contestation of the meaning of Whiteness, reflected, for example, in the history of the US Supreme Court's treatment of Whiteness in immigration law, where we see that "Whiteness is a social construction whose composition changes throughout time and place," granted to particular social groups or rescinded according to the political exigencies of the moment.[34] This line of thought suggests that the signs of threatened innocence that Portilla was observing in 1952 were not, in fact, signs of a historical shift in the existential foundation of the nation, as he claimed, but were simply par for the course.[35]

Perhaps Portilla was simply misled by the common illusion that one's own time is more historically significant than it truly is. But on the other hand, perhaps the present moment always has the potential to be what the Greeks called a *krísis*—the turning point in a disease, in which the patient will either succumb or recover. Today, as social movements in the US are finding new ways to bring the distorting effects of privilege into public awareness, in hopes of teaching the innocent world to see its own innocence with suspicion, only time will tell whether these efforts are simply a continuation of the nation's perpetual fixation upon its own moral status—or the beginning of something new.

Notes

1. This information about the context of the article's production is provided in the introduction to Portilla's anthology, *La fenomenología del relajo y otros ensayos*, 11.

2. There are some signs that Portilla perceives a need to provide evidential support for his implicit claim that his observations are, in fact, representative of widely pervasive trends. For example, he assures the reader that he could provide "innumerable" examples of the kinds of trends he has identified: "That the US American world becomes fully comprehensible from the postulate of innocence is something that can be verified by innumerable facts, more or less complex" [143].

3. The Christian Bible depicts Jesus as a martyr who offered human beings a chance to redeem themselves from their subjection to sin, guilt, and death, but was rejected and murdered by those he was trying to save. For this reason, Jesus has almost always been depicted with a loving but sad expression.

4. According to Portilla, "Pragmatism can, without serious alteration, be reduced to the following formula, which has been coined by the US American philosopher, Patrick Romanell: 'The truth of an idea (proposition, belief, hypothesis) depends on the practical value of its results.' This means that both the truth and the *real meaning* of an idea must be sought in its consequences for action, i.e., its *effectiveness*." In response, Portilla says: "Pragmatism can only be sustained under the assumption that men will propose only morally valid ends. It is only within a community composed of substantially virtuous men that it is possible to postulate the action of men as a criterion of the good and of truth" [150].

5. "Only on the assumption of innocence does it become possible to face the future openly and confidently as happens in the disturbing doctrine of manifest destiny that you see with the annexation of Texas" [155].

6. "I believe that the proliferation of literature on sexual matters can be explained by the fact that everything concerning sex resists being clearly integrated in a perspective of total innocence, and it is thus necessary to return [to the topic] again and again in a sort of vertigo of fascination. It is precisely this character of proliferation to infinity, of production in a series, that gives meaning to the detective story in the US. Faced with the irrefutable fact of crime, there is nothing so comforting as the detective novel. . . . Psychoanalysis and the detective novel can therefore be interpreted as a technical domestication of evil, but such domestication can only occur when an innocent world has previously been postulated. Banishing evil to the periphery of being and controlling it with psychological and police techniques, all that remains is, literally, to wash our hands" [147–148].

7. The kind of controlled experiment that may lend some support to some of Portilla's hypotheses is described, for example, in E. L. Uhlmann, T. A. Poehlman, D. Tannenbaum, and J. A. Bargh, "Implicit Puritanism in American moral cognition," *Journal of Experimental Social Psychology* 47 (2011): 312–320. This study compared random groups of US Americans to British, Canadian, and Asian American groups and found "evidence that the judgments and behaviors of contemporary Americans are implicitly influenced by traditional Puritan-Protestant values regarding work and sex."

8. I am grateful to Manuel Vargas and Clinton Tolley at the UCSD Mexican Philosophy Lab for their help in clarifying this line of thought.

9. For a rich source of discussion about this and related issues, see Kalpana Ram and Christopher Houston, *Phenomenology in Anthropology: A Sense of Perspective* (Bloomington: Indiana University Press, 2015).

10. As Heidegger puts it: "The fact that this sort of thing can matter to us is grounded in our attunement." Heidegger, *Being and Time*, 176.

11. Hans B. Schmid, *Plural Action: Essays in Philosophy and Social Science* (Dordrecht, Netherlands: Springer Science & Business Media, 2009), 69.

12. Portilla, "Phenomenology of Relajo," 145.

13. Ibid., 198.

14. Ibid.

15. For more on the *relajiento* and *apretado*, see chapter 2.

16. Heidegger's classic formulation of the definition of "world" is as follows: "That wherein Dasein understands itself beforehand . . . [and] in terms of which it has let entities be encountered beforehand." Heidegger, *Being and Time*, 86. "Dasein" is Heidegger's term for creatures like us, i.e., creatures that make sense of reality in the existentially inflected ways that human beings do.

17. William Blattner, *Heidegger's* Being and Time: *A Reader's Guide* (London: Continuum, 2006), 63.

18. Thus, in the full passage that I cited above, Heidegger connects the class of experience made possible by this fearful attunement to the corresponding feature of the world such an attunement reveals: "The fact that this sort of thing can matter to us is grounded in our attunement; and as an attunement [the concern for safety and security] has already disclosed the world—as something by which we can be threatened, for instance." Heidegger, *Being and Time*, 176.

19. The concept of a live option is famously articulated by William James, who illustrates his conception of this kind of possibility with the example of a religious person considering the belief system of another faith. Even if a Christian can make sense of the views of his Muslim counterpart, he says, so that the Muslim's belief system is perfectly intelligible, nonetheless the Christian is likely to find that these ideas do not make an "electric connection with [his] nature" and "refuse to scintillate with any credibility at all. As an hypothesis it is completely dead." William James, "The Will to Believe," in *The Will to Believe and Other Essays in Popular Philosophy, Vol. 6* (Cambridge, MA: Harvard University Press, 1979), 199.

20. Thanks to Lori Gallegos de Castillo for making this connection.

21. See Heidegger's discussion of care (*Sorge*), and its "equiprimordial" constitutive elements of discourse (*Rede*), mood (*Befindlichkeit*), and understanding (*Verstehen*). Heidegger, *Being and Time*, 375, 293, 277.

22. Jonathan Lear, *Radical Hope: Ethics in the Face of Cultural Devastation* (Cambridge, MA: Harvard University Press, 2006).

23. Miranda Fricker, *Epistemic Injustice: Power and the Ethics of Knowing* (Oxford: Oxford University Press, 2007).

24. This formulation is adapted from Robin DiAngelo's discussion of "White fragility," which she defines as "a state in which even a minimum amount of racial stress becomes intolerable, triggering a range of defensive moves." Robin DiAngelo, "White Fragility," *International Journal of Critical Pedagogy* 3, no. 3 (2011): 54–70.

25. The reader may be surprised by Portilla's characterization of such panty raids as "naive and playful," when such activities were undoubtedly frightening to many of the women targeted by these brazen displays of misogyny and the impunity with which men could violate women's boundaries. However, because this passage is located in an essay criticizing the hypocritical and dangerous "innocence" of US Americans, I suspect that Portilla is being ironic in this char-acterization—i.e., that although those who participated in such activities viewed themselves as merely being naive and playful, Portilla thinks we ought to assess such individuals more harshly. That said, such passages highlight the problematic fact that, as discussed in the introduction, Portilla fails to engage with women or issues of gender in his writing. For more on the history of panty raids, see Beth Bailey, "From panty raids to revolution: Youth and authority, 1950–1970," in *Generations of Youth: Youth Cultures and History in Twentieth-Century Amer-ica*, eds. Joe Alan Austin and Michael Willard (New York: New York University Press, 1998), 187–204.

26. Thanks to Andrea Pitts for calling attention to this point. For a discus-sion of Mexican and Chicana philosophers that harmonizes with the critique of Portilla I offer in this section, see Andrea Pitts, "Toward an Aesthetics of Race: Bridging the Writings of Gloria Anzaldúa and José Vasconcelos," *Inter-American Journal of Philosophy* 5, no. 1 (2012): 80–100.

27. For an excellent comparison of slavery and its aftermath in the US and other societies, see Orlando Patterson, *Slavery and Social Death* (Cambridge, MA: Harvard University Press, 1982).

28. Cornel West, "My Intellectual Vocation," in *The Cornel West Reader* (New York: Civitas Books, 2000), 20.

29. West, "Prophetic Christian as Organic Intellectual: Martin Luther King, Jr." in *The Cornel West Reader*, 429.

30. West, "Introduction." in *The Cornel West Reader*, xix.

31. For excellent articulations of this view, see Gloria Anzaldúa, *Border-lands/La Frontera* (San Francisco: Aunt Lute, 1987). See also Mariana Ortega, *In-Between: Latina Feminist Phenomenology, Multiplicity, and the Self* (Albany, NY: SUNY Press, 2016).

32. See, for example, David S. Owen, "Towards a Critical Theory of White-ness," *Philosophy and Social Criticism* 33, no. 2 (2007): 203–222.

33. Thanks to Shannon Sullivan for suggesting this point. For further dis-cussion, see Shannon Sullivan, *"White Innocence: Paradoxes of Colonialism and*

Race by Gloria Wekker," *philoSOPHIA: A Journal of Continental Feminism* 7, no. 2 (2017): 363–367.

34. Jose Jorge Mendoza, "Illegal: White Supremacy and Immigration: Core Issues and Emerging Trends," in *The Ethics and Politics of Immigration: Core Issues and Emerging Trends*, ed. Alex Sager (London: Rowman & Littlefield International, 2016), 201–220.

35. On the other hand, the Immigration and Naturalization Act of 1952 abolished the use of racial restrictions in immigration and naturalization statutes. This provides some reason to think that there *was* something about this period of history—which coincided, of course, with the so-called "civil rights era"—that was historically important for White society and may have constituted something of a crisis for innocence. My point, however, is that this is simply a "crisis" that never ends. Thanks to Lori Gallegos de Castillo for these points.

Part III

On "Thomas Mann and German Irrationalism"

Chapter 5

From Irrationalism to Complacency for the Death of the Other

Carlos Alberto Sánchez

Portilla is a philosopher of seriousness; a defender of reason; a humanist who believes that human excellence is possible, even if it hides behind *relajo* and other collective nihilisms.

When we read his critique of *relajo* in his "Phenomenology of Relajo," we hear a philosopher anxiously advocating for rationality and correct action. *Relajo*, as "the suspension of seriousness," is *a* consequence of the overthrow of rationality by a modern capitalist consumerism where what matters is what is most enjoyable, even if that is *doing nothing* and believing in nothing.

Portilla's critique of irrationalism continues in his essay on Thomas Mann, "Thomas Mann and German Irrationalism" (see the appendix). According to Portilla, irrationalism, as we find it in, most prominently, Arthur Schopenhauer and Friedrich Nietzsche, intended to elevate vital human values—the value of life, the passions, instincts—over and against the value traditionally placed on reason by humanist philosophies. In Schopenhauer, for instance, reason, as the search for meaning and transcendence, was now subordinated to the Will, as the irrational, indefatigable striving *to live*, which, in its striving, ultimately revealed the meaninglessness of life and the "will to nothingness." The failures of reason to locate meaning, and the recognition that the will was a purposeless striving, meant that the best course of human action was asceticism, a letting-go of the desire for meaning and a surrender to the irrationalism of the Will. But asceticism, as the triumph of irrational vitalism, was ultimately a "moral stance" that "develops out of compassion" with the recognition that all suffering is shared in common in a meaningless world.[1]

The twentieth century, however, saw a perversion of this sort of irrational vitalism. Irrationalism in the twentieth century was associated not with an affirmation of life or an asceticism of the will, but mainly with that which preceded the ascetic moral stance, namely, a view of life as absurd and meaningless. In the first part of the twentieth century, and in the shadow of Nietzsche, anti-rational vitalism became an *affirmation* of nihilism and death, an irrationalism without compassion or surrender. Ultimately, coming to terms with the meaninglessness of existence would lead not to asceticism, but to violence.

The triumph of nihilistic irrationalism had serious human consequences. The genocidal politics of National Socialism—the brutal instrumentality of the concentration camps—was one of these. Since the negation of reason signaled a rejection of humanism, which in turn signaled the denial of the value of personhood, the value of the human, and an affirmation of death, it was irrationalism that made possible the complacency before the death of other that shocked the world after World War II. It is in this context, and in this tradition, that Portilla locates and criticizes Thomas Mann's version of irrationalism.

In what follows, I'd like to think with and after Portilla about the value of death and the consequences that follow from such the axiological inversion that subsumes reason and life to nihilistic irrationalism and death. This will be a meditation *alongside* Portilla, and I proceed, first, by considering Portilla's critique of Mann's irrationalism; secondly, I briefly summarize the Mexican idea of death as we find it in post-Revolutionary Mexican thought; thirdly, I reconstruct Portilla's critique of the Mexican idea of death based on his critique of the German idea; and, finally, I think *beyond* Portilla and consider his remarks in light of violence and death in twenty-first-century Mexico.

1. On Thomas Mann

"Thomas Mann y el irracionalismo aleman" was delivered as a lecture at a conference on literary themes in 1962. At the start of his presentation Portilla dramatically announces that "[in this lecture], the dead lion [Thomas Mann] is delivered to the maw of the living dog [Portilla]" [183].[2] From the start, we are told that Portilla will ravenously tear Mann to shreds—or, at least, that this is his intention. The focus of the living dog's attack is Mann's irrationalism, or that disdain of reason common to existentialist thinkers of the time. But, according to Portilla, Mann's irrationalism is specifically German and particularly pernicious. He writes:

> The tradition of German irrationalism . . . can be characterized in a summary and elemental way in several postulates found in the work of Thomas Mann. These postulates are: the primacy of life and the irrational over intelligence and reason; the primacy of death over life; the primacy of disease over health; and the primacy of the individual and the unique over the common and the universal.
>
> In the course of time, these postulates would be expressed in the collective life of Germany as that degraded form of superiority belonging to the Germanic race, with its core of anti-Semitism and anti-Christianity, and the pretension, equally absurd and monstrous, to inaugurate a new millennial period of human history. [188]

The source of Portilla's reading of Mann are Mann's various novels, such as *The Magic Mountain* and *Death in Venice*. There, Portilla finds echoes of Nietzsche, Schopenhauer, and Wagner, especially in Mann's advocacy of an irrational vitalism that privileges the following: (1) irrationalism over reason, (2) death over life, (3) disease over health, and (4) the particular over the universal. While postulates (1) and (4) are also found in non-German thinkers such as Søren Kierkegaard, Albert Camus, Blaise Pascal, and José Ortega y Gasset, Portilla's critique of Mann focuses on the cultural and *historical* consequences of (1) irrationalist vitalism and (2) the privilege given to death at the expense of life. This historical critique is announced in the phrase "in the course of time," in which, he says, these "postulates" devolve into anti-Semitism, anti-Christianity, and the unwarranted ("monstrous") Germanic belief in its own historical privilege and exceptionalism.

A closer look at postulates (1) and (2) will bring Portilla's critique of Mann into focus.

1.1. On Reason and Irrationalism

The concept of reason is hard to pin down. Rather than rigorously define it, modern philosophers after the Enlightenment go to great lengths to affirm an unequivocal "faith in reason." From Descartes to Kant, having "faith in reason" means that human beings can confidently appeal to their own naturally endowed intellect in the project of comprehending the harmonious, comprehensive ordering of the universe and its laws. "Reason" itself, however, is known only *via negativa*, in terms of what it cannot do—namely, go beyond its limits in experience (for instance, Kant's famous critique of "pure reason"). However, for humanists, reason and the ability to reason, that is, basic rationality, are essential to being human, and thus the proper use of reason is thought to be the distinguishing characteristic of civilized, self-governing and self-determining peoples and societies. In the history of philosophy, Socrates himself represents the ideal of the rational citizen, capable of formulating questions about self, society, and her place in the cosmos. Negatively, Aristotle's barbarian represents the non-rational subject. Here is a creature defined by excess, violence, chaos, and limitation (in speech, foresight, and understanding); the barbarian is the epitome of irrationality, and this irrationality helps observers make sense of his brutality and his backwardness. However, after Nietzsche, Schopenhauer, and other proto-existentialists, irrationalism as a philosophical posture means that looking for order or harmony in the universe is a fool's errand, that life is lived in the now, that everything is, indeed, chaos, violence, and meaninglessness, and that our "rational" faculties" can never give us the kind of access to "truth" that the history of philosophy seemingly took for granted.

In the "Phenomenology of Relajo," Portilla chastises his fellow Mexicans for their lack of commitment to truth, clarity, seriousness, and responsibility; in short, he criticizes Mexican culture for its irrationality. Among the goals of the "Phenomenology," one is to "warn the youth about the dangers of the lack of seriousness."[3] *Relajo* is a lack of seriousness, it is the ground of irresponsibility, which itself initiates, for an individual and for a culture, "a slow process of self-destruction."[4] The purpose of philosophy, according to Portilla, is to bring about "a clear consciousness" of who they are and what they must do.[5] This clear consciousness is rationality. As a philosopher, Portilla understands his role, then, as one of "promoting reason in a specific society, of clearly putting before the collective consciousness the ultimate base of its thinking, of its feeling, and of its acting."[6] In this way, *reason* is what is most desired for the salvation of specific, situated communities. Aside from making possible a clear consciousness of what is most immediate to situated peoples, reason and rationality have a more significant purpose, that of allowing a culture or an individual to "view existence as a totality," to acquire a perspective that, ultimately, serves as the basis for morality and responsibility. Without this ability to "relate to existence as a whole," as "a unitary whole," morality is not possible, as the "whole," the "unitary," remains out of view.[7]

For this reason, I read Portilla's critique of irrationalism in "Thomas Mann and German Irrationalism" as framed by his views on seriousness, clarity, and moral responsibility that we find in his "Phenomenology."[8] In the essay on Mann, Portilla faults the German literary giant for advocating that disdain of reason that leads to nihilistic attitudes such as *relajo* or to more impactful attitudes such as a lack of sympathy for others (a lack of sympathy that translates to an inability to see the "unitary whole" on which moral responsibility rests). While the "Phenomenology" is written so as to "warn of the dangers" of irrationalism (and apathy), a warning directed specifically to a Mexican "Nietzschean generation *avant la lettre*,"[9] one that had given itself over to a process of self-destruction, Portilla's faulting of Mann has more to do with what has already taken place, with the consequences that have already had a regrettable historical impact on humanity: the catastrophe of the holocaust. And more than faulting Mann, Portilla is now warning us all; it is a warning to all readers that only reason can save us, and its denial or inversion can only bring death. Of course, Portilla is not blaming Mann for the millions dead; neither is he implicating him in the Nazi ideology that made this possible. His complaint is that Mann, as a man of clarity and morality, should have repudiated irrationalism the moment that he saw it transform itself into a necro-politics.

Portilla finds the origin of German irrationalism in Martin Luther, who in his world-historical (to use a Hegelian phrase) protestation against the Roman Catholic Church in 1517, declared faith (and not reason) as the only direct access to God. Reason had lost its privilege and had no role to play in man's communication with the Divine (as it did in someone like St. Thomas Aquinas, who, although he recognized the limits of reason and affirmed the priority of faith over it, did not deny reason the possibility of knowing the truth of religious claims, even if incompletely[10]). Portilla writes, "The Lutheran believer finds his certainty within, not in a logical system of truths or in an external authority represented by the Church, but only in the personal call of God" [188]. Portilla locates the beginning of the historical revolt against reason in that turn to inwardness made possible by Luther, which likewise implied a revolt against logic and external authorities (the institution of the Church); this revolt, moreover, required an affirmation of values that exist independently of our ability to justify them with reasons, that stand outside the realm of reason, or that go against what a humanistic conception of the rational would approve. Some of these *irrational* values that are now affirmed are the values of "greatness," "power," "destruction," and "death."

But the affirmation of these values does not lead to a more vital culture, to a more realistic conception of the human being, or to any sort of ethics capable of strengthening community. The affirmation of these values leads to politics, a politics that is far from ethical and, one could say, the opposite of morality. Portilla criticizes Thomas Mann for not recognizing the slippery slope of his own irrationalism. He writes:

> [Thomas Mann] loves the nineteenth century "for its pessimism and for its musical communion with night and death" and the criterion of this love, his reason, is "greatness." Can a more radical declaration of irrationalist faith be imagined? What values are these? Night, death, pessimism, and greatness! We are one step away from the cry: "Long live death!" One step away from *Nacht und Nebel*. Night and fog. I do not need to explain to you what these two words mean. [190]

While the term *Nacht und Nebel* is one we find in Richard Wagner's *Das Rheingold*, Portilla here alludes to Hitler's directive in 1945 to imprison and murder political dissidents under the cover of "night and fog," a directive that Portilla locates on the consequential chain that begins with a previous commitment to or "declaration of irrationalist faith."[11] If the "criterion" of justification for one's actions is the pursuit of greatness, a courageous will to nothingness, or the fearless recognition of the meaninglessness of life, then demanding the death of the other (Hitler's *Nacht und Nebel*), or being complacent before that death, is properly, while irrationally, justified. That is, if the criterion for my actions is greatness, then what *appears* to devalue greatness (my own or my culture's) must be sacrificed or removed. Recognizing such a morally problematic connection prompts Portilla to declare that these values are not the values of community, of love, or of human flourishing. Similarly to his critique of relajo in the "Phenomenology," Portilla's complaint against Mann seems to be that the great German writer has dogmatically adopted a cultural attitude of nihilism before the value of life that can only lead, and has already led, to death. In the "Phenomenology" Portilla referred to such a cultural attitude as a "Nietzscheanism avant la lettre," one likewise rooted in a disdain of reason and the dogmatic giving-oneself-over-to-irresponsibility and the suspension of seriousness.

1.2. On Death

While the irrationalism of Nietzsche and, later, of Ortega y Gasset is a version of vitalism, a belief that life has an intentionality and a potentiality all its own, Portilla believes that German irrationalism, especially that version advocated by Mann, mirrors that of National Socialism—i.e., it mirrors a denial of life where the slogan "Long live death!" expresses the anti-human and anti-ethical politics of an entire culture.

The value given to death by German irrationalism is problematic for obvious reasons, the most obvious of which is that it may lead to social or personal complacency before the death or the suffering of the other. Since, in this schema, the thought of death empowers and authenticates (as in Heidegger's *Being and Time*), the real, actual death of the other is witnessed in a fog of moral ambivalence, or not witnessed through the lens of morality at all but rather in an attitude of acceptance or helplessness. Portilla imagines a critic of his reading of Mann who would argue that Mann was only speaking poetically or metaphorically about death, that the consequences of endowing value to death were beyond his imaginings. Anticipating such criticism, Portilla points to one of Mann's characters in *The Magic Mountain*, Hans Castorp. Portilla insists that the words spoken by Castorp reflect Mann's own beliefs on the meaning and value of death. Portilla cites Castorp,

> who declares . . . in somewhat ambiguous terms his fidelity to death and, at the same time, his decision not to grant it any power over his thoughts. "Death is a great power," he tells us. "I want to keep fidelity to death in my heart, but I want to clearly remember that fidelity to death and to the past is nothing but vice, dark and antihuman voluptuousness when it governs our thinking and our conduct." [190–191]

According to Portilla's reading, this evidences Mann's awareness of the power of this idea, expressed by Castorp as a desire *not* to grant it influence over his thinking since he knows that it is "dark and antihuman voluptuousness" that cnds by influencing behavior. This passage also points to Mann's irrationalism, one that has precipitated a value inversion where the *idea* of death contains a "great power" that can govern conduct and thinking—at its worse, a powerful idea that, in its antihuman voluptuousness, makes one complacent for the other's death.

Portilla continues, with perhaps his most direct condemnation of the immorality of irrationalism and of Mann's role in advancing it:

> I confess that I do not understand at all what this fidelity to death means, if it is not a disguised way to take sides against the human, against the neighbor in his most concrete sense. It is hatred of man and a secret will for destruction. Nothing keeps this destruction from beginning with self-destruction. This dark and antihuman voluptuousness governed the thinking of Germany for a century, before governing its conduct during the fifteen most criminal and inhuman years in the history of man. [191]

Here we get a clearer sense of Portilla's ethical commitments as well as his politics. As an ethical philosopher, he considers hate for and violence toward the concrete other "antihuman" and destructive, but likewise hate and violence toward the self. As a political philosopher, he sees the "secret will for man's destruction" as the point at which consent and complacency must end, the point at which something must be done for the sake of the "human species."

In his critique of Mann, Portilla is clear: Mann contributed through irrationalism to the "fifteen most criminal and inhuman years in the entire history of the human species." But perhaps Mann did not realize the consequences of irrationalism on *concrete* persons; or, perhaps, irrationalism does not understand that it is no longer dealing with abstract humanity when it devalues life. Life in its concreteness is always the life of a concrete person. If fidelity to death means an inversion of the value of life, then the life to be devalued will be a concrete life, a real life, and the most concrete way to devalue this life will be to murder the concrete other. This disregard for the concrete existence of the neighbor is dangerous and irresponsible. It is dangerous for whoever does not speak against it. But it is also dangerous for whoever does. Portilla suggests that the first victim of the devaluation of life could be the one who pledges loyalty to death, since "nothing keeps this destruction from beginning with self-destruction." The "antihuman voluptuousness" of a fidelity to death, this blind romanticizing of nothingness and destruction, in denying the value of life denies it absolutely—no life is more valuable than death—so that its only consequence will be deadly and, ultimately, genocidal.

Mann is not to blame, of course, for those fifteen years of death and criminality. But he lent voice to a philosophy of death that certainly justified it. Portilla, lunging at the "dead lion's" throat like the ravenous dog he proclaims to be, proclaims his verdict:

> Yes. Let us say it at once. It seems to us that the context of ideas, the spiritual atmosphere in which the work of Thomas Mann moves, is exactly the same as that of National Socialism. . . . we will not find in his work philosophical principles that could have been opposed to National Socialism. This bourgeois, intelligent, and cultured man does not participate in the barbaric orgy. But how can we not see that the philosophical foundations of his work and the spiritual climate that it reflects are the same as those in the name of which National Socialism tried to found a superior order that would govern the world for the next thousand years? [191–192]

What is strange about Portilla's critique of Mann's apparent infatuation with death is that the position he criticizes is of a similar kind, if not identical, to a Mexican idea of death with which I'm certain he was familiar. It was an idea of death as ancient as Mexico itself and one that in Portilla's own time was elaborated by none other than Octavio Paz and Emilio Uranga, two figures that he was intimately familiar with, the latter being his closest friend and fellow member of Grupo Hiperión, and the former being the future Nobel Prize winner and author of *El laberinto de la soledad.*

2. The Mexican Idea of Death

In *The Labyrinth of Solitude,* Octavio Paz writes: "there are two attitudes toward death: one, pointing forward, that conceives of it as creation; the other, pointing backward, that expresses itself as a fascination with nothingness or as a nostalgia for limbo."[12] Paz goes on to say that the attitude that points forward is characteristic of European and North American cultures; the backward-pointing attitude characterizes Mexican and Latin American ideas of death. We will call the forward-pointing attitude the *instrumental attitude*; the backward-pointing attitude will be referred to as the *historical attitude*.[13]

To say that one's attitude toward death is instrumental is to say that death, my death and death in general, is something that *will happen*; it is an event of the future, always on the horizon and always a possibility. Its presence makes possible creation in the now, since the prospect of a looming death forces one to labor while one can; thus, Paz says that this attitude is creative. The historical attitude, on the other hand, is one that holds that death is a permanent presence, a limbo, or a perpetual recovery of a past annihilation, a nostalgia lived in the present as an accumulation of the past.

The first, forward-pointing, instrumental attitude is neatly described by Sigmund Freud when he says, "The goal of all life is death."[14] This means, for Freud at least, that life is a steady progress *toward* death. As a goal, or a destination, death motivates life *forward*. The relationship between life and death is summarized by the cultural anthropologist Ernest Becker in *The Denial of Death*: "[T]he idea of death, the fear of it, haunts the human animal like nothing else; it is a mainspring of human activity—activity designed largely to avoid the fatality of death, to overcome it by denying in some way that it is the final destiny of man."[15] As a "mainspring of human activity" it is "creation" in Paz's bifurcation above.

The second, historical, attitude appears most poignantly in the Mexican poetry, literature, art, and philosophy of the twentieth century. Although this attitude reflects a relation to and with the past, it is a past that is present or made present in everyday existence. The poet Xavier Villaurrutia sings,

> If you are everywhere
> in the water and in the earth
> in the air that engulfs me
> . . . in the breath I take
> in my confusing blood
> could you not be, Death, in my life,
> water, fire, dust, and breath?[16]

In a similar vein, and a few decades later, Portilla's colleague in Grupo Hiperión, Emilio Uranga, theorizes: "For the Mexican, death is . . . an everyday accomplishment [*un hecho cotidiano*] . . . all would agree that for the Mexican death is familiar. Our people coexist with death."[17] Both Uranga and Villaurrutia lend voice to a view that holds that death is not an inevitable event that will befall me in a near or distant future, but, rather, that death is a happening in the now, codified in the social space as an "everyday," "familiar," presence. As such, it is not a "goal," as it is for Freud, but an "accomplishment" of the past and repeated in the present. What the Mexican attitude toward death, as we find it in Paz, Villaurrutia, and Uranga, implies is that in Mexico there is a coexistence with death. For his part, Paz sees death as a presence that makes possible the very intelligibility of life: "Death defines life. . . . Our deaths illuminate our lives. If our deaths lack meaning, our lives also lacked it."[18] To be defined by death is to be captured by it, as in a glow or a halo. It is all around, inescapable and personal. That is why a meaningless death can only correspond to a meaningless life—by defining life, death shares in life's significance or lack thereof. Coexistence and connection allude to an intimacy and identity with death; the case is different with Becker's idea of death, one that evokes separation and distance, which is why death, Becker says, "haunts the human animal like nothing else."[19]

A classic study of Mexican art published by Anita Brenner in 1929, *Idols Behind Altars*, recounts Mexico's "strange" relation to death:

> This familiarity with death is shocking to the European. But where death is so much at home in Mexico, he [*sic*] is no longer a dreaded and a flattered guest. . . . The city jabs slyly at him, makes a clown of him. It belittles him for his trumped-up value. . . . Except as a physical phenomenon, death itself is disregarded.[20]

We can guess that what is "shocking to the European" is the lack of similarities between her own conception of death and what she finds in the Mexican home, street, and marketplace. The shock, as all shocks, is due to coming face-to-face with the unexpected and different. More accurately, it is due to the unresolved double bind that keeps the European from finding reason in what is not *the same*, thus, in the act of surprise, *marginalizing* it as barbaric or, in the best case, *poetic hyperbole*.

In *Death and the Idea of Mexico*, Claudio Lomnitz declares that "death in Mexico gets a very different rap."[21] And, given the peculiarities of its colonial history, it should. What makes the rap different is its tone, which represents a strange relationship to death, one of both familiarity and indifference. According to Lomnitz, for instance, death is part of the national spirit to such an extent that it has become one of "Mexico's national totems."[22] Taking up a place alongside representations of the patriot Benito Juárez and the Virgin of Guadalupe, death, or the representation of death, occupies a privileged position in the Mexican national consciousness as a symbol of national identity. However, unlike the Virgin (who represents hope and devotion) and Juárez (who represents law and reason), death "has a more nihilistic and lighthearted component."[23] In other words, death is not an event to be feared, but a presence to behold and admire. To admire death is to regard living itself with a nihilistic attitude, to mock it or mock those who, for whatever reason, are absorbed in their own lives, disregarding its limitations and its finitude. Thus, as a national symbol, or national sign, death represents an all-encompassing value that, instead of unifying, as totems are meant to do, divides and separates—or, in mockery, constantly threatens to separate. The presence of death becomes a constant reminder that our errands are fool's errands, that our lives, full of sound and fury as they may be, ultimately signify nothing. So the rap that death gets in Mexico might be different to those who exist beyond its socio-political borders and are thus unencumbered by its history, but there is nothing *different* or strange about death's rap for Mexicans themselves.

Uranga makes this point in reference to the United States: "For the North American [*el norteamericano*], death is a reality that must be hidden, a phenomenon that is silenced and masked as much as possible so that it will not disturb, with its impertinence, the flow of a life that unfolds in radical dedication to [self]-realization and work."[24] The Mexican's relationship to death is, plainly put, out in the open. The reality of death is not hidden, or masked; death itself forbids this, as it is what defines life. And Mexicans realize and accept this intimate arrangement and they "coexist with death."[25] But these are platitudes. In Uranga's philosophical program, the question deals with this familiarity, with the apparent everydayness of death.

Uranga echoes Paz, Zea, and Brenner in his estimation that Mexican death "corresponds to a global project of life."[26] This means that the clue as to why the Mexican possesses this idea of death is hidden in the Mexican's idea of *life* itself. The Mexican idea of life, or his conception of life, is rooted in the historical experience of the conquest, colonization, and centuries of failed attempts to assimilate to the European, and later, North American, utopias—and this would be why Mexican death is both of the past and always a very old version of itself in the present. But being rooted in such an unyielding history allows Mexicans access to insights unavailable to the *norteamericanos*, for instance, that while life always begins, it never ends, it never wraps up, it never concludes. In other words, life's ends are not meant to be fulfilled. As Uranga puts it, "the life of the Mexican is always consumed but never consummated [*la vida del Mexican se consume siempre, pero nunca se consuma*]."[27] The reason that life will never be consummated is given historically, in Mexico's history of interruptions, and, as such, in the history of projects begun and left unfinished, since, Uranga notes, "life is always on the verge of being cut down [*tronchada*]."[28] And, since life is always on the verge of interruption, then there is no reason to take it seriously—this lack of seriousness is, Uranga tells us, found in the Mexican attitude toward *both* life and death. Uranga summarizes the Mexican idea of death in the following passage from an essay published in 1950:

> The abyss between life and death is not insurmountable; rather, there is an imperceptible passage from one to the other. Death is familiar to us, just as our own lives; we approach death, and we understand it [as we understand our lives]. And the manner in which we take ourselves seriously or in jest, that way in which we coexist in life, is also the way in which we approach death. The Mexican posits vitality in death, charges it with existential significance and in such a way recovers it and dislodges from it that value that others put on it, who dehumanize it and alienate it, displacing it from life. When we affirm that death, for the Mexican, is a symbol of his own life we mean to suggest that he (the Mexican) recognizes himself in death, which means that everything that belongs to death as its own peculiarity is laid claim to by the Mexican's very existence.[29]

This, of course, is the opposite of saying that thinking about death motivates me to act (what Becker tells us above, and what Brenner suggests). According to Uranga, death doesn't motivate me at all, since, like my own life, it lacks any tangible promise of fulfillment.

In the context of the "Mexican idea of death," we are justified in asking about the motivations of Portilla's claims against Mann. If his own contemporaries held a similar view of death to Mann's, an irrationalist idea that seems to devalue life and affirm the value of death, is there a different motive, or different reasons, to his critique? Paz's, Villaurrutia's, and Uranga's conception of death reflect a particular cultural phenomenon, one in which death is affirmed as a constant presence, a *fait accompli*, just as in Mann. Becker's, and to some extent Freud's, characterization reflects a more generalized "Western" attitude that places death, as the "mainspring of human activity," squarely on par with other events to be realized at a future time. Is this what Portilla seeks to articulate? A Western attitude consistent with his humanism and his belief in reason?

3. On Complacency

The question confronting us from the previous section is the following: why does Portilla ignore the historical inversion of the value of life in Mexico in his critique of Thomas Mann? Consider the following passage from his lecture on Mann:

> Death as a tremendous mystery, as an ennobling experience of a metaphysical rank higher than life itself, is one of the central themes of German irrationalism. There is a tendency in this philosophy to revere death as something sacred, as a higher value. This monstrous inversion of vital values admits of all nuances, but is concentrated in two attitudes: the refined cult of one's own death, in the sense that it is adequate or appropriate to the life of the individual—death as a crown, as a diadem of life, as we find in Rainer Maria Rilke, who had the grace to die from an infection caused when the thorn of a flower pinched his finger. And the slightly less refined cult of death expressed in the fascist cry of "Long live death!" and in the skulls that adorned the helmets and epaulets of select Nazi troops. Between one and the other attitude there is not much difference. If I am happy to live for death, it is then easy for me to be complacent with the death of the other, or, at least, to be so that the death of the other does not bother me that much. [189–190]

We note first that Portilla makes it clear that "death" as a "mystery" and "ennobling experience of a metaphysical rank" is "central" to German irrationalism. This, as we saw in the previous section, is false. It is not central to German irrationalism; it is found also in Mexican romantic poetry of Villaurutia, the cultural philosophy of Paz, and the phenomenological insights of Portila's fellow Hiperión, Emilio Uranga—*none of whom were irrationalists.*

Secondly, we insist that the "monstrous inversion of vital values" is not unique to Mann or to Germany. Like Paz and Uranga, Portilla recognizes two attitudes toward death resulting from the German commitment to irrationalism, one more refined than the other: the first, death as a representation of life (what Octavio Paz meant when he said, "tell me how you die and I will tell you who you are"), and the second, "less refined," attitude that is more of a worldview, that colors life in its actuality. Both attitudes are nihilistic for Portilla and both run counter to a proper moral stance, since "if I am happy to live for death . . . then it is easy for me to be complacent with the death of the other."

Here, of course, Portilla has in mind the atrocities of the Holocaust, placing partial blame for their occurrence on an irrationalist philosophy that Mann endorses. These atrocities were made possible by a complacency with the death of the other, a complacency adopted by the German people themselves. The French-Lithuanian philosopher Emmanuel Levinas held a similar view, namely, that complacency with the death of the other was partly responsible for the atrocities of concentration camps. For Levinas, however, it was not irrationalism that doomed the Jews to their deaths, or a philosophy of death that elevated it above life, but an instrumental *rationality* that valued *knowledge* above all else, which meant that the very life of the other (the matter of ethics) was always an afterthought of reason.[30] However, for both Levinas and Portilla, complacency before the other's death is the end result.

For his part, Levinas suggests that such complacency is rooted in thinking of death as a personal event, characterizing the impossibility of all possibilities *for me.* If my death is what makes my life possible in the now and in the future (if it is "creative"), then the other's death will lack significance, since it has nothing to do with me. But Levinas argues that we do not experience our own death at all, that our own death is an impossible event; that what we experience is, in fact, only the death of the other. And like the other, death is a mystery. That is, the mystery of death is that it is given in itself as an *other* (a not-I) that cannot be comprehended, whose approach I cannot know or anticipate; similarly, the other *person* is an other (a not-I) that cannot be comprehended, whose approach I cannot know or anticipate. These two mysteries are one; the other is the other's death.[31] Levinas writes in *Time and the Other*:

> The Other as Other is not only an alter ego: the Other is what
> I myself am not. The Other is this, not because of the Other's
> character, or physiognomy, or psychology, but because of the
> Other's very alterity. The Other is, for example, the weak, the
> poor, "the widow and the orphan."[32]

If I can only know the mystery of death by knowing the other of death, then the other's death *will* matter to me. The other as mystery means that I cannot conceptualize her, but must be responsible for her *life*. Against all complacency, Levinas says,

> The Ego as hostage to the other person is precisely called to
> answer for [her] death. This responsibility is for the Other
> in the ego, independent of every engagement ever taken by
> this ego and of all that would have ever been accessible to its
> initiative and its freedom, independent of everything that in
> the Other could have "regarded" this ego.[33]

In simpler terms, I am beholden to the other by the mere fact of her appearance before me (I am her "hostage"). She exists, and because she exists and she exists within the space of my ego's regard, I am responsible for her life, and, thus, I am called "to answer" for her death—I am responsible for her wellbeing. This originary responsibility means that I cannot be complacent.

An idea of death that sees death indifferently or as something to be revered without appeal to, or in relation to, the other, will ultimately lead to a complacency for the other's death. As Levinas suggest, however, tying death to the other is the way to overcoming this complacency, an overcoming via an original responsibility for the other, which means that death is always attached to the person of the other, death is always personal—it is always the death of the other. And this is perhaps the most significant criticism of those philosophies of death, like Mann's, Uranga's, or Paz's, namely, that taken to their extreme they lead to complacency with the death of the other. The other's death should always be accompanied by surprise and shock, but this can happen only if death itself is unexpected, feared, and not inserted into the normality of the everyday.

4. Considerations *after* Portilla

Toward the end of the lecture, Portilla asks, "At this point you will rightly wonder: What does all this have to do with Thomas Mann?" His answer suggests that it has less to do with Mann and more to do with a cultural or historical commitment to irrationalism and the consequences of such a commitment. "I ask myself this question in another form," he continues. "I wonder: Why did this disciple of Schopenhauer and Nietzsche not follow them to the last consequences of their thought? Why did Thomas Mann not join the crusade against reason and against the 'Jewish spirit' that according to Nietzsche had poisoned the very fountains of human life?" [195]. His answer is that, as a "fortunate inconsistency" [195], Thomas Mann simply confused irrationalism with Christian faith (although the latter was a "universalist and rationalist . . . humanistic current" [196]), but failed to follow either commitments to the anti-Semitic, death-obsessed, "Hitlerian horror" [196] of the second World War. This leads Portilla to question *how* one could be committed to irrationalism *and* still pretend to be a humanist, as Mann seems to have done. If irrationalism leads to the worship of the value of death, then any pretension to humanism is necessarily empty given the complacency with the death of the other that may ultimately follow.

At this point our reflection shifts to considerations beyond Portilla and to other applications of his critique. But before doing going further, we ask: Is a causal correlation established between irrationalism and complacency for the death of the other? The answer is no. The idea that a devaluing of the value of reason ultimately leads to the concentration camp falls apart when we consider that the genocidal technologies of the Third Reich were ultra-rational—witnessed in those "criminal years" was the triumph of what Max Horkheimer described as "instrumental reason" (a blind means-to-end rationality) and not, as Portilla claims, of irrationalism (anti-reason).[34] Nevertheless, lacking this correlation we are still left with the fact of a complacency for the death of the other that Portilla finds offensive to our very humanity.

Where does this complacency originate? With Portilla we could say that it originates in the inversion of the value of life, in the proclamation "Long live death!" that finds an echo in the Mexican idea of death. If life loses its meaning, then the death of the other is not going to matter as much as if it did have meaning. If death claims that meaning, then complacency before that death comes much easier.

A quick example from our own time: contemporary Mexican narco-culture gives us a glimpse into the consequences that Portilla imagined for a culture overtaken by the cult of death. In this context, Mexican and German philosophies of death have had similar consequences in that in the value inversion of life and death, death—the destruction of the other—has become an accepted commonplace. This is especially the case in the culture of narcotics trafficking. Also known as "narco-culture," this is a violent culture, where death is an omniscient, everyday reality. Songs are written about narco-culture as a cultural space; films glorify it; and newspapers insert it into the national conversation as a space of death and destruction that reflects what Lomnitz called "Mexico's national totem," i.e., death itself. In this cultural space, the value of life seems to have been supplanted, not by a glorification of death, but by a will to death, an indifference to it. With over 250,000 cartel-related killings since December 11 of 2006,[35] the evidence of this will to nothingness is overwhelming. Complacency for the death of the other is the rule, and not the exception. A recent discovery of a number of mass graves (*narcofosas*) in central Mexico (an all-too-common method of body disposal for the cartels) prompted the British journalist Ioan Grillo to publicly confess, in a *New York Times* column covering the grisly discovery, that he was "dumbstruck by the extent to which normal life seems to carry on next door to such terrors."[36] Normal life carries on because death is too familiar, social protestations lead nowhere, and together, familiarity and helplessness lead to complacency in the face of everyday terror.

While we certainly cannot make any direct causal connections between any particular *philosophy of death* or any perverted view of reason and the genocidal Nazi years or the contemporary narco atrocities, what is clear is that any displacement in the value of life has consequences. Portilla's ethical intuition is right in this respect: If we devalue that which makes the person a person (in his case, reason), then their death will cause no alarm. But just as Portilla can't say that Mann is complicit with the Nazis for their horrors, because he wasn't, neither can we say that the Mexican philosophies of death promoted by Paz and Uranga, for instance, have anything to do with the thousands dead in the narco-wars.

Portilla ends his reflections on Mann by telling us that he simply cannot figure out how a man of Mann's stature and intelligence would ever succumb to the antihumanism of irrationalism. Neither can he explain how an entire culture—especially one with such a rich humanist tradition in philosophy and the arts, the home of Goethe, Beethoven, and

Hegel—how such a people would stand idly by as the Nazis perpetrated their horrific crimes. He ends:

> Can we expect that one day this sinister ambiguity will be finally uprooted and banished from modern culture? In any case, I'm afraid that it will not be men like Thomas Mann who will help carry out this task. In contemporary Germany, and even beyond its borders, under the ashes of prosperity, the embers of the will to power, hatred of reason, and fidelity to death are still alive, and it is not impossible that they may one day invade the world with a terrifying wave. [198]

Portilla's pessimism here betrays a faith in the power of reason that he certainly suggests he has and that wished Thomas Mann would have elevated to the level of action. Nevertheless, we can say that Portilla's prophetic insight into the coming of that terrifying wave of anti-reason and fidelity to death has been realized. Everywhere we see these manifest as terrorism, neoliberalism, or populism, and everywhere we are asked to be complacent and antihuman, in other words, to be grateful for our advancements and to accept that innocents have to die for progress (and victory).

Too bad both of these lions, Mann and Portilla, are now dead and so can't say more. In our case, we leave Portilla here, in these pages, to be devoured by other ravenous dogs to come.

Notes

1. The case that Schopenhauer's notion of asceticism is a "moral stance" in which an "identification with the suffering of others" takes place is fascinating and helps us understand the differences Portilla saw between nineteenth- and twentieth-century irrationalism. For a more contemporary reading, see João Contâncio, "Nietzsche and Schopenhauer: On Nihilism and the Ascetic 'Will to Nothingness,'" in *The Palgrave Schopenhauer Handbook*, ed. Sandra Shapshay (London: Palgrave McMillan, 2017), 425–446.

2. Jorge Portilla, "Thomas Mann and German Irrationalism," translated by Carlos Alberto Sánchez and Francisco Gallegos. Translation included in the appendix. Page numbers in brackets refer to the 1984 Spanish edition of this work included in *Fenomenología del relajo y otros ensayos*.

3. Portilla, "Phenomenology of Relajo," 125–126.

4. Ibid.

5. Ibid., 126.

6. Ibid.

7. Ibid., 184.

8. It is not known when "Phenomenology of Relajo" was actually written. It could be the case that the "Thomas Mann" essay was written first, and thus we could read the "Phenomenology" as an extension of that lecture, or that the "Phenomenology" was written first, in which case we could read Portilla's "other" essays through the lens of the "Phenomenology." However, the sustained phenomenological reflections of the latter, its length, breath, and richness, justify us reading the "other" essays through its conceptual lens.

9. Portilla, "Phenomenology of Relajo," 126.

10. See Thomas Aquinas, *Selected Writings*, ed. Ralph McInerny (New York: Penguin Classics, 1999).

11. See Jackson Spielvogel, *Hitler and Nazi Germany: A History* (London: Routledge, 2004).

12. Paz, *The Labyrinth of Solitude*, 61.

13. See Carlos Alberto Sánchez, "Death and the Colonial Difference: An Analysis of a Mexican Idea," *Journal of Philosophy of Life* 3, no. 3 (2013): 168–189.

14. Sigmund Freud, *Beyond the Pleasure Principle*, trans. J. Strachey (New York: Hogarth Press, 1950), 50.

15. Ernest Becker, *The Denial of Death* (New York: The Free Press, 1973), xvii.

16. Xavier Villaurrutia, "Décima Muerte," 1933, accessed December 12, 2008, http://amediavoz.com/villaurrutia.htm. The untranslated stanza goes as follows: "Si en todas partes estás, / en el agua y en la tierra, / en el aire que me encierra / y en el incendio voraz; / y si a todas partes vas / conmigo en el pensamiento, / en el soplo de mi aliento / y en mi sangre confundida / ¿no serás, Muerte, en mi vida, / agua, fuego, polvo y viento?" This is my translation.

17. Emilio Uranga, "El tema de la muerte en la filosofía contemporánea," *México en la cultura*, October 29, 1950, 64.

18. Paz, *The Labyrinth of Solitude*, 51.

19. Becker, *The Denial of Death*, xvii.

20. Anita Brenner, *Idols Behind Altars: The Story of the Mexican Spirit* (New York: Beacon Press, 1970), 25–26.

21. Claudio Lomnitz, *Death and the Idea of Mexico* (New York: Zone Books, 2005), 20.

22. Ibid., 43.

23. Ibid., 21. Further on, he writes: "The three great totems of Mexican national history—Guadalupe, Juárez, and the playful skeleton—correspond, as national signs, to three different version of the social contract. In the first case, Mexico was represented as having been born out of a relation of loyalty and filiation with the *virgin morena*. The Mexican nation was her particular community of

devotees, and the compact that kept the nation together was its Marian devotion. In the case of the Juárez totem, the Mexican nation was born again, after a long battle with its internal and foreign enemies, in a social compact between citizens committed to the rule of law and reason. . . . Death emerged as a national totem in the aftermath of the Mexican Revolution" (43).

24. Uranga, "El tema de la muerte," 64.

25. Ibid.

26. Ibid., 65.

27. Ibid.

28. Ibid., 66.

29. Ibid., 65.

30. See Emmanuel Levinas, "Diachrony and Representation," in *Time and the Other*, trans. Richard A. Cohen (Pittsburgh: Duquesne University Press, 1987): 97–120.

31. Levinas, *Time and the Other*, 70.

32. Ibid., 83.

33. Levinas, "Diachrony and Representation," 107.

34. For more on "instrumental reason," see Max Horkheimer, *Eclipse of Reason* (New York: Bloomsbury Academic, 2013).

35. See "Estrategia fallida: 250.000 asesinatos en México desde el inicio de la "guerra contra el narco," *RT News*, May 24, 2018, https://actualidad.rt.com/actualidad/272788-mexico-llega-250000-asesinatos-inicio-guerra-narcotrafico.

36. Ioan Grillo, "The Paradox of Mexico's Mass Graves," *New York Times*, July 19, 2017, www.nytimes.com/2017/07/19/opinion/mexico-mass-grave-drug-cartel.html.

Chapter 6

Portilla's Hope

Phenomenological Flourishing and Affective Liberation

Francisco Gallegos

The previous chapter discussed Portilla's argument in "Thomas Mann and German Irrationalism" that Mann's novels can be used as a lens through which to examine "the intellectual and affective climate" of Germany in the nineteenth and early twentieth centuries. As we saw, Portilla articulates this view in a provocative manner, advancing the thesis that Mann's work expresses and even celebrates the same basic existential orientation that produced Nazism. This thesis is controversial, because Mann was a celebrated social critic and philanthropist, as well as a Nobel Prize laureate in Literature, who fled Germany in 1933 and, on the outbreak of World War II, conducted monthly anti-Nazi broadcasts on the BBC.[1] Despite these admirable features of Mann's biography, Portilla's view is clear:

> Thomas Mann, trained in the school of Schopenhauer, Wagner, and Nietzsche, was certainly not a Nazi or a Hitler collaborator. From the first moment, the man Thomas Mann, the writer, the artist, revolted against the wave of savagery that flooded Germany and predicted the final triumph of democracy. But we will not find in his work philosophical principles that could have opposed National Socialism. This bourgeois, intelligent, and cultured man does not participate in the barbaric orgy. But how can we not see that the philosophical foundations of

his work and the spiritual climate that it reflects are the same
as those in the name of which National Socialism tried to
found a superior order that would govern the world for the
next thousand years? [192]

But while Portilla clearly repudiates Mann's philosophical perspective, the central purpose of his essay is not to disparage Mann. Rather, Portilla's more ambitious aim in this text, in my view, is to use Mann's work as a means of tackling one of the most difficult questions facing contemporary social and political theorists—namely, how was it possible that the democratic nation of Germany could support Hitler and participate so enthusiastically in the fascism, imperialism, and genocide that he orchestrated? How could such a thing have happened?

In order to answer this question, Portilla turns to the conceptual framework of phenomenological nationalism (discussed in chapter 2) that I have argued is central to his phenomenological social theory (discussed in chapter 4). From this perspective, he suggests that everyday life in pre-war Germany took place within a distinctive "world," or context of significance, that altered how individual Germans experienced and made sense of the things they encountered. This world constituted a distinctive "space of possibilities," in the sense that the meaning things had within this world was shaped in advance by a certain set of interpretations about what thoughts, feelings, and actions would be reasonable, fitting, and viable. Of course, within this space of possibilities, a wide variety of positions were available to individuals—just as a soccer field, together with the rules and traditions of soccer, constitutes a "field of play" within which a wide variety of maneuvers and strategies are possible to players. However, all of the various positions that individual Germans took up—including the position that Mann took as a critic of Hitler—were ways of responding to things *as they showed up within a common context of significance*. Thus, although Mann certainly responded to things in a more admirable way that many of his countrymen, a close examination of his work shows that Mann remained firmly located within the same world, that he shared the same underlying context of significance as that which made shockingly brutal behaviors and attitudes appear to many Germans as reasonable, fitting, and viable.

In short, Portilla argues that if we read between the lines of Mann's novels, we can discern a "spiritual atmosphere" that is "exactly the same as that of National Socialism" [191]. As we will see, Portilla views this spiritual atmosphere as one that is structured by an affective attunement that is focused on the concern of *meaningfulness,* and especially the threat of a *loss of meaning*—the possibility that human life is ultimately meaningless in the vastness of a violent and uncaring cosmos. Whatever we conclude about Portilla's argument, his analysis deserves our serious consideration. For as Portilla eloquently notes in the essay's final passage, the war against Hitler may be over, but the kind of threat that Hitler represented endures. "In contemporary Germany," he says, "and even beyond its borders, under the ashes of prosperity, the embers of the will to power, hatred of reason, and fidelity to death are still alive, and it is not impossible that they may one day invade the world with a terrifying wave" [198]. If this is correct, then it is urgent that we gain a better understanding of the existential conditions that made Nazism possible.

I will return to the practical urgency of Portilla's critique of Mann in the final section of this chapter. Before arriving there, however, I want to highlight some aspects of this text that are likely to be obscured by the dramatic, real-world stakes of the essay's subject matter. My central claim in this chapter is that—in addition to whatever insights the essay may offer into the conditions of the possibility of Nazism and the ways that nationality can influence our experience—this essay, written just one year before Portilla's premature death, is of significant scholarly importance for understanding Portilla's philosophical system as a whole.

As noted previously, Portilla never had the opportunity to organize his thinking in the form of a book-length treatise; all we have from him are essays and newspaper columns, many of which respond to current events or the various topics that captured the interest of his intellectual circle. Within these formats, Portilla was able to launch incisive and philosophically sophisticated critiques, but he was not able to articulate the *positive vision* that motivated these critiques, the social and political ideals that he cherished, in comparison to which he found current social and political reality criticizable. In "Thomas Mann and German Irrationalism," Portilla does not explicitly articulate his positive vision, but he *does* express unusually vehement disdain for the values that, in his view, underlie Mann's novels. As he puts it, "the intellectual and affective climate of [Mann's] work is deeply unpleasant to me. And more than unpleasant, I would say that it deeply disgusts me" [183]. I argue that we can extract from this disgust the positive ideals that implicitly guide Portilla's engagement in social and political thought. Simply put, what Portilla hopes for is the *opposite* of what he sees in pre-war Germany.

What Portilla sees in pre-war Germany—in a tradition of thought that, he suggests, has roots as far back as Luther and can be glimpsed in Freud and in Romantics like Rilke, but which comes into full flower in the work of Schopenhauer, Wagner, and Nietzsche—is an "irrationalism" that endorses the following "postulates": "the primacy of life and the irrational over intelligence and reason; the primacy of death over life; the primacy of disease over health; and the primacy of the individual and the unique over the common and the universal" [188]. With the aid of these thinkers, he says, "Germany produced a kind of original cultural personality that was, in a certain way, exceptional, departing from the rational, Christian, and universalist spirit of the European tradition" [187–188]. On this basis, then, I offer the following interpretive conjecture: If the writings of these German thinkers elicit deep disgust from Portilla, it is because Portilla believes wholeheartedly in the "rational, Christian, and universalist spirit of the European tradition." In other words, Portilla's core political values are rationalism, Christianity, and universalism.

These core values give Portilla a political perspective that, in my view, is akin to what Cornel West calls *Christian democratic socialism*.[2] This political viewpoint is optimistic where "German irrationalism" is pessimistic. German irrationalism holds that reality is neither rational nor conducive to the maintenance of happy and healthy human communities. Those who see reality in this pessimistic manner may very well endorse fascism, concluding that political order is always tenuous and so must be imposed by force and fiercely protected from the constant threat of disorder. In contrast, Christian democratic socialism is guided by the belief that reality is rational, and its rationality is manifest and accessible to ordinary people, who therefore can be trusted to participate in governing themselves. Likewise, Christian democratic socialism holds that the logic of life is not perverse, but offers the possibility of love, abundance, forgiveness, and redemption, in addition to hardship, tragedy, unfairness, and evil—*if* we work together and care for those in need.

One attractive feature of this interpretation of Portilla's politics is that it connects his political philosophy with his interest in phenomenology in a profound way. If reality is inherently irrational and inhumane, as German irrationalism holds, then acquiring more knowledge of reality promises to bring only further grounds for political pessimism. But if, to the contrary, reality is inherently rational and relatively humane, then we need only to learn how to attend to reality and see it clearly in order to be able to transcend the provincial biases and irrational projections that prevent us from understanding one another, so that we may collaborate productively to address our shared aspirations and challenges. And, of course, learning how to attend to reality and see it clearly is precisely what Portilla thinks phenomenology helps us to accomplish. In this way, phenomenology provides both the *motivation* and the *means* for social and political transformation.

In what follows, I further develop this interpretation of Portilla's positive political vision, highlighting connections between Portilla's approach to phenomenology and the political ideals that appear to guide his work. In section 1, I return to Portilla's masterpiece, "Phenomenology of Relajo," in order to draw out the ethical and political ideals that orient and motivate Portilla's work. In section 2, I step back and consider Portilla's analysis of pre-war Germany, as well as his investigations of Mexico and the US, in light of my interpretative account of Portilla's positive vision. By doing so, I argue, we can identify some of the most crucial challenges facing those who yearn for the healing of our nation: liberation from the moods that have held sway in our collective lives for decades, distorting our relationships to one another and to the worlds we share, undermining our ability to flourish as sense-makers.

1. Phenomenological Flourishing

My interpretation of Portilla's positive political vision is inspired by Aristotle, who, unlike Portilla, philosophized in a systematic fashion, so that his views can be organized as a neat progression from metaphysics, to ethics, to politics. According to Aristotle, reality is teleological in nature, and every kind of thing has a particular function; therefore, for human beings, virtue lies in the development of the capacities required for the excellent performance of the human function, i.e., the development of the capacities that allow human beings to flourish as the kind of creatures they are; and, therefore, the best political arrangements are those that cultivate and express human flourishing. In this section I argue that if there is a philosophical system that implicitly grounds Portilla's thought, it is one that is marked by his consistent emphasis on *phenomenology* and the central importance of *affect*. Thus, instead of a true metaphysics, Portilla offers a view about how meaning is experienced, according to which meaning is disclosed by our emotional responses to the things we encounter. In other words, our reality is meaningful to the extent that we are able to perceive and respond emotionally to the beauty of the beautiful, the joyfulness of what is joyful, the injustice of what is unjust, the sadness of what is sad, and so on. On the basis of this view about the nature of meaning, Portilla's work points us toward a quasi-ethical ideal that I call "phenomenological flourishing," a kind of wellbeing consisting in the development of our capacities to disclose meaning. As we will see, flourishing in this sense centrally involves the skillful navigation of moods in order to be able to disclose the meaning of the things we encounter. From this perspective, the best political arrangements will be those that nourish and reflect our capacities to disclose meaning. In the current political context, pursuing this ideal will require that nations be liberated from entrenched affective attunements that undermine individuals' capacities to skillfully navigate moods and disclose the full range of meanings that the world has to offer.

Let us begin, then, with Portilla's view of the nature of reality, or more precisely, the nature of our experience of meaning. In "Phenomenology of Relajo," Portilla touches on three fundamental features of meaningful experience. First, meaning consists in the evaluative properties that things have in the context of a situation. Portilla uses the term "value" to refer to evaluative properties, but what he has in mind is not a belief or principle (as when we praise a person's "strong family values"), but simply the way something *matters*. Examples of values (i.e., meanings or matterings) that he offers include such things as the *gracefulness* displayed in a dance performance, the *joyousness* of a celebration, the *solemnity* of a ceremony, the *fascinating quality* of a university lecture, or the *gratification* found in an "orderly and creative conversation."[3] Second, Portilla argues that such meaning is experienced as originating externally to us, in the world itself, rather than as being a mere subjective projection. Our experience of meaning is thus marked by a certain passivity, in the sense that we find ourselves suddenly subjected to "the call of value," the experience of being *called upon* to respond appropriately to the way things matter.[4] Third, despite originating outside us, meaning requires our cooperation in order for it to come fully into existence and remain real and present in the world. We cooperate with meaning and aid in its realization primarily by responding emotionally to it in an appropriate way, allowing ourselves to be immersed in the meaningfulness of the experience and to be gripped or moved by the way it matters.[5]

In sum, Portilla holds that the world is meaningful, and while its meaning is not a mere subjective projection, nevertheless the meaningfulness of the world requires our sincere cooperation in order for it to be realized. As Portilla puts it:

> All value, when grasped, appears surrounded by an aura of demands, endowed with a certain weight and with certain gravity that brings it from its pure ideality toward the world of reality. The value solicits its realization. The mere grasping of the value carries with it the fulfillment of that demand, of that call to its own realization in the world; and in order for this demand—which appears in the objective realm of the lived experience of the value—to be realized, the subject, in turn, performs an act, a movement of loyalty [to the value] that is a kind of "yes," like an affirmative response.[6]

Responding emotionally in this way to the call of value constitutes what Portilla terms "seriousness," i.e., taking the meaning of the object or event seriously.

> This answer, this "yes" that corresponds—by means of the subjective aspect of the grasping of the value—to the objective demand with which it presents itself, is an intimate movement of loyalty and commitment. This is seriousness. When, in an immediate and direct (nonreflexive) way, I pronounce that "yes" inside myself, when I give an adequate response to the demand for actualization inherent to the value, I tacitly commit myself to a behavior, I mortgage my future behavior, making it agree beforehand with that demand: I take the value seriously. Seriousness is the intimate and deep commitment to which I make a pledge with myself in order to maintain a value within existence.[7]

The *political* implications of these points are profound. If value is not merely subjective, but requires our cooperation in order for it to be realized, then we have reason to work together to construct the social and spiritual conditions that make meaning possible.

To illustrate Portilla's conception of the experience of meaning—as well as the political implications of his view—consider his example of the gracefulness of a dance performance. Portilla notes that the gracefulness of the dance is not something that the dancer alone has complete control over. Instead, in order for gracefulness truly to shine forth from the dance, there must be cooperation from an *audience*, who must direct their attention to the performance quietly and with interest, allowing themselves to become immersed in it and moved by its beauty.[8]

> For example, the gracefulness of a dancer is something almost tangible, but at the same time it requires the attention of an audience to be able to unfurl itself in the fullness of its possibilities. It requires the attention of one or two people who anticipate the graceful movements as something expected, necessary, and "logical," and which nevertheless surprises [them] as an absolute creation, as an absolutely unpredictable novelty. Gracefulness, undoubtedly, rests on the dance technique—learned laboriously by the performer—but also on recognition by the spectator. In a certain sense, it is a collective endeavor directed from within by a tacit agreement between performer and audience. It emerges, precarious and vulnerable, like a burgeoning that lays root in the field of harmony among dancers, musicians, and spectators, and it survives as something definitive, perfect, and stimulating in the memory of all these groups. This gracefulness cannot attain the stability and solidity of the "thing-value." Its evanescent reality has required the support of multiple generosities, and it rests on this support.[9]

In this experience of gracefulness becoming realized through the cooperation of the dancer and the audience, Portilla sees the possibility of genuine community—the generous cooperation of people, both with one another and with a precarious but real meaning that transcends the particular individuals involved and gathers them together in appreciation of what matters.

Portilla's views regarding the nature of meaningful experience shape the way he assesses the character traits and dispositions of individuals. Whereas Aristotle focused on moral virtues and vices in relation to the ideal of human flourishing, Portilla focuses on the emotional dispositions that affect a person's capacity to respond to meaning and thereby flourish in a phenomenological sense. However, as mentioned above, Portilla's ideal of phenomenological flourishing is implicit in the text and expressed *via negativa* in his critiques of characters whom he sees as exhibiting a stunted capacity for meaning-disclosure. In such critiques, we see an implicit view that there is an important kind of wellbeing that consists in the development of our capacities to reveal and respond to what matters in the situation at hand.

In "Phenomenology of Relajo," for example, Portilla criticizes the *relajiento* and *apretado* (discussed in some detail in chapters 1 and 2)— not for their moral vices, but for their stunted capacity to disclose the meaning of what they encounter. Each of these characters is unable to respond emotionally to the full range of ways that things can matter, and so they are often unable to participate in collective endeavors to bring forth the meaningful possibilities that are incipient within a situation. These characters are emotionally inhibited in different ways. The *relajiento* is not serious enough but, rather, compulsively enacts a "suspension of seriousness," typically by joking around constantly, refusing to allow himself to be moved by any kind of meaning besides the bitter humor that can be found in futile endeavors. The *apretado*, on the other hand, is too serious about a narrow range of meanings to be able to take other kinds of meaning seriously. In particular, the *apretado* is fixated on propriety and status, and as a result, he is too uptight to allow himself to be moved by any meaning besides that which confers importance on his own social role.

In both cases, the result is that these individuals are largely insensible to the incredible wealth of meaning in the world, and therefore live small, stunted lives, tormented by a deep, spiritual suffering and a profound isolation from others. In the case of the *relajiento,* because he "refuses to take anything seriously, to commit to anything," his time on earth does not take the shape of a developing and unfolding human life, but is merely a collection of relatively meaningless moments, each unrelated to the others. As Portilla puts it:

> A "relajiento" is, literally, an individual without a future. The "relajiento" lives perpetually turned toward that very close past from which the present has just emerged, to laughingly negate its content. . . . The "relajiento" assumes no responsibility for anything; he doesn't risk doing anything; he is simply a good-humored witness of the banality of life.[10]

The good humor of the *relajiento*, however, is a mask that only thinly disguises a "deep melancholy that is only revealed in secret confidences" and a "nihilism" that, over time, becomes compulsive and "mechanical," making him vulnerable to "an acute sense of failure" as well as to "resentment and to all forms of suicide."[11] While the *relajiento* makes for a good drinking buddy, and he may therefore spend a good deal of time "laughing heartily" with his companions, he cannot cooperate wholeheartedly with others in the realization a transcendent value, and for this reason, he is permanently cut off from the experience of genuine community.[12]

The fate of the *apretado* is not much better, as his emotional fixation on social status quickly becomes a prison.

> In this way, "apretado" individuals are slaves of others: slaves of the dispossessed, whom they fear but whom they need in order to be "apretado" and distinguished; slaves of the possessors, whom they fear and flatter; slaves of appearances to which they subjugate their entire lives; slaves of their apparent virtues and of their maxims, which they consider threatened by negation since "apretado" individuals are immersed in a world of negations. They are continually obligated to stand up for these virtues and maxims, since casting doubt on them is equivalent to casting doubt on themselves. They are slaves of property, doomed to pursue it or to simulate it in order to be valuable, or—to say the same thing—in order to be. "Apretado" individuals are the living denial of freedom.[13]

Like the *relajiento*, the *apretado* is permanently cut off from experiencing genuine community with others. While healthy relationships involve vulnerability, in the sense of being open to being touched and even changed by the other, the *apretado* is too self-important and uptight to admit being vulnerable and in need of what the other can provide, and for this reason he is unable to participate in meaningful interchange and dialog with others.[14] In the absence of healthy and vibrant relationships built on mutual appreciation of a transcendent meaning, the *apretado* must rely on artificial, institutional structures—and ultimately violence—in order to maintain his place in the social order.[15]

On the basis of Portilla's critique of these characters, we can postulate that phenomenological flourishing requires the skillful navigation of moods in order to respond appropriately to the meaning of the situation at hand, and, when called upon to do so, to participate with others in bringing that meaning into fruition. This skill, I argue, will involve making use of both "seriousness" and "the suspension of seriousness," without being captured by either of these extremes. For example, returning to Portilla's description of the gracefulness of the dance performance, we can imagine that as the audience enters the theater, each of these individuals has recently been immersed in a different situation, and that some of these previous situations were frustrating, some were joyful, some were sad, and so on. Therefore, in order to make themselves ready to become immersed in the meaning of the performance, the members of the audience must "suspend" their responsiveness to that previous situation. If, for instance, a person remains gripped by a mood of irritability after struggling for a half hour to find a parking spot near the theater, they will not able to be moved emotionally by the gracefulness of the dance. After detaching from their previous moods and thus making themselves sufficiently open to the meaning of the present situation, members of the audience must be willing and able to let themselves be gripped by the meaning of the performance and to do what they can to deepen and intensify their responsiveness to it. This may include taking a variety of actions to *protect* the mood that enables the performance to work, and to *repair* the mood if it should be disrupted by a momentary distraction—activities that are constitutive of taking the performance and the gracefulness of the dance "seriously." But at same time, they cannot become so immersed in this particular meaning that they become completely unresponsive to other meanings that may emerge as the situation develops or changes. If the members of the audience take the dance performance too seriously, they will become *apretados*, uptight theater snobs who cannot appreciate the many other kinds of things that matter, apart from what matters about the performance.

In this way, the navigation of moods involves a constant dance of detachment and immersion as we attune and re-attune ourselves to the meaning of the situations we encounter over time, so that we are able to appreciate and respond appropriately to the diverse ways that things can matter. We can describe this quasi-ethical ideal of phenomenological flourishing in a number of different ways. As an ideal of *emotional agency*, it involves the development of the capacities associated with the various modes of sense-making described in chapter 4—cognitive, linguistic, social, and practical. As an ideal of *emotional maturity*, it involves the development of the psychosocial stamina that enables us to resist the temptation to resort to defensive maneuvers when faced with meanings that make us uncomfortable. As an ideal of *emotional freedom*, it involves the development of a kind of flexible and resilient emotional agency not only within individuals, but also within entire communities. For as we have seen, the meaning of things depends on their context of significance, and this context of significance is constituted in large part by the traditions and institutions that enable us to think, speak, feel, and act in the ways that we do. To this extent, our sense-making capacities are inherently social in nature—and indeed, not merely social, but also *national*. Thus, although Portilla does not say so explicitly, there is one idea that is never far from the surface of his essays: that if we hope to see the development of emotional freedom among individuals, we must work for the *affective liberation* of the nations to which they belong.

2. Affective Liberation

In Portilla's essays, we find that the central political task of our time is finding a way to dissolve the rigid and harmful affective attunements that grip our nations—such as the profound *zozobra* that Portilla saw in Mexico, the *threatened innocence* he saw in the United States, and the deep sense of *meaninglessness* he saw in Germany. On Portilla's view, such affective attunements structure the context of significance within which the events of everyday life in the nation gain their meaning, altering what possibilities show up as live options. By contributing to the tendency of individuals within the nation to be over-sensitive to some concerns and under-sensitive to others, these national affective attunements undermine individuals' ability to respond flexibly and appropriately to the many ways that things can matter. As a result, they subvert the phenomenological flourishing of individuals and choke off the lifeblood of community—the experience of cooperating with others in the realization of a transcendent and evanescent value. As these experiences of collective meaning-disclosure become less frequent and less intense, individuals within a nation lose the ability to experience themselves as being a genuine community. In place of true coexistence, we increasingly find its degraded counterpart—the mere cohabitation of individuals within an artificial territorial boundary. When the interests of faction and self are the only interests that make any real sense, national life becomes disoriented, and the nation finds itself vulnerable to the influence of strongmen who promise a return to order. But, of course, this promise is as empty as it is dangerous, because in the absence of the *existential order* found in genuine community, the order of political institutions must always be violently imposed.

By way of conclusion, then, let us reflect on where these rigid, national affective attunements might come from, and what might be done to overcome them. A helpful place to start to understand the tendency of nations to succumb to the grip of problematic affective attunements, in my view, is Portilla's analysis of the experience of meaning. According to Portilla, all values—that is, all of the evaluative properties of things that are actually present in our experience—are evanescent, fragile, and temporary. Values emerge into existence, and if we cooperate in their realization by responding emotionally to them, they may blossom, shine forth, and remain for some time, but ultimately, they will disappear, as what matters in the present situation will inevitably develop and change. Meaning is thus unstable, unpredictable, and beyond any person's control. Even if we orchestrate situations that are conducive to emergence of a certain kind of meaning, our ability to do so does not constitute any personal power to produce meaning on our own. The context of significance that makes the emergence of meaning possible includes other people, who are beyond our control; moreover, it includes social institutions that are being constantly negotiated and subjected to the many forces of historical change.

The result of all this is a profound and inescapable *existential vulnerability* that consists in the fact that the values that give our lives meaning are always subject to "suspension" in ways that we cannot control. This fact gives rise to some of the most difficult challenges that we face as human beings, challenges related to the delicate work of balancing immersion and detachment. For example, how can we be wholeheartedly committed to something, yet remain flexible, adaptable, and resilient, ready to give it up when needed? How can we create strong identities without then becoming prisoners of those identities? In order to avoid the pain and suffering generated by our existential vulnerability, we are constantly tempted to resort to one of two basic defensive strategies: to become overly attached or overly detached. In the first case, we refuse to accept that values are evanescent, and like the *apretado*, we act as though our cherished values were stable and solid "things." In the second case, we protect ourselves from the pain of the disappearance of values by keeping ourselves detached and invulnerable, refusing, like the *relajiento*, to take them seriously. As we have seen, resorting to either one of these defensive strategies comes at an enormous spiritual cost. Nevertheless, it requires admirable courage and support for anyone to be able to avoid the temptation to try to protect themselves from their existential vulnerability in these ways.

With this in mind, we can see that the situation is exponentially more difficult for those who have experienced traumatically painful encounters with existential vulnerability, especially when they are young. If a young person is confronted with the fact that any value can be suspended—that the context of significance their lives and identities depend on can be suddenly taken from them, and neither they nor anyone else has the power to secure or guarantee any particular meaning—the devastating impact of this experience can shape their character for many years. Such trauma can push a person to adopt one of the two basic defensive strategies, attachment or detachment, as a stable part of their personality, or to cycle endlessly between these two opposite extremes. Judith Herman describes the latter outcome in psychological terms in her classic text, *Trauma and Recovery*.

> The conflict between the will to deny horrible events [i.e., excessive detachment] and the will to proclaim them aloud [i.e., excessive attachment] is the central dialectic of psychological trauma. . . . The psychological distress symptoms of traumatized people simultaneously call attention to the existence of an unspeakable secret and deflect attention from it. This is most apparent in the way traumatized people alternate between feeling numb and reliving the event. The dialectic of trauma gives rise to complicated, sometimes uncanny alterations of consciousness, which George Orwell, one of the committed truth-tellers of our century, called "doublethink," and which mental health professionals, searching for calm, precise language, call "dissociation."[16]

As Herman's text makes clear, when the pain of existential vulnerability becomes traumatic, it becomes difficult for a person to navigate moods with flexibility and resilience, especially with regard to the particular values or concerns most directly associated with their trauma. Instead of a skillful dance of immersion and detachment, we find internal strife and polarization.

Is it possible that, like individuals, nations, too, can develop conflicted and polarized emotional dispositions in response to traumatic confrontations with existential vulnerability that take place early in their histories? Perhaps extraordinarily painful experiences, occurring at an impressionable time in the nation's history, can disrupt the development of a community's sense-making capacities, thereby shaping its shared context of significance for generations to come. Did something occur during the birth of the Mexican nation that can be understood as an extraordinary and traumatic confrontation with the inescapable insecurity of identity, and with our basic insufficiency as human beings, whose lives are located on just this side of non-existence? Did something happen during the formation of the United States that constituted a traumatic encounter with the possibility of our own sin and evil? Was the German nation wounded by an early glimpse of the ultimate groundlessness of meaning, leading to an endless circling around "the problem of . . . the 'why' of the very meaning of life" [187]?

If this line of inquiry is on the right track, it may shed light on some of the challenges faced by those who seek to intervene into the cultural politics of their nation. If a nation is gripped by a rigid and problematic affective attunement that originated in an early traumatic experience, distorting the nation's relationship to a certain kind of value or concern, the healing of this nation will require a collective *desensitization* to the urgency of this value or concern. Only when the value or concern in question is not experienced as a matter of life or death will it be possible for individuals to avoid succumbing to the temptation to use defensive strategies to cope with the intensity that arises whenever it appears that the value or concern is at stake. But accomplishing such a desensitization without resorting to those same defensive strategies will be quite tricky. For example, if it is true that pre-war Germany was in the midst of a profound confrontation with the possibility of meaninglessness, then what it needed most was to realize that this concern, while real, is not all-important, but is simply one concern among many that deserve our attention. What the German nation needed was to hear the message, "Do not worry so much about the possibility meaninglessness." But how could a person communicate such a message? Those who tried to communicate this message in a level-headed and measured way were likely to find that they were totally unable to connect with a society that was gripped by the apparent urgency of the concern. In the context of that urgency, the only messages that were likely to make sense were those that were more extreme, such as a straightforward embrace of nihilism ("Do not worry about meaninglessness—because life is totally and irrevocably meaningless anyway, so there is no point worrying about it!") or a straightforward denial of nihilism and an embrace of some fundamental and stable value ("Do not worry about meaninglessness—because our movement will guarantee the meaningfulness of your existence!").

What, then, will help to loosen the grip of an affective attunement that is undermining the phenomenological flourishing of a nation? In the case of traumatized individuals, what appears to help is to learn about the nature and manifestations of trauma in general, and to come to understand one's own traumatic experience in particular, so that one is able to put the experience into a narrative that can be shared with others. According to Herman, healing from trauma has the following elements:

> First, the physiological symptoms of post-traumatic stress disorder have been brought within manageable limits. Second, the person is able to bear the feelings associated with traumatic memories. Third, the person has authority over her memories; she can elect both to remember the trauma and to put memory aside. Fourth, the memory of the traumatic event is a coherent narrative, linked with feeling. Fifth, the person's damaged self-esteem has been restored. Sixth, the person's important relationships have been reestablished. Seventh and finally, the person has reconstructed a coherent system of meaning and belief that encompasses the story of trauma.[17]

If the healing of nations is similar, then perhaps philosophy can play an important role in the process of constructing an understanding of what happened to the nation, how that past experience continues to shape the life of the nation, and what larger system of meaning could integrate this trauma in a more balanced way.

Indeed, if there is one overarching goal of Portilla's philosophical work, it is to use the power of language to contribute to the healing of nations. This hope is articulated in a passage from "Phenomenology of Relajo" that has already been cited, but which we may better appreciate now, at the end of this inquiry.

> From this point of view, philosophy has the function of promoting reason in a specific society, of clearly putting before the collective consciousness the ultimate base of its thinking, of its feeling, and of its acting. Philosophy, to the extent that it is a "logos" on humankind, performs an educating and a liberating function. Through it, what is concealed and tacit becomes present and explicit, and something can be transformed by its enlightening action. . . . The word can pull me

out of the magma of the situation and allow me to act in a manner contrary to the objective currents of obligation that flow from it. In a direction opposite to that of psychological habit, tradition, class interest, and so on, the truth sets me free, and perhaps the ultimate sense of all authentic philosophy is this liberating operation of "logos."[18]

As human beings, our lives are always poised at the edge of the abyss, subjected to the sudden suspension of the meanings that form the only ground we have. In our fear we often clutch at whatever assurances are closest to hand, regardless of whether doing so helps us to flourish. Portilla has an extraordinary appreciation for this painful aspect of the human condition, and his work teaches us to look here, with sympathy, to understand the ultimate source of our political woes. Thus while his essays may appear at first glance to be entirely critical of the nations and characters he discusses, we must remember that what motivates Portilla's inquiry in each instance is a sincere commitment to use the power of the word to help communities be more free—to discover and return to those places where values can emerge into existence before our eyes, uniting us in appreciation and commitment, giving dignity to our collective struggle to find the meaning of our experience.

Notes

1. Hermann Kurzke, *Thomas Mann: Life as a Work of Art: A Biography*, trans. Leslie Willson (Princeton, NJ: Princeton University Press, 2002).

2. Cornel West, "The Making of an American Radical of African American Descent" in *The Cornel West Reader*, 3–19.

3. Portilla, "Phenomenology of Relajo," 145.

4. Ibid., 142.

5. Describing the experience of emotional immersion in response to meaning, Portilla offers the example of "enraged individuals who 'feel,' in the cenesthesia of their rage, in the contraction of their bowels, the hatefulness of their enemy or of the offense. Enraged individuals, in effect, *sink into* their rage; they let it flow like a current of bodily sensations that manifest the hatefulness of what provoked the rage; they *let themselves be led* by the rage precisely to make the abominable [aspects] of the motive more embodied and more tangible—which serves at the same time as a legitimization of the violence of their emotion." Portilla, "Phenomenology of Relajo," 155.

6. Portilla, "Phenomenology of Relajo," 129.

7. Ibid.

8. The notion that meaning "shines forth" in this way is central to the view defended in Hubert Dreyfus and Sean Kelly, *All Things Shining: Reading the Western Classics to Find Meaning in a Secular Age* (New York: Simon and Schuster, 2011).

9. Portilla, "Phenomenology of Relajo," p. 145.

10. Ibid., 147.

11. Ibid., 149.

12. Ibid., 148.

13. Ibid., 146.

14. "Dialogue is impossible with an 'apretado' individual. Genuine dialogue presupposes the transcendence and the evanescence of value; but when value is there—completely made out of flesh and English cashmere—the only thing left to do is listen attentively and assent respectfully, or dissent—but not a lot and only with the greatest possible prudence." Portilla, "Phenomenology of Relajo," 197.

15. "Deep down, 'apretado' individuals love order more than freedom. Order is that stable situation of society that allows these individuals to play the exclusivity game and to give themselves the pleasure of embodying value." Portilla, "Phenomenology of Relajo," 196.

16. Judith Herman, *Trauma and Recovery: The Aftermath of Violence—From Domestic Abuse to Political Terror* (London: Hachette UK, 2015), 1.

17. Herman, *Trauma and Recovery*, 213.

18. Portilla, "Phenomenology of Relajo," 127.

"Critique of Criticism"
"The Spiritual Crisis of the United States"
"Thomas Mann and German Irrationalism"

BY JORGE PORTILLA

Critique of Criticism[1]

Jorge Portilla

Translated by Francisco Gallegos and
Carlos Alberto Sánchez

The dispute, badly formulated and imprecise, over Mexican literature that has been unfolding since the famous "roundtable" held in Bellas Artes some months ago offers excellent material for reflection to anyone interested in the spiritual situation of Mexico.[2] The scope of this situation is clear to anyone who has realized the extent to which problems surrounding community, its structure, its constitution, and its destiny, occupy a central place in contemporary philosophy.

In Mexico, as one would expect in regard to any problem of the spirit, the spiritual aspects that are conditioned by the structure of our community are also becoming more evident. The ground of *living* communal relations that can be found in *every* aspect of human life is increasingly obvious, and this ostensible presence of the specifically social in everything is undoubtedly one of the essential features that characterizes the height of our times. The ostensibility [*la ostensibilidad*] of community is today an indication of the level reached everywhere in philosophical, scientific, and everyday consciousness.

But when a structure of the community is made visible as a constituent feature or as a ground of all human action and thought, this also begins to expose the deceptions that the beneficiaries of the "social system" could get away with in the era of naive individualism.

One of these deceptions is rehearsed every day in Mexico, that of a certain "Literary Criticism" that is neither literary nor criticism, but a crude condemnation of some writers in the name of the Mexican Nation. A literary criticism that is expressed in interviews, in gossip columns, in conversations in the café, which is more in the atmosphere than on paper, and with respect to which it is necessary to highlight certain points so as to not end up drowning in it or, at least, being a silent accomplice [159].

Clearly no one writes for himself. It is evident that the act of writing, even if one keeps the writing in a safe, is an outline for communication; it is the outline for a possible dialog where the interlocutor, or at least the concrete witness, is, in the end, the critic. And it is equally true that the writer, even if he does not address himself or intends not to address himself to a community, even if he merely proposes to display to others the marvels of his interiority, remains "situated" in that community, constrained first of all by the language in which he writes, and establishes himself, whether he wants it or not, within a certain attitude and in a certain place within it. Society is a permanent field, a dimension of existence that can be evaded by no one, and even less by the writer who has left an objective testimony of his being in his work. But neither can critics, nor even critics who prosecute writers, take the social as the basis for their criticism. It is not enough to make oneself disinterested in the life of the community itself in order to cease to be situated in it, certainly. But neither is the appeal to society enough to be situated in it in the form that one would wish, just as it is not enough to say that one is in the right to actually be in the right. One can speak loudly as a representative of the "people" or the "proletariat" without actually becoming a representative.

The community is the atmosphere in which both the writer and the critic breathe, and the act of simply condemning the writer, in the name of the community, is a folly and an act of bad faith.

Condemnation is foolishness, especially in this case, because it is nothing more than an exorcism, a magical gesture that pretends to expel the writer from the community for whom he writes. But magic is ineffective. Octavio Paz, Juan José Arreola, Juan Rulfo, Carlos Fuentes, Garibay, Burns, etc., cannot be expelled from the Mexican community by calling them English or French or xenophiles [*extranjerizante*]. They cannot be expelled from our cultural community, not even by executing them all so as to remove them from the world of the living, because their work, whether good or bad, is *constituent* of that cultural community. To expel them would have to involve eliminating them physically and also destroying their work in an auto-da-fé with the express approval of the nation. But this is, at least, [160] improbable.

If the critic's denial is not this magical act of expulsion, but an order to be silent, a "silence yourself" that the critic directs to the writer, then it is an act of bad faith, because language and communication are used to deny someone the right to speak. Criticism, then, is no longer critical but personal, and the audience is deceived when it is asked to accept it as criticism, because it is no longer criticism but a personal matter.

In either case, the critic is supposed to be a representative of the society in whose name he condemns. But this assumption introduces an element that diverts criticism from its original intention. Things take on the aspect of a nationalist McCarthyism, since the reasons put forward are not properly aesthetic, but rather reasons of cultural politics. On one side are the good guys and their representative, the critic; and on the other are the bad guys and their spokesperson, the writer. And the aesthetic or literary criteria of "literary" criticism, where are they?

It is useless to try to figure any of this out. We find only the bereaved censor of the Mexican nation who knows what is and what is not in the best interest of the nation and which, in the name of this national interest—never defined by him in clear terms—vetoes the communicative effort of the writer.

What can the accusation (which is not a critical judgment) of "xeno-phile" [*extranjerizante*] mean to a Mexican writer? Obviously it means that this foreign writer has no right to address Mexicans. Put another way: it means that this foreign writer is not, properly speaking, a Mexican writer, and that he is not a Mexican writer simply because he writes in the manner of the French, English, Spanish, or American writers.

This presupposes the previous acceptance that Mexico is not a nation anymore, that it is not a participant of the universal community, but a sealed repository of human culture. That we have nothing in common with men of other nationalities. This assumes that Mexico *is* or *possesses* a specific good that is put in danger by the communicative action of the foreign writer; and, furthermore, that Mexicans possess an excellence that can be contaminated by contact with that which is alien to it [161].

Thus, to the internal negation of the Mexican community within the dialog between the critic and the writer, there must be added, *necessarily*, the external negation of the human community, the community from which Mexico has been removed. Certainly, Mexico has been removed from the human community for the sake of a certain excellence, for the sake of a certain absolute value belonging to Mexicanness itself. It is obvious to the critic that what the xenophile *sees* as valuable "outside" of our repository must be "inside." But how to find it if we have begun our search by defining it negatively? What is this Mexican excellence that xenophiles do not see, but that the nationalists do see, even though they have never told us much about it? They invite us to contemplate Mexican excellence and want the writers to use their talents to mine this priceless value. But why would they not benefit themselves with their discovery? Why do they not take advantage of that mine themselves?

Perhaps because they have begun to define it negatively, as non-English, non-French, non-Spanish, non-Yankee, etc., and, unfortunately, a sum of negations cannot yield a positive result. The negation of universality, masked behind the negation of particularity, cannot transform itself into something positive, and hence the notorious infertility of all nationalisms—of *all* nationalisms, including the Mexican. Because, in the best of cases, if we convert the negation of universality into the affirmation of particularity, we would affirm as excellent a Mexican particularity. But which one? This particularity cannot be geographical, since, in human affairs, geography cannot be decisive as a source of value. It would have to be a cultural particularity. But culture is nothing but the concrete expression of the *universal.* Our search for the particular would have to take us to that which could particularize culture, give it local color. The source of this peculiar color would have to be race.

Race is the only thing that can offer sufficient guarantees of peculiarity. From the racial point of view, the most active and fruitful aspect of our history, the mestizo aspect, offers a danger, since to affirm it is to imply the affirmation of a "piece" of the Spanish; however, we all agree that what race has of value comes from our indigenous "blood." [162] What are the excellences of the indigenous people? The answer is: that they are indigenous. But this is exactly what Hitler said about the Germans. The Germans were excellent because they were Germans. If we appeal to the indigenous cultural past, then we are doing what Mussolini did when he appealed to the imperial past of Rome to prove Italian "superiority," and when Hitler appealed to "Germanness," polluted by Rome and Christianity, to arouse Germany's homicidal and anti-universalist enthusiasm. When a group of people begins to consider itself wonderful because of what it has of its "own" and what makes it "different," it is already preparing the destruction of other peoples. But this is no longer "culture"; this is war.

The denial of universality, implicit in the vague, nationalist "criticism," leads us to fall into the negative hollowness of nationalism, in the same obtuse racism of Hitler, which has marked, moreover, the most infertile epoch of German culture and, perhaps, the erasure of Germany's distinguished cultural past.

To condemn the effort of a Mexican writer by saying "That has already been done in France or in the United States" is to appeal to nationalism, which is latent in Mexicans as it is in men of all nationalities; it is a dirty game. It is to condemn Mexicans to singularity, which, in addition to being demagogic, is to go against culture as a manifestation of universality and fraternity.

But it does have an advantage for the critic. This criticism can signify that the one who implements it is a sensible man who will not be deceived. He is much better than the writer he criticizes. And how does he demonstrate it? He demonstrates this by not writing like Proust, nor like Joyce, nor like Faulkner. He does not write like them because he does not want to. All he wants is to give a critique whose ultimate and real meaning is to invite the writer not to write.

The result is silence; it is a criticism that shrugs its shoulders, that closes the dialog and opens the region of solitude, of discouragement, and of infertility. There is no real answer for the writer: there is no orientation, no direction to follow in terms of his art. If someone happens upon a good path for our self-understanding, like Rulfo, neutralizing popular language until [163] it becomes a literary instrument capable of expressing certain states of what we might call our national spirit, or like Arreola who does this with a clean, agile prose full of spirit, the conatus of *national* lucidity found in these fortunate discoveries dies in the middle of the absurd discussion about which of these writers is "better." Criticism becomes an obtuse bar dispute with no end. If Rulfo is "better" than Arreola *because* he is more Mexican, why must he not be "worse" than Pancho Villa, who was, no doubt, more Mexican than Rulfo? And why should not Arreola be much "better" than Kafka, since Arreola is Mexican?

The voice of the critic, distant and imprecise, sounds once again and we hear it speak of "struggle against imperialism." But as it speaks, bad faith once again reappears. Now criticism wants the writer to be a political writer. It points to a theme. It condemns the writer as a writer because he does not deal with politics, because he does not give a historical-universal direction to his writings. The writer is baffled, does not know what to answer. Maybe he does not feel inclined to deal with issues he has no expertise in. He is not interested in the philosophy of history, and he does not know how to put the philosophy of history into a story that recounts the vicissitudes of a farmer or the love affairs of the young petit bourgeois. On the other hand, he has nothing at his disposal to oppose the struggle against imperialism, and he oscillates between, on the one hand, a feeling of guilt before the critic who, without supporting it himself, throws the weight of history and the destiny of man at him, and, on the other, protest against incomprehension and the violations against his rights as an artist. The dispute is complicated, partly because it is not clearly formulated and partly because it is tied to terror: Who would want to appear before the poor and exploited Mexican people as a defender of imperialism?

The critic deploys the terrorism of the social, as in another time, and in another respect, other critics exercised the terrorism of science or that of freedom. In fact, this criticism is simple and overwhelming. He criticizes the writer for what he does not do, and not for what he does. Against this charge there is no possible defense. The writer finds in it a monstrous negative image of himself in which he does not recognize himself. It shows him, or rather, it hits him over the head with what he is not, without appreciating the value of what he is. His guilt is infinite and without appeal [164]. The critic, on the other hand, is a mass of positivity and innocence; he is what the writer should strive to be.

The way this strange and wonderful transformation is done is simple: The writer has not trumpeted his anti-imperialist views, he does not recount the struggle of the people or the proletariat for the sake of man's freedom, *therefore* he is the enemy of the people, of the proletariat, and of man. He is a traitor sold for Yankee gold and, for that reason, also a bad writer. His accuser must be a hero of the resistance and serving the cause; *after all*, he exposes the villainous writer and is, perhaps, an excellent writer himself, as evidenced by the fact the he does literary criticism. The result of the criticism is twofold: It creates an enemy of the proletariat, which it exposes and annihilates in the very act of creating it, and also creates a proletarian defender who continues to exist afterwards, with the clear conscience of a just man.

The dirty game is obvious. What we have here is criticism in a void. A man is judged for what he does not do. It would be as valid to condemn an archaeologist for not being a mathematician or a physiologist for not being an engineer. The *not* is an inexhaustible source of guilt. Certainly, political judgment is more universalizable than professional judgment, but, in any case, it should fall on positive political acts and not on a literary work as such. Here we have, in reality, a political judgment passing itself off as a literary judgment, with which someone is freed from the effort of judging according to the things themselves and, along the way, confirms his position as the beneficiary of a political attitude that he presents as literary excellence.

If you talk about politics from the standpoint of literature and talk about literature from the standpoint of politics, things become unclear, and someone will be left with the vague impression that the writer is a bad Mexican, an imperialist, and a bad writer, and that the critic, on the other hand, is an honest man who is not easily fooled. The political judgment seems true because it distracts from the literary question. The literary judgment, in turn, seems true because it diverts attention to the infinite field of negations and to politics, and the critic [165] can pass himself off as an honest man.

In reality, this way of judging gets everything wrong. It is false that those writers condemned by the gossip of the salon that calls itself "leftist" are enemies of the working classes and partisans of imperialism. It is false that not thematizing anti-imperialism diminishes their quality as writers. It is false that critics, in exercising their badly named criticism, are in reality performing a useful labor in the service of the working classes or their interests.

In the assumption that the opinion of the critics is capable of informing the opinion of the working classes—which is extremely doubtful; in the assumption that this entire dispute is really about something more than a vulgar pretense of prestige on the part of the critics; all of that is in the heart of the "bourgeoisie" and without any real or tangible reference to the working classes being against the writers we have mentioned, or those writers being against the working classes. It is not enough to call someone a traitor for him to be one in reality. And if any of them ever became an actual informant or agent of imperialism, his role as agent or informant would come from a positive act of commitment or a positive commitment to some imperialist body, but not from the fact of not creating literature with a certain theme.

If Juan José Arreola were to accuse one of his critics before the Investigative Committee of the American Senate, affirming, for example, that the critic is a dangerous man who threatens the peace of the continent, this would make him an informant, but not a bad writer of prose.

And if a critic accuses Octavio Paz of being an Agent of Imperialism, Paz will not become such an agent on that account, but neither will the accuser become a good poet. Besides, nobody wins anything in all of this. Recrimination is absolutely useless.

What sense, then, can these sorts of judgments have? In truth, their origin lies in the false position of the critic with respect to his own ends and his own perspectives.

Undoubtedly imperialism is a reality, as is economic oppression and the struggle against it throughout the world [166].

But this struggle, which seen as a whole appears unified, gives itself, from an individual point of view, as a mosaic of innumerable possibilities. It becomes an indeterminate number of possible tasks. One can be in it, cooperate with it in a thousand different ways, assuming a task generally oriented by the meaning of that struggle. One can effectively oppose the advance of imperialism from any point of view. Anyone can do something in this sense—from an incidental act, to the sacrifice of one's own life for the advent of a better world or for the improvement of the existing one. One can put all one's efforts to lend reality, to give body, to a movement aimed at promoting justice in the world.

But one can also take advantage of the world's movement toward justice so as to serve oneself [*darse cuerpo a sí mismo*]. In this way one finds a thousand easy ways to justify oneself. When declaring oneself a defender of justice it may *seem* that one is really doing something to bring it about, and in this way one can come to believe oneself to be a righteous man. It is evident, however, that it is not enough to declare that one is something in order to become that thing in reality; but the declaration also offers an easy path to self-justification. There is a very easy way to give substance to one's own self-righteousness: Denounce that which is evil—in this case, the imperialist.

The true anti-imperialist is irresistibly compelled to be the watch-dog [*a la vocación de gendarme*]. Just like his well-known counter-figure: the anti-communist. The two are destined to frantically wave their flag, whether or not it is necessary. The lack of real foundations for their own talents compels them to uncover evil everywhere, since what makes us good is to defeat the bad guys. If one cannot find the evil one needs so as to be good, then one invents it. It is not difficult to do so, since for any lack of positive reasons, negative ones will always be at hand. The field of the "*not*" is infinite.

Here is offered the same structure that the great American playwright Arthur Miller has emphasized in his drama about the Salem witch hunts:

The good judge: "You're a witch . . ."

The bad woman: "But I do not even know what a witch is . . ." [167]

The good judge: So then how do you know that you're *not* a witch?

This is the key to everything. At bottom it is all about Manichaeism, that sad ally of stupidity and insufficiency, which allows some to become respectable and righteous; a Manichaeism that allows "hatred of evil" to turn into "love of the good," for which it has to invent both good and evil. That is, it has to lie. For Manichaeism everything is clear as long as we renounce our need for clarity; for this reason, it is the weapon of the mediocre and the father of bad faith. But it is also everywhere the true enemy that is capable of crushing those rare individuals who today, as always, represent the only hope of peace in the world: men of goodwill.

The Spiritual Crisis of the United States[3]

Jorge Portilla

Translated by Francisco Gallegos and
Carlos Alberto Sánchez

It is already commonplace in contemporary philosophizing to say that all reflective thinking comes from a natural world that determines it. All scientific thinking comes from a world not scientifically constructed. In the same way, discussions regarding the cultural world of a nation open up a field of reality determined by the point of view of the one who is discussing it, and an essential aspect of that point of view is the national origin of the observer.

That this is to the detriment of the objectivity of those judgments formulated about a particular national world by a person who is alien to that world is a matter that does not concern us here; the fact is that such judgments are continually formulated, and not a few of them—in very bitter terms, I may add—have been aimed at our country. These are things about which nothing can be done.

On the other hand, all Mexicans are presented with the need at one time or another, and by the nature of things themselves, to take a position that is as clear as possible regarding the historical facts of our northern neighbor. The need to take such a position is based, it seems to me, on the fact that the United States always appears to us in the form of a radical "otherness," to say it with the happy neologism of Antonio Machado. The ultimate foundations of the US American civilization [*civilización norteamericana*] are almost absolutely strange to us, however impressive and even plausible the results may seem to us.

The effort to understand the peculiar US American way of being is thus imposed on us as a first step towards adopting a lucid and well-defined attitude toward US American culture, and it is on the basis of this radical feeling of strangeness and as a result of that will to understand that we profile the fact of the US American crisis and its scope.

Succinctly put, we believe that what is in crisis is precisely the very foundation of US American life as such—the foundation of what [140] in the US they have come to call *The American Way of Life*.[4]

What this foundation is, and in what sense it can be said to be in crisis, is, therefore, what I will try to clarify in what follows.

In an issue of *Time* magazine for May 19, 1952, there appeared in the section of "Religion" an article titled: "Requested: The American Smile." It reads:

"Dr. Hubert Eaton, a 70-year-old director of California's Forest Lawn Cemetery, is a cheerful man. In his creed, inscribed on a plaque in Forest Lawn, he wrote: 'I believe above all in a Christ who smiles and who loves you and I.'" Forest Lawn itself boasts of "bright and joyful private sleep rooms . . ." (this is what they call the tombs) "the beautiful views of the green meadows and tall trees . . ."—these things apparently reinforce Dr. Eaton's theology. But Dr. Eaton, who has filled the cemetery with a mass of paintings and religious statuary (including a replica of Michelangelo's *David* with a fig leaf), has not found an image of Christ that looks sufficiently happy to accommodate his convictions.

Dr. Eaton's best artistic acquisitions have come from Italy. Last year he offered a prize of one million lire ($1600 USD) to the artist that could achieve the most suitable *close up*[5] portrait of a smiling Christ. The jury was constituted by five Italian experts.

"A few days ago," continues *Time*, "director Eaton arrived in Florence to examine the paintings submitted by thirteen of the 32 Italian artists invited to participate in the contest. When the pictures were uncovered it was clear that someone had made a mistake. Six of the portraits did not smile at all. The rest had, at best, a faint smirk."

Eaton commented: "Nothing is good enough for Forest Lawn, as you see." He added: "all these paintings, even the smiling ones, look sad and definitely European. What I need is a radiant Christ who looks upward with an inner light of joy and hope; I want a Christ with an American face." The judges gave their decision, withdrew the prize money, and gave each artist a consolation prize of 100,000 [141] lire. Next year a new competition will be held. Eaton said he will continue to call for new contests until he gets what he wants.

It is undeniable that this whole thing is very original, and it is almost certain that Dr. Eaton's strange pretense has not occurred to anyone outside the United States.

But it is not necessary to discuss this, what matters here is that we can extract, from this pilgrim's story, a principal category for the interpretation of the US American way of life.

This category is found in our story as a presupposition without which the claim of the director of Forest Lawn would be impossible.

Indeed, the unusual demand, which, besides, is apparently so difficult to fulfill, that Christ smiles, delicately overlooks the fact of Christ's passion and the manner of his death. It radically ignores the difficult nuances of the relationship between the historical Jesus and the humanity of the men who followed him and those who killed him. It erases the *sense* of Christ's appearance in history, the sense of His life and His death.

This *sense* that motivates His appearance in history, His life and His death, is none other than *sin*, or if you prefer *evil* or the fall of the man. In between man in general and the man, Jesus of Galilee, we find this scandalous, irrational, uncontrollable fact, which is *evil*, and which transforms the relationship between any man and Jesus into a difficult and delicate matter whatever may be the attitude that is taken before his immense presence. These attitudes oscillate between those of St. Paul and those of Nietzsche, passing through those corresponding to the German idealists Kant and Hegel. The good director of Forest Lawn, however, takes a completely different and absolutely *sui generis* attitude. He wants a smiling Christ and wants to see this comforting smile on an American face.

This means that Dr. Eaton knows nothing of evil, neither of sin nor of man's fall, nor of the need for redemption that is bought at the price of Christ's death. That is, it means that Dr. Eaton is *innocent*.

Well, it would seem that innocence is precisely that category that ultimately founds the US American way of life.

But here it is necessary to correct a misinterpretation that may arise from the anecdote with which I have illustrated my [142] hypothesis.

When I say that innocence, that is, the absolute unfamiliarity [*extrañeza*] of evil, is the *foundation* of the *American Way of Life*, I mean that the idea of innocence *serves* to make sense of almost every particular nuance of that way of life, as I hope to show later.

This does not mean, of course, that every US American, taken individually, will take himself as innocent from blame, let alone that this *objective belief* is accepted as true, so to speak, and found everywhere in the innumerable forms and interpretations of life and man that characterize US American culture.

I take here the word *innocence* in its more general sense of unfamiliarity with evil; he is innocent who is not defiled by evil in general or by sin in particular. An innocent world will thus be that world in which evil has not penetrated, where evil has not corrupted the root of life itself.

We enter, therefore, into our interpretation without further details, which besides are not suitable in the short space of this conference.

The first noticeable characteristic one can attribute to the United States, visible even for those who have never visited that country, is the ubiquitous presence of *quantification*. Before you are told anything else, you are told the number of library volumes, the costs and sizes of buildings, or the number of times you could wrap the world in wire. The tendency to apply the category of quantity has many aspects and can be interpreted in several ways. It has been said that its origin lies in the fact that the US is a capitalist economy and the corresponding tendency to *value* everything, a tendency proper to any nation of merchants. It could also be interpreted as originating from scientific thought, or as belonging to a nation of builders in which measurement, the quantification of reality, is a necessary starting point.

But these explanations do not elucidate the fact that quantity (volume, cost, dimension) serves in the US as a criterion of value. The surprising insistence that such a building of such a height should be the *highest* in the world, for example, points to a tendency to identify the *most* with the *best*; this is not merely the valuation beloved by merchants; [143] behind it there is a US American satisfaction with his world.

The US American seems to take quantity as the abstract and pure form of his own excellence, as an aseptic symbol of superiority, blessed with a certain scientific air.

It is not our intention to reproach anyone; all peoples seek these comforting symbols. What interests us is to underline the fact that the US American has taken as his symbol precisely the category of quantity; he reads his own excellence in a quantitative comparison.

Explanations for the origin of this phenomenon may be more or less valid, but what matters to us is not a genetic explanation but, rather, *to make clear or highlight a condition of possibility*; we say therefore that the condition of possibility for considering quantity as the criterion of value is precisely an innocent world.

Indeed, in a world where evil does not penetrate, any *increase* can only be an *increase of good*. Any affirmation of quantitative superiority is then the realization of *genuine* superiority. The mere consciousness of a great magnitude is bound, in this hypothesis, to the consciousness of a superior good.

In a world conscious of evil, magnitude does not say anything; it is axiologically mute and may even take on a sinister aspect. Consider, for example, the dimension of apocalyptic beasts in the Tower of Babel, or the somber aura of giants in Greek mythology or the world of Germanic sagas.

That the US American world becomes fully comprehensible from the postulate of innocence is something that can be verified by innumerable facts, more or less complex—perhaps less characteristic than the tendency toward quantification, that is to say, less known in the world outside the US, but which may help to characterize it with the same profundity.

Among other defining aspects of the US American way of life, some of the most important appear in the field of filmmaking, in an excessive interest in so-called sexual "problems," the interest in, and monstrous proliferation of, psychological or psychoanalytical literature, the equally monstrous proliferation of the detective novel, and finally, hygiene, that is, the obsession with bodily cleanliness [144].

Of course there are manifestations of higher rank such as pragmatism. Pragmatism is the philosophical expression of the US, and this is recognized around the world. Philosophers from the US and elsewhere may disagree on everything, but they agree that pragmatism is a characteristically US American philosophy. The basis of this identification is not very clear, but it is something that one instinctively intuits, in the same way that we guess the kinship of two people by the identical spirit in certain gestures. But about this we will not make a judgment; we will simply point out that pragmatism fits the same interpretation that we propose for the other, more quotidian aspects (of life in the US), and I think even here we have seen certain signs of crisis.

Two features of filmmaking reveal the conception of the US American world as a field of innocence, leaving aside the films in which this is the actual theme, such *Mr. Deeds Goes to Town*, or *You Can't Take It With You*; the first, of lesser importance, is the confrontation between the US American world and the outside world with the theme of the US American hero abroad; the other is the inevitable happy ending, about which we will speak later.

This confrontation appears, if we exaggerate just a bit, as the contrast between paradise and the "outer darkness, where there is weeping and the gnashing of teeth."

The US American hero always appears justified; he is the center that determines the sense of the world that surrounds him, and in determining this sense he becomes the lord of that world. The "others" cannot take a point of view on him that is not easily surpassed by the most basic moral judgment, and precisely by a moral judgment; the others are *evil*, they desire evil. The US American hero wants the good, and more than desiring it, it can be said that he embodies it—this is his strength; his weakness is that he sits precisely in the "outer darkness" where evil has an important place and therefore can corner him and put him in difficulties so serious that they can only be overcome with the providential arrival of steel angels, aerial fortresses, which at the end of the film appear as a glorious and roaring symbol of light and the good, cleanliness and order.

The contrast between the two worlds is always [145] depressing for non-US Americans, and the *genetic explanation* of this pious US American interpretation can be found in the Calvinist and Puritan origins of that nation. Calvinism condemned wealth as the end of human life with great violence, but it was also a doctrine that reinforced economic virtues and ultimately viewed wealth not as a path for salvation but as an indubitable sign of predestination.

R. A. Tawney, in a chapter entitled "The Triumph of the Economic Virtues" from his *Religion and the Rise of Capitalism*, writes that "Convinced that character is everything and circumstances nothing, [the Puritan] sees in the poverty of those that fall on the road not a misfortune to be pitied and helped, but a moral fault to be condemned, and in wealth not an object of suspicion, which can be abused like other gifts, but a blessing that rewards the triumph of energy and will. Tempered by self-examination, self-discipline, self-control, he is the practical ascetic who wins his victories not in the cloister, but on the battlefield, in the stock market, and in the marketplace."

We venture as a hypothesis regarding the origin of the US American way of life a second moment of secularization, which was the secularism of Calvinism with respect to the Catholic world. It would seem that the US American world is a secularized Puritanism that has largely forgotten its Protestant, Calvinistic, and Puritan origins, and has become a kind of terrestrial paradise, a strange form of modern immanentism that for some reason preserves as living relics the virtues that Tawney calls economic.

In fact, the outside world appears in US American cinema as generally composed of poor, therefore bad, and naturally filthy and stupid men, incapable of such audacious and apt actions as that of US American heroes. They can be nice, cheerful, with big mustaches and exaggerated gestures, but they are incapable of industry and at most sell apples or sing passionate songs accompanied by their guitar like the grasshopper of the story.

I want to insist for the last time on the fact that what we care to emphasize is not that individual US Americans believe themselves to represent [146] excellence—all the peoples of the world have the same pretension—but, rather, that the US American in general finds his excellence in this peculiar feeling of purity [*incontaminación*], of unfamiliarity with the somber facts of existence, facts which are supposed to be absent from US American life.

The vexing issue of the vulgar view of the outside world in cinema raises the problem of how evil occurs in the US, since it is evident that the thesis of US American innocence cannot mean that this nation is actually paradise.

Let us note in passing that if there is no sin in paradise, then there should be no death, which is the result of sin and evil. But certainly there is death in the US, even if it appears there is not much, because we cannot fully believe Norman Vincent Peale, the New York preacher who has published a brochure with the title *Not Death at All*.[6]

Well, as there really is death, there is also evil, and with this we address the question of the great interest in psychoanalysis, in so-called sexual problems, and the proliferation of the detective novel.

Whatever one may think of psychoanalysis as a therapeutic technique or as an anthropology, it is true that from a moral point of view it is, or it can be, a system of excuses.

It is obvious that at the level of individual psychology, the unconscious is a kind of other self, a Mr. Hyde, which psychoanalysis is capable of taming by means of an adequate technique. Taken as an anthropology, psychoanalysis cleverly conceals everything problematic from traditional ethics. It simply eliminates the theory of freedom, the theory of ends, and the problem of evil.

The ego is, on the one hand, innocent of the excesses of the "id," but in addition these excesses can be controlled with a rational technique. In its first aspect, it is undoubtedly an excuse and allows one to assume wayward impulses in a horizon of innocence, and in its second aspect, it turns evil into something controllable, into a passing and superficial phenomenon that does not affect the very core of personality, since the "id," despite being an annoying guest of the psyche, is conceived as radically strange, like a relic of a subhuman world that can be *eliminated* and *controlled* [147].

Psychoanalysis thus reveals itself as an excellent instrument guaranteeing innocence at the level of individual life, and the impressive volume of psychoanalytic literature in the US begins to make sense in the light of our hypothesis.

It would be tempting here to draw a parallel between the role of the unconscious in individual psychic life and that of black men in social life, and to show precisely how the refusal of the White man to assume his guilt before the man of color in America's dark racial conflict is the ultimate basis of racial discrimination.

But, on the one hand, to present an interpretation of the racial problem of the United States in the framework of the concepts of psychoanalysis would mean simplifying the terms of a very serious problem; on the other, it is not our intention to solve the internal problems of the US, but to outline a first attempt at interpretation from the point of view of our own [Mexican] circumstances.

We note, however, that the basis of racial discrimination is precisely that refusal of the White man to assume his guilt.

In connection with the role of psychoanalysis is the continued allusion to sexual matters under the neutral title of "sex" in newspapers and magazines and in the innumerable books that solemnly offer to solve the problems of sex in a scientific manner.

But where this innocence of the sexuality seems to reach its critical point is in the famous Kinsey report that intends to inform people about the "sexual behavior of the human male."[7] In this extraordinary book we find all the splendor of that "innocence of becoming" Nietzsche speaks about, at the same time a *postulate and expression* of modern science's neutral attitude toward the moral world.

Let us overlook the naive and playful assaults in which young college students seize the most intimate garments of their companions for no other purpose than to display them innocently in the light of day.

I believe that the proliferation of literature on sexual matters can be explained by the fact that everything concerning sex resists being clearly integrated in a perspective of total innocence, and it is thus necessary to return [to the topic] again and again [148] in a sort of vertigo of fascination.

It is precisely this character of proliferation to infinity, of *production in a series,* that gives meaning to the detective story in the US. Faced with the irrefutable fact of crime, there is nothing so comforting as the detective novel.

Not only do we see there that the one who commits the crime pays, and that every criminal ends up falling into the hands of the police, but we are also able to master one of the most disturbing apparitions of evil (crime) through technical procedures. With the same daily insistence with which newspapers talk about the presence of crime in society, the detective novels remind one that there is a whole scientific world, with laboratories full of precision instruments and perfectly trained and capable men who keep crime on the periphery of the world.

If we compare the treatment of this issue with Dostoyevsky's *Crime and Punishment,* where the topic of evil as crime is treated in all its depth, the meaning of the US American detective novel becomes clearer to us.

Psychoanalysis and the detective novel can therefore be interpreted as a technical domestication of evil, but such domestication can only occur when an innocent world has previously been postulated. Banishing evil to the periphery of being and controlling it with psychological and police techniques, all that remains is, literally, to wash our hands.

From an uncontaminated spiritual world we see the sacramental value of water and soap, as well as other more sophisticated products, such as chlorophyll-based deodorants for all conceivable uses. The *last, most humble and contemptible* vestige of evil, *grime,* is the easiest to remove.

Certainly the lament of Saint Paul—"the good that I want, I do not do, but I practice the very evil that I do not want. Wretched man that I am! Who will set me free from the body of this death?"—does not find resonance in the United States.[8]

So far I have tried to verify the value of a hypothesis by interpreting, in its light, facts that in our eyes appear as characteristically North American and that pertain to the structure of daily life in that nation [149].

But its value can be extended to an interpretation of the US American philosophy *par excellence,* pragmatism. About that point, I regret that lack of space does not allow me to give the subject the treatment I would have wanted. But I believe that in a more detailed analysis of the content of this philosophical tendency, our hypothesis would not only be confirmed, but its validity would become even more evident.

Pragmatism can, without serious alteration, be reduced to the following formula, which has been coined by the US American philosopher

Patrick Romanell[9]: "The truth of an idea (proposition, belief, hypothesis) depends on the practical value of its results."

This means that both the truth and the *real meaning* of an idea must be sought in its consequences for action, i.e., its *effectiveness*.

Both Pierce and James Dewey place action, effectiveness, as a criterion of verification of all possible truth; that is, they claim that the ultimate verification of a truth is the conduct that it inspires or determines, and no one doubts the possibility of building an entire philosophical system within the horizon of this postulate. But there is a fundamental ambiguity here, because it happens that a criterion has been previously assumed that decides about the action.

For if the truth of an idea is said to depend on the practical value of the results of the idea, if the verification of a truth depends on the conduct that it inspires or determines, the excellence of such behavior, then on what does it expend? If the truth of an idea depends on its effectiveness, we can ask: effectiveness *for what*?

But pragmatism is precisely the philosophy that refuses to answer the latter questions, because another of its postulates is that the world of action is automatically regulated, that is, that action is the source of its own criteria of value.

In the words of John Dewey, there is a certain "power of *experience* itself to provide its own necessary principles of belief and action," that is, "experience and life can regulate themselves." (see John Dewey, *What I Believe*, chapter 1).

The most obvious interpretation is that pragmatism [150] is the philosophy proper to an active people, but this interpretation in being true does not sufficiently cohere with the facts.

What is implied in such a conception is a naive trust that everything will go well. To refer truth to its practical results is possible only on the assumption that the practical results will eventually reflect the Truth with a capital "T". That is, it is possible only on the naive belief that man will not lose his way. The truth depends on behavior, but the criterion of that behavior, not expressed philosophically but revealed in this conception itself, is the good diffused in a world where evil has no place.

Pragmatism can only be sustained under the assumption that men will propose only morally valid ends. It is only within a community composed of substantially virtuous men that it is possible to postulate the action of men as a criterion of the good and of truth.

Pragmatism is representative, on a more respectable level, of the same world in which we find the *Happy Ending* of US American filmmaking. Relatively speaking, both pragmatism and cinema respond to the most serious questions by saying that everything will work out.

Pragmatism, however, has ceased to be the dominant philosophy in US American universities, and there are even some philosophy professors, such as the notable professor from Chicago, Mortimer Adler, who have attacked it with surprising violence.

This general abandonment of pragmatism, *although significant*, is only a hint of the crisis of innocence and optimism beginning to become evident in the US.

The crisis begins to take shape in certain paradoxes whose profile acquires more precise contours as the international history of the postwar period unfolds.

It is becoming increasingly clear that the guiding ideals of US history that led this nation to optimism and an unwavering confidence in them have placed it before the outside world as the bearer of a program of hegemony reinforced by unprecedented military might. An armed nation with the most destructive instruments in history, forced [151] to impose on the world its own ideals, *excellent as they may be*, can hardly preserve the aura of innocence that colors the US American way life.

On the other hand, the outside world does not seem to accept with any sort of joy the rose-colored perspective of North American regulation. The guilty world resists adopting the solutions of the innocent world, and this causes great perplexity for the Americans.

To put it in the terminology of an eminent US American philosopher: "every individual with sensibility (in the US) finds himself in relation to a structure that is never confirmed in the vicissitudes of recent history." That is, the categories that from within US American life suffice for a complete understanding of everything, seem to fail in their function when it comes to interpreting the entirety of contemporary history.

The third paradox, the most serious in our view, appears in the light of the US American claim to defend spiritual values in the face of the threat of materialism.

"The question of materialism," Reinhold Niebuhr tells us in his excellent *The Irony of American History*, "gives rise to certain ironic consequences in our dispute with communism. . . . Perhaps the Communists are not *in the philosophical sense* as consistently materialistic as they pretend to be. They support the idea of a 'dialectic' or 'logic' underlying nature and history, which means that a *rational* sense and structure extends along the entirety of reality. Despite the constant emphasis on 'human dignity' in our own liberal culture, our predominantly naturalist bias often results in views on human nature in which the dignity of man is very clear."

"In the meantime," he adds, "we are immersed in a historical situation in which the paradise of our domestic security is suspended in the hell of global insecurity."

These ironic paradoxes or situations, as Niebuhr says, are objective configurations which, insofar as they are known in the US, give rise to certain attitudes or dispositions, and it is these reactions that can be interpreted as symptoms of crisis [152]. Several levels can be distinguished among them, and in the highest it would be necessary to place the study of Reinhold Niebuhr mentioned above. In this remarkable work, the New York philosopher, in trying to clarify the position of America in the world community, makes clear the pretension of the founders of that nation and of the theorists of its politics.

"The purpose was," he says, "to start a new beginning in a corrupt world . . ."

New England came to be described by US American ideologists as "the place where the Lord would create a new heaven and a new earth."

His description of the spirit that animated the founders and ideologists is condensed in the title of the second chapter of his book, "The Innocent Nation in an Innocent World."

The result is the profound mismatch between the US American world and the outside world, and the content of the book revolves around the possibilities of correcting this mismatch, that is, of achieving community, coexistence as a means of escaping the ironies of US American history, that is to say of the paradoxes that arise from the position of the United States in the contemporary world.

In recognizing this mismatch, Niebuhr performs a movement of reflection about the history of his country, seeking precisely the origin of a fault, a fissure that explains the situation; that is, he undertakes a review of the spiritual foundations of America with a critical spirit, i.e., with a non-dogmatic spirit (a radically different attitude from naive confidence in traditional values).

We cannot outline here a sketch of the profound and lucid course of his research; what interest us is only to highlight the fact that the content of the work involves in its author the abandonment of the dogmatic attitude toward the values embodied in US American life.

In our view, Niebuhr's is a description of the US American situation precisely in its character of crisis, *because what we have here is a crisis of foundations*, and a crisis is only worthy of the name when it affects or puts into question the validity of something fundamental. On the surface, only problems occur. A problem is a contradiction more apparent than real, one that resolves [153] itself with certain axioms or assumptions; but when these same axioms or assumptions become doubtful or unjustifiable, one can no longer speak of problems but of crisis.

Indeed, Niebuhr manages to save US American ideals of democracy, freedom, and dignity of the individual, but he finds that the need to accept a politics of power to defend such values, which are constitutive of the nation, makes it impossible to maintain the atmosphere in which they flourished. The nation that at one point represented a new beginning in a corrupt world now seems to corrupt itself in the act of imposing on the world its most valued assets.

If we were to compare the attitude of Prof. Niebuhr to the proponents of the doctrine of Manifest Destiny, which takes the American nation as a civilizing force, we could see how Niebuhr represents a moment of crisis, and precisely a crisis of the innocence we are talking about.

At a rather less respectable level than the Columbia professor, we find the dogmatic attitude of propaganda that pervades all advertising media, according to which we must defend the threatened US American way of life.

Why defend the American way of life and not just speak rather of freedom or human rights?

More than any other point this one appears to be the one that reveals more than anything the crisis of US American consciousness. Indeed, only the vulnerable can be defended and, at the very same moment in which the necessity to defend a form of life appears, so does the insufficiency of that form of life. Precisely in this defensive attitude does the US American confesses himself to be bothered *by the look* or *the criticism* of something foreign, something not American. Faced with this threatening action from the exterior, one can justify any attitude regarding any *thing, ideal, value*, or *principle*, but doing so threatens innocence itself, because innocence is by definition invulnerable, and what is invulnerable does not require any defense whatsoever.

Until recently the feeling of innocence was accompanied by an aura of invulnerability that manifested itself in [154] the way in which, for example, Bernard Shaw's insolence was tolerated when directed against the US, and the idea that to succeed as a writer in the US the most direct way was to elegantly insult Americans.

There are good reasons therefore to assume that if US Americans now consider themselves vulnerable *as Americans,* this is certainly a sign that the assumption of innocence of the US American world, if not completely gone, at least is beginning to lose its efficacy. I do not mean to say, then, that the main tenet of US American life has ceased being innocence and has become guilt. This would not be a crisis but a conversion. Vulnerability is certainly not synonymous with guilt, but both one and the other are phenomena of the same family and have the same existential foundation. This foundation is none other than the finiteness or deficiency of human existence that the Germans call debt (*Schuld*) and the French call lack (*manque*). Concepts such as *finitude, deficiency, vulnerability,* lack, fault, blame, all have a close relationship that is immediately perceived.

And so US American vulnerability, as a presupposition for the defense of the *US American Way of Life,* is threatened by an *imminent* guilt. Said in familiar language, this means that the defense of the *American Way of Life* has its roots in the fear of the US to assume any guilt; meanwhile it launches more atomic bombs or simply unleashes a war that in the eyes of the world makes its virtues suspect. And this is a spiritual crisis in the US because what is at stake is precisely this *innocence,* this absolute justification found in the spirit that animated the founders of the nation and that has diffused itself into every corner of its existence.

We could accumulate data that highlights this bad faith present in the US, such as the spontaneous creation of committees that undertake nothing less than the censorship of libraries. Then there were the articles of faith that accused books of subversiveness or of having been written by authors suspected of having "un-American views." [155] These small spontaneous inquisitions clearly contradict the most fundamental feature of the US American spirit, precisely in that they pretend to defend a vague US American orthodoxy.

This is another example of the foundational crisis of which we speak. But the crisis becomes more evident when we consider the profound change in temporal perspective that is involved in all these events. One of the features that North American philosophers emphasize more than any other in pragmatism is the openness of this philosophical attitude toward the future.

Indeed, to refer the validity of an idea or proposition to its practical results involves placing the meaning of truth in the future. If we take pragmatism as an expression of the US American spirit, we find a correlation between the philosophical attitude of pragmatism and the open, optimistic, and futurizing spirit of US American culture.

But a defense of the *American Way of Life* reveals a shift of emphasis that goes *from the future to past*, since the lifestyle of a nation is something that is taken as already over and done with, something that can be found in the past and not in the future.

Only on the assumption of innocence does it become possible to face the future openly and confidently as happens in the disturbing doctrine of Manifest Destiny that you see with the annexation of Texas. But abandoning the protentive [*futurizante*] attitude for a retentive attitude [*una actitud retentiva*] is a clear indication of at least some difficulty in holding the assumptions of innocence.

What the United States appears to now show the world is not an indeterminate future as a common task, but its own past as the source for self-justification. In this perspective, the future is closed, and there is instead an opening to the past. However, talk of a "closed future" is just another way of indicating that which we have indicated in our talk of crisis.

We can summarize all this as follows:

The spiritual crisis of the United States is primarily manifested in the fact of a particular maladjustment between [156] North America and the rest of the world, including between its allies and its enemies. The root of such maladjustment can be found in that fundamental underlying feeling of innocence, seen as typical of the US American way of life but as strange to every other country the world over. The crisis is *expressed*, in turn, in the way in which the United States is aware of this maladjustment and in its willingness to defend that vague set of goods that constitute the "American way of life." This shows that the United States has to some extent lost the claim to absolute justification that is at the origin of its history; thus, we have characterized that confluence of elements as representing the crisis of US American innocence.

It remains alien to our purpose to point to solutions or ways out of the crisis.

What we can say is that if the resolution of the crisis is understood in terms of America's participation in that guilt common to all humanity, a guilt that would be fully accepted by that nation, then we can also say that such a solution involves a conversion capable of subverting the very foundations of that culture, and, of course, this seems highly unlikely.

For this reason it would perhaps be legitimate to anticipate a change in attitude regarding their foreign policy in the sense of an honest and open politics of power that has no pretentions of justification. But that anticipation can only be confirmed or disproved by future facts themselves.

This seems to us to be, broadly speaking, the picture of US American spiritual life at present.

These reflections were made possible by meditations on Mexican reality initiated by the Grupo Hiperión in 1949 and continued, with varying degrees of rigor and with more or less success, until today. My reflections on the facts described here have been determined by my prior attention to the characteristics of our Mexican cultural world.

The US American characteristics of innocence, substantiality, [157] and optimism have been noticeable from a consciousness of characteristics contrary to guilt, accidentality, insufficiency, and, in general, the sense of finitude that seem to inform the specific manifestations of our own [Mexican] world.

The United States appears to us, then, to confirm that first impression of "otherness" about which we spoke at the start of this reflection, and it does so in the form of a stark contrast that affects the deepest roots of the life of both peoples.

What does this contrast mean, and, in view of that meaning, what should be the proper attitude of Mexicans toward the US American world? These are questions whose solution will be proposed after the clarification of the meaning of our history, which the Grupo Hiperión and its teachers, Samuel Ramos, José Gaos, and Leopoldo Zea, have proposed as an urgent task of Mexican philosophy.

Thomas Mann and German Irrationalism[10]

JORGE PORTILLA

TRANSLATED BY FRANCISCO GALLEGOS AND
CARLOS ALBERTO SÁNCHEZ

I have the floor on Thomas Mann. For forty minutes, that man of genius is at my mercy. I can do with him as I please; I can praise him or I can denounce him. I can talk about him intelligently or stupidly.

The dead lion is delivered to the maw of the living dog.

This is one of the great flaws, perhaps one of the inevitable flaws of what we might call the culture of the university. We small men have to shine a light on great men. Naturally, we cannot perform this operation without shrinking them. "One more century of readers and the spirit will stink," says Nietzsche somewhere. I fear that in the present exposition I am going to shrink Thomas Mann, and I will, perhaps, make the spirit exude the bad odor that is characteristic of our time of passive readers and of writers without genius and without a love of man.

I think that against this degradation of great men by small professors, there is an antidote: admiration. If we admire a man, our speech about him does not diminish him. Admiration emboldens us and makes us rise to the occasion. Admiration is the "eros" that unifies small and great men. Admiration shortens distances and allows us to speak reasonably, if not adequately, of men who greatly exceed us. Admiration, however, does not mean, in any way, sympathy. There can be an admiration in sympathy and agreement, but there can also be admiration in antipathy and discord.

The latter sense of this word describes my admiration for Thomas Mann.

My admiration for him is great, but his thought, or, rather, the intellectual and affective climate of his work is deeply unpleasant to me. And more than unpleasant, I would say that it deeply disgusts me. If I have agreed to come before you to speak about him, it is because at one time my feelings were precisely the opposite, and because this double experience permits me not to consider myself entirely disqualified to present to you my thoughts about him [184].

A Personal Reading

But how can we boil down all of Thomas Mann's thoughts, which cover all aspects of human experience, in a few minutes? This cannot be done even if we take the easy way of abundant citations, because this would require a careful rereading of an oceanic oeuvre where, in addition, phrases and passages which bring everything together in a clear sense are rare. The expression "Northern fog" comes to mind. Mann's style is a morose, meticulous reflection, full of twists and turns, of doubts and interrogations, where clear and distinct ideas, precise ideas, definitive judgments are conspicuous by their absence. Thus, we enter a state close to that of despair as soon as we try to find out clearly and precisely what Thomas Mann thought about some of the great issues that represent our main concerns in the middle of the twentieth century.

In view of these difficulties I have had no choice but to attend to my personal experience with Thomas Mann in order to extract the material for what follows.

I believe I have the right to do so. After all, while aspiring to absolute objectivity, any discourse about the work of Thomas Mann would likewise make a selection of topics and themes, in which it would be extremely difficult to separate the objective from the subjective motivations.

With this in mind, I will speak about Thomas Mann from my experience and from other philosophical and spiritual experiences connected with his work.

Many years ago, more than twenty, I read Mann for the first time. First, *Death in Venice*, a novel of aestheticism, decadence, and death. Then, *The Magic Mountain*, a novel about spiritual crisis, disease, and death. Later, *Doctor Faustus*. Mann spoke a language that was familiar to me, and in his books I found, if not an answer, certainly a deep harmony with my adolescent anxieties.

It happens that before reading him I had already discovered, with immense joy, German philosophy, which introduced me to what I believed were the deep and obscure aspects of reality.

My enthusiasm was explicable. I was badly educated, as are all Mexicans who have completed their secondary education, in which nobody, absolutely nobody, [185] learns anything, anything at all important. Judging from what my junior high and high school teachers had taught me, the world was not much more than a story told by an idiot, full of sound and fury, signifying nothing.

It was then that I discovered a book by Arthur Schopenhauer, which was translated into Spanish, that bore the complicated title of *On the Fourfold Root of the Principle of Sufficient Reason.* Then I read *The World as Will and Representation.*

From Schopenhauer to Nietzsche

Schopenhauer provided me, for the first time in my life, the possibility of attaining a coherent conception of reality. His philosophy seemed to me to be a wisdom that was concrete and attached to the eternal and daily problems that constitute the substratum of all human experience. More than as a scholarly explanation of the world, it was presented as an interpretation of life scrutinized in its most intimate realities. Because life is the first reality, previous to all thought, to all knowledge, to all philosophical doctrine. Life can exist and continue without thought, but thought cannot occur without life. Philosophy, according to Schopenhauer, could propose theories and give lessons, but in the end it is life that decides and uses intelligence, even genius, so as to place it at the service of its secret purposes or, to use Schopenhauer's own expression, "at the service of the Will."

Knowledge, the "representation" of the world, is something that comes later, an addition, a perfected tool, a light that the will has ignited to orient itself in the search of what can satisfy it. This Will, the ultimate substratum of universal reality, prior to human intelligence, is already manifested in nature: in plants, by the ingenious and oriented mechanism of its structure; in the animal, by the moving perfection of its limbs, by the surprising adaptation of its organs to a diet, by the variety of its offensive and defensive weapons, by the infallibility of its instinct and by the subtlety of its stratagems. When contemplating the inexhaustible diversity of these forms, horrible or comic, each one shaped by desire, one imagines them as capricious inventions of an insane or delirious demiurge. Finally, in man, the Will bestows the luxury of an intelligence that fabricates instruments and [186] weapons with which man compensates for his natural weakness. The Will rises up to reason, which allows it, by means of concepts and words, to store all the experience of the species and substitute the immediate present of the animal for an abstract and fictitious world of memory and anticipation, which extends human power to infinity.

However, regardless of how great the richness and extension of knowledge, it remains a delayed, precarious, intermittent function, attached to a nervous system, to a material organ whose vicissitudes it must necessarily obey and partake in. Reason is at the service of a Will that secretly sustains it, moves it, and uses it, but whose mystery remains hidden.

However, this mystery can be revealed. This Will, which in nature was unconscious, blind, or masked, can become conscious [*clarividente*] in man, at least under certain conditions. The somnambulist awakens abruptly and ceases to be a victim of suggestion. The blindfold on his eyes and the secret of the Will is manifested in its tragic cruelty. But this revelation is due not to science, nor to knowledge of external reality, but to a metaphysical intuition that reveals to man the inner reality of life, the hidden meaning of the drama, at the same time as the misfortune of the innumerable existences in which life is bound by bonds and sympathies that originate at the very root of being.

Behind the world as representation, which is merely its decoration, the external curtain of knowledge, where intelligence reigns as mistress and lady, the world is discovered as Will, and there the problem of values is posed, that is to say: the "why" of the very meaning of life.

By discovering in Will the substratum of reality, man becomes aware of the formidable disproportion that exists between the ends pursued by Will and the incalculable suffering, or the crimes, that are the price of an always ephemeral triumph, of a happiness that always disappoints. At the same time, the absolute irrationality of this blind Will is revealed, which is identical to the insatiable egoisms in which Will has divided itself, fascinated by the illusion of number. It is a fierce Will that destroys itself with its own claws and sets traps everywhere, traps into which it itself constantly rushes [187].

This fevered illusion of desire reaches its climax in the instinct of reproduction, in the love between the sexes. It is called the "Will of the Species," and it is able to leave blind the most clear-sighted, calculating individual, to force him to perpetuate the painful and always blameworthy error that is existence, condemning him in advance to suffering and death. It is an eternal and everyday drama that will start again perpetually as long as the blind man wants to live, which can nonetheless come to a happy ending thanks to the miracle that nature had not wanted or expected: the birth of the redeeming genius. The forms under which this miracle occurs are many: the asceticism of holiness, the intellectual heroism of thought, art that presents to life a kind of incorruptible mirror where it recognizes itself in its tragic depths. In all these manifestations, the genius always represents an anomaly of nature, a kind of disease, a monstrosity in virtue of the excess of that cognitive faculty in which an exceptional state of heroic or meditative detachment is affirmed. The genius strips man of his violent instincts, of his egoistic desires, to guide him to renunciation, to liberation and nirvana, to that eternal wisdom in which the profound thinkers of all times have recognized the supreme end of the painful trial that human life represents for every man.

Schopenhauer's masterpiece, *The World as Will and Representation*, appeared in 1819 to total indifference and silence by a public interested above all in the philosophy of Hegel and in the revolutionary movement that culminated and failed in 1848. It was after this date that the philosophy of this caustic and misanthropic thinker acquired a formidable popularity and prevalence in the spiritual life of Germany. The pessimistic irrationalism of Schopenhauer would animate the life and work of two other German geniuses of the nineteenth century: Wagner and Nietzsche.

In ways that we cannot examine in detail here, this "cheap" [*barata*] philosophy, this vision of the world that was within reach of all intellectual abilities, this simplistic and elementary conception of things, was going to provide a point of departure for Wagner's messianic Germanism and Nietzsche's anti-Christianity.

Through the work of these three men, Germany produced a [188] kind of original cultural personality that was, in a certain way, exceptional, departing from the rational, Christian, and universalist spirit of the European tradition. Nietzsche's work can be defined as a critique of those three founding principles of our civilization.

Mann in the Tradition of Irrationalism

In many places in his work, Thomas Mann declares himself a disciple of these three men, but it is very difficult to specify what he takes from each one of them. It is impossible, moreover, to make a summary synthesis of the thought of Nietzsche or Wagner, among other reasons because their thought is tedious and contradictory, and because it is in continuous transformation, without us being able to discover in it an organic and coherent development in the sense demanded by reason and logic.

The tradition of German irrationalism, however, can be characterized in a summary and elemental way in several postulates found in the work of Thomas Mann. These postulates are: the primacy of life and the irrational over intelligence and reason; the primacy of death over life; the primacy of disease over health; and the primacy of the individual and the unique over the common and the universal.

In the course of time, these postulates would be expressed in the collective life of Germany as that degraded form of superiority belonging to the Germanic race, with its core of anti-Semitism and anti-Christianity, and the pretension, equally absurd and monstrous, to inaugurate a new millennial period of human history.

The primacy of the irrational is nothing new in Germany, not even in Schopenhauer. It comes from Luther, whose theology departs from Scholasticism. The fundamental problem of Scholasticism was the problem of the knowledge of God within the framework of traditional Platonic and Aristotelian philosophy. In opposition to this rational principle of knowledge, Luther offers an irrational principle of a chemically pure faith. For him, believing did not at all imply knowing. The Lutheran believer finds his certainty within, not in a logical system of truths or in an external authority represented by the Church, but only in the personal call of God. The Reformation was a violent disruption of Aristotelian and Platonic theology just as German culture disrupted Greco-Roman civilization.

There is a passage in *The Magic Mountain* that seems to have been written together with Luther and Schopenhauer: " 'Faith is the organ of knowledge' [189] says Naphta, 'the intellect is secondary. Your science without premises is a myth. There is always a kind of faith, a conception of the world, an idea, in a word: a will; and the task of reason is to interpret it, to demonstrate it always in all cases. . . . Truth is that which is in man's interest. In him all of nature is concentrated, and all of nature is made for him. He is the measure of all things, and his salvation is the criterion of truth.' " Settembrini rebels against this way of seeing and dismisses it as pragmatist, but he cannot oppose to it a more valuable theory of knowledge. Could we say that Thomas Mann favors Naphta's definition? We know at least that Hans Castorp instinctively channels Mann's philosophical speculations about the salvation of man.

Aschenbach, the hero of *Death in Venice*, makes a pact with the destructive forces and abandons himself to his evil power. Hans Castorp stands resolutely on the side of civilized man and his interests. After having listened at length to the radical ideas expressed by Naphta and Settembrini, he concludes that the way to salvation passes through man and respects the primacy of the concrete person.

From the endless disputes of Naphta and Settembrini in *The Magic Mountain*, Hans Castorp comes to a conclusion that, to me, seems to express the thought of Thomas Mann at its most profound. But let us return to what we have called the primacy of death.

Death as a tremendous mystery, as an ennobling experience of a metaphysical rank higher than life itself, is one of the central themes of German irrationalism. There is a tendency in this philosophy to revere death as something sacred, as a higher value. This monstrous inversion of vital values admits of all nuances, but it is concentrated in two attitudes: the refined cult of one's own death, in the sense that it is adequate or appropriate to the life of the individual—death as a crown, as a diadem of life, as we find in Rainer Maria Rilke, who had the grace to die from an infection caused when the thorn of a flower pinched his finger. And the slightly less refined cult of death expressed in the fascist cry of "Long live death!" and in the skulls that adorned the helmets and epaulettes of select Nazi troops. Between one and the other attitude there is not much difference. If I am [190] happy to live for death, it is then easy for me to be complacent with the death of the other, or, at least, to be so that the death of the other does not bother me too much.

In a study on Freud in 1929, we find in Mann a declaration of love for German Romanticism that is distinguished precisely by its love of the pathological. He says: "The nineteenth century was not Romantic only in its first half. Throughout its decades, its scientific pride was compensated and even surpassed by its pessimism and by its musical communion with night and death; for this reason we love it, and we defend it against the contempt expressed by the present time, infinitely less great."

This paragraph shows us the context of ideas in which we find the thought of Thomas Mann. He loves the nineteenth century "for its pessimism and for its musical communion with night and death," and the criterion of this love, his reason, is "greatness." Can a more radical declaration of irrationalist faith be imagined? What values are these? Night, death, pessimism, and greatness! We are one step away from the cry: "Long live death!" One step away from *Nacht und Nebel*. Night and fog. I do not need to explain to you what these two words mean.

The primacy of the irrational and of death are always latent in the work of Mann, but they are expressed with particular perfection in that passage from *The Magic Mountain* that without a doubt you are all familiar with: Hans Castorp's declaration of love to Clawdia. "Love, you know," says Hans, "the body, love, and death, those three things are one and the same. For the body is disease and voluptuousness and that which brings death. Yes, they are both carnal, love and death, and that is their terror and their enormous attraction. But death is, on the one hand, a thing of ill repute, immodest, which makes one blush with shame; on the other hand, it is a very solemn and very majestic thing, *much higher than the living life that earns money and fills the belly: much more venerable than progress, which brags about time—because it is history and nobility and piety and the eternal and sacred that makes us take off our hats and walk on tiptoes . . .*"

Certainly, this is not Thomas Mann's last word on the matter. Not even the last words of Hans Castorp, who declares a few pages later, in somewhat ambiguous terms, [191] his fidelity to death and, at the same time, his decision not to grant it any power over his thoughts. "Death is a great power," he tells us. "I want to keep fidelity to death in my heart, but I want to clearly remember that fidelity to death and to the past is nothing but vice, dark and antihuman voluptuousness, when it governs our thinking and our conduct."

Note the contradictory nature of this statement. I confess that I do not entirely understand what this fidelity to death means, if it is not a disguised way to take sides against the human, against the neighbor in his most concrete sense. It is hatred of man and a secret will for destruction. Nothing keeps this destruction from beginning with self-destruction. This dark and antihuman voluptuousness governed the thinking of Germany for a century, before governing its conduct during the fifteen most criminal and inhuman years in the history of man.

Yes. Let us say it at once. It seems to us that the context of ideas, the spiritual atmosphere in which the work of Thomas Mann moves, is exactly the same as that of National Socialism.

Several volumes would be necessary to show how the philosophical constructions—if one can speak of "constructions" in this case—of Schopenhauer, Wagner, and Nietzsche, plowed and fertilized the field where National Socialist ideology would flourish, and how German Romanticism, which culminates in these thinkers, prepared the unprecedented degradation of the spirit of a people until it was ready to humiliate and submit itself to the absolute authority of a band of gangsters as stupid as they were cunning. I will not go into detail as to how this became possible. But it is not difficult to see that a philosophy that eliminates reason and dialogue as ultimate authorities, eliminates also the criterion of its own hierarchy and opens the doors to its own degradation.

Already in Nietzsche, philosophy becomes a real orgy of brilliant observations, of grotesque prophetic attitudes, and of utterly crass vulgarities, where contradiction is not an obstacle for anything, since truth is only what the will to power consecrates as such, and where reason is only a ploy of the slaves to destroy the "universe of the masters" or is an expression of the weakness [192] and the resentment of the Jews; a Semitic trap that has infected Europe through the most subtle of perversions: Christianity.

Another of the mysteries of German thought is the veneration and predilection for Friedrich Nietzsche. "I will never forget," Thomas Mann tells us, "how much my personal dispositions have been educated, exalted, and deepened by Nietzsche's psychological passion. I speak in *Tonio Kröger* of the 'disgust of knowledge.' It is an excellently Nietzschean expression, and the youthful disenchantment expressed in it highlights the similarities between the natures of Hamlet and Nietzsche, in which my temperament is recognized as in a mirror, a nature called to knowledge without having been born truly for knowledge."

Thomas Mann, trained in the school of Schopenhauer, Wagner, and Nietzsche, was certainly not a Nazi or a Hitler collaborator. From the first moment, the man Thomas Mann, the writer, the artist, revolted against the wave of savagery that flooded Germany and predicted the final triumph of democracy. But we will not find in his work philosophical principles that could have opposed National Socialism. This bourgeois, intelligent, and cultured man does not participate in the barbaric orgy. But how can we not see that the philosophical foundations of his work and the spiritual climate that it reflects are the same as those in the name of which National Socialism tried to found a superior order that would govern the world for the next thousand years?

How can a man proclaim himself a disciple of Nietzsche and not be anti-Semitic and anti-Christian? The issue about which Nazism expressed itself with more violence and with a more criminal irrationality was, without a doubt, anti-Semitism and an anti-Christianity implicit in it, which did not come out to the open because the war prevented it; without doubt, however, it would have been brought to the light of day if we stick to the testimonies that survive regarding Hitler's views and his source of inspiration: Nietzsche's *Genealogy of Morals* and *The Will to Power*.

Christianity became a reaction against Judaism. It fought fiercely against Judaism during the time of its first expansion. Nietzsche, however, perceives in Christianity a continuity of Judaism, a profound kinship. And he's right: We Christians, according to the expression of Pope [193] Pius XI, are Jews in spirit.

But how does Friedrich Nietzsche see things? In his eyes, it is Jewish cunning that put the Christian ideal on the historical scene. The religion of Christ is for him nothing more than an immense act of revenge perpetrated by the Jews against the splendors of the ancient world. The Israelites have executed their designs with a supreme Machiavellianism: they crucified the founder of Christianity and denied their own religion with the hope that other peoples would fall without suspicion into the trap set for them. I leave it to your good judgment to measure the acumen of this vision of things: Jewish thought, exasperated, advanced behind a strange and masked phantasm called Jesus, a wonderful means of seduction imagined by Israel to serve its resentment.

Let us admire here, says Charles Andler in his monumental spiritual biography of Nietzsche, the black magic of this great secret politics of hatred. At one stroke, the deadly poison distilled by the Jewish soul spread throughout the body of mankind. Europe, America, and Africa alike have been Jewish since then. Because Christianity is not, as one might think, "a movement against the Semitic instinct, but its consequence, one more conclusion of its terrifying logic"—it is an "emancipated form of Judaism," but Judaism nonetheless; it constitutes the revenge of Israel.

Take, for example, the Christian God, this God of the poor, of sinners, of the sick. He is a "good" God, God of a degenerate race, pale ideal of a declining life. Will we oppose His kind nature to the just nature of the God of Israel? In no way. In one way or another, we are in the presence of the same "moral" God. God who is at the same time just and good, who by those two traits together opposes the aggressive god, the strong, brave, arrogant god, the god who is at times evil to the noble people, where life ascends. Wherever He goes in the world and whatever the number of those who adhere to him, this God remains a Jew and his kingdom remains a ghetto kingdom.

The objection should not be raised that Plato, and later Aristotle, had already conceived of a God who could be considered, at least in certain respects, as an ancestor of the Christian God. Insofar as this Greek God appears as transcendent, that is to say, alien to life and to the healthy passions [194] of this world, he himself is the fruit of a first contamination of Hellenism by the Jewish spirit. Plato, the anti-Hellene, this Semite by instinct, is "the great bridge that leads to corruption" (Nietzsche, *The Birth of Tragedy*).

With the Jewish God, Christianity accepted the Jewish idea of salvation, so as to impose itself on other peoples of the world. It is the Jewish idea of sin. The Jewish idea of sacrifice. It is all of Jewish morality in its fundamental inspiration; morality of resentment, morality of the weak and of the slaves, that is substituted for the heroic morality of the Greeks. Christian charity is a Jewish charity incubated under the ashes of humility and misery in the small circles of the diaspora. The sign of the Cross is the symbol of the transmutation of all ancient values fraudulently conducted by the Jewish spirit.

Nietzsche particularly hates the Apostle Paul—"this ambitious and untimely soul, this spirit full of superstition and cunning," this ominous bigot, this forger, this archetype of the genius of hate—for the decisive role he played in the formation of the new cult. Nietzsche denounces him, like he does Socrates, for being a decadent. Before Paul there was only a handful of sectarians whose influence was not assured. Jesus was for Paul a simple "theme" of his music. Paul is thus "the inventor of Christianity," through whom the Jewish people, or rather the Jewish priestly caste, could march onward toward the spiritual conquest of the world.

With Nietzsche comes the time to operate a new transmutation of values. Time to reject not only the dogmas and precepts of Christianity but, more radically, the type of soul that has engendered them. On the ruins of an abolished Christianity there had to rise, finally, a thought finally purified, purified of the Jewish spirit.

This is the root of the National Socialist Reich's claim to have the right to found a new thousand-year period in the history of man. From this perspective, the pretension to carry out a colossal transmutation of values under the sign of the swastika makes sense. Would it be disrespectful to Nietzsche to say that National Socialist thought lacked a Jewish morality and Jewish spirit?

The previous paragraphs on Judaism and Christianity I have taken from *The Birth of Tragedy* and *The Genealogy* [195] *of Morals* and *The Will to Power* of Friedrich Nietzsche.

Now I cite Hitler's views on this subject: "The most sensational event in the ancient world," says the Führer, "was the mobilization of the sub-world against the established order. This business of Christianity had to do as much with religion as Marxist socialism had to do with the solution to social problems. The ideas represented by Jewish Christianity were strictly unthinkable for Roman minds. For the Romans, the gods were familiar images. It is difficult to know if they had an exact idea of the beyond. For them, eternal life was personified in living things and consisted of a perpetual renewal. They had conceptions quite close to those that were common between the Japanese and the Chinese when the swastika made its appearance among those peoples.

"The Jew, who fraudulently introduced Christianity into the ancient world to ruin it, has reopened the same gap in modern times by taking as a pretext, this time, the social question. It's the same trick as before. Just as Saul became Saint Paul, Mordecai became Karl Marx."

Here is another disciple of Nietzsche. The quotes could be multiplied, and we would find the same ideas, the same language, and sometimes the same expressions.

At this point you will rightly wonder: What does all this have to do with Thomas Mann? I ask myself this question in another form. I wonder: Why did this disciple of Schopenhauer and Nietzsche not follow them to the last consequences of their thought? Why did Thomas Mann not join the crusade against reason and against the "Jewish spirit" that according to Nietzsche had poisoned the very fountains of human life?

I find no other answer than to say that it may be a fortunate inconsistency. Because Mann, as far as I know, never thoroughly reviewed the foundations of his conception of the world and of life. In his struggle against National Socialism he limited himself to using Christian principles in which he half-believed, as one believes in a fable favorable to life, and on some occasions he spoke, without fully clarifying his thought, of a false German revolution and of a true Russian revolution, but he never asked himself in depth why [196] the German revolution was false and the Russian true.

The Hitlerian horror and the war were necessary so that this spirit, which could hardly be called lucid, would come to the realization that the particularist and irrational National Socialist ideology equally denied the two universalist and rationalist conceptual frameworks that constitute the two great humanistic currents of our day: Christianity and socialism.

From the blind will to live, as a substratum of the reality of the will to power as the ultimate criterion of truth and morality, and of the notions of ascending life and descending life, the idea of a race of masters had to arise, those bearers of a superior morality, and of a race of slaves equally bearing, for Nietzsche, the degenerate ideas of Christianity and socialism.

In 1937, Mann published an essay entitled "Christianity and Socialism,"[11] from which I cite some paragraphs: "Man [i.e., Hitler] who confuses truth and lies pretends to overthrow Christianity." (As he makes this criticism, Mann forgets that for his teacher, Nietzsche, true philosophy is beyond binary opposites: good and evil, truth and falsehood.) "One can leave open the question of whether or not historical evolution demands that Christianity be overcome. But it must be said, however, that if someone is disqualified to decide the level of morality to which humanity has come thanks to Christianity, how can one pretend to have overcome it, without rising above it? And that is not what we can expect from the propagandists who announce its decline. Goethe said to Eckerman, 'The human spirit will not surpass the moral elevation attained by Christianity as it shines in the Gospels, yet today some revolutionary literati imagine that they have finished with it. It is an unprecedented impudence. Christianity has been a demand which has itself been exceedingly high and exceedingly pure, in such a way that it has not been able to become anything other than a moral judgment that clarifies consciences. But its discipline has never been so necessary as in our time, when ignorance and barbarism are affirmed in all their horror, precisely for those who claim to have overcome Christianity.'" Note now that Mann resorts to Goethe to ground the value of Christianity. Now Mann will ground [197] socialism in Nietzsche:

"Materialism may have an idealistic and religious foundation more real than the pretentious sentimentality of those who despise matter. It does not mean in any way a lowering of the spirit; it means the will to penetrate matter with humanity, which expresses itself so well in the magnificent sentence of Nietzsche: 'We want to impregnate Nature with humanity . . . we want to take from it what we need in order to dream beyond man.' This is an expression of the highest humanity, of the highest love for man and of his elevation above himself. It is the word of an authentic artist. For has art ever done anything other than impregnate the nature of humanity, take from it what it needed to elevate it, to enrich life in the creative act? In art, the spirit loves matter. It testifies to the desire to give a form and meaning to life. Yes, that natural instinct exists. I know an expression of the great individualist Nietzsche that emits a very socialist sound: 'Sin against the earth is the most terrible sin. . . . Do not hide your head in the sand of celestial things, but carry it proudly, this terrestrial head, which creates the sense of the earth.' That is the materialism of the spirit; it is the return of the religious man to earth, to that which, for us, represents the Cosmos. And socialism is nothing other than the decision, which is imposed on us as a duty, not to turn our gaze towards the metaphysical clouds and flee from the most urgent demands of the material universe, of social and collective life, but to be with those who want to give a sense to the earth, a human sense."

At the age of 75, in 1950, Mann published an essay titled "My Time," in which he seems to see clearly the relation between irrationalism and the advent of German fascism. He says: "Nihilism, which Nietzsche had predicted as inevitable, *and which had to be fulfilled as a form of intellectual life during the Second World War*, was already prepared in the far reaches of the intellect, for instance, in the writings of Ernst Junger. Someone who understood it has called National Socialism the revolution of nihilism—which it was, mixed with sinister beliefs in the inhuman, in the pre-rational and chthonic element, in the earth, in the people, in the blood, in the past, and in death." [198] He adds, "It is not that these specific elements of the age have been completely new in my maturity as a man. But I want to say this: we, old men, have known the reaction against liberalism and rationalism in a form that was still that of an extreme culture; a bleak game played by humanism itself, as a pessimism that expressed itself in the prose of our great epoch of humanistic culture and whose proud misanthropy never abjured respect for the idea, the superior vocation, the dignity of man. I speak of Schopenhauer and also of Nietzsche, who learned from the former and transformed his own pessimism into a Dionysian lyricism but who, even in apostasy, continued to be his disciple; a humanist, even in his most strident and painful eccentricities, placing in the center of his philosophy the elevation of the human being, his future, his liberation from moral humiliations."

Is this not amazing? Five years after the end of the second war, Thomas Mann reiterates his faith in the humanism of Schopenhauer and Nietzsche—a German humanism in which at each step the most extreme levels of inhumanity are clearly perceptible.

I finish here my considerations on Thomas Mann. It produces vertigo to delve deeper into the mystery of German irrationalism, the bottom of which is not to be found. Every time we think we are on firm ground, and find a way out, a new contradiction, a new affirmation of the primacy of the irrational plunges us into the abyss of unreason.

Madness, which was Nietzsche's illness, praised by Mann as the source of his genius, at one point seized an entire people. And the same man who so often addressed himself to Nietzsche and invited him to abandon his arrogant and homicidal madness, at the end of his days declared his fidelity to the irrationalist and antihuman tradition of nineteenth-century Germany.

Can we expect that one day this sinister ambiguity will be finally uprooted and banished from modern culture? In any case, I'm afraid that it will not be men like Thomas Mann who will help carry out this task. In contemporary Germany, and even beyond its borders, under the ashes of prosperity, the embers of the will to power, hatred of reason, and fidelity to death are still alive, and it is not impossible that they may one day invade the world with a terrifying wave.

Notes to Appendix

1. Jorge Portilla, "La Critica de la Critica," in *Fenomenología del relajo y otro ensayos* (México: Fondo de Cultura Económica, 1984), 158–167. Originally published in *Revista Mexicana de Literatura*, September–October 1955. Pagination in brackets corresponds to the 1984 edition.

2. The Palace of Fine Arts (Palacio de Bellas Artes) has for almost a century served as the artistic and cultural center of Mexico. That a "roundtable" on the state of Mexican literature was held there suggests that it was an event of great significance and one certain to evoke a strong reaction from Mexico's most prominent intellectuals, as it does here from Portilla.

3. Jorge Portilla, "La Crisis Espiritual de los Estados Unidos," in *Fenomenología del relajo y otros ensayos* (México: Fondo de Cultura Economica, 1984), 139–157. Originally published in *Cuadernos Americanos* in 1952. Pagination in brackets refers to the 1984 edition.

4. In English in the original.

5. In English in the original.

6. See Norman Vincent Peale, *Not Death at All* (New York: Prentice Hall, 1949)—Translators.

7. See Alfred Kinsey, Wardell Pomeroy, and Clyde Martin, *Sexual Behavior in the Human Male* (Philadelphia: Saunders, 1948); also, Kinsey, Pomeroy, Martin, and Paul Gebhard, *Sexual Behavior in the Human Female* (Philadelphia: Saunders, 1953). These sociological studies were highly controversial books in their time as they openly discussed subject matter previously thought taboo. In the original, Portilla misspells Kinsey as "Quincey," which we have corrected here—Translators.

8. See Romans 7:19 and 7:24—Translators.

9. Patrick Romanell is the author of the influential *The Making of the Mexican Mind*, the first comprehensive commentary on the history of philosophy in Mexico, focusing specifically on philosophy in twentieth-century Mexico.

See Patrick Romanell, *The Making of the Mexican Mind* (Lincoln: University of Nebraska Press, 1952)—Translators.

10. Jorge Portilla, "Thomas Mann y el irracionalismo alemán," in *Fenomenología del relajo y otros ensayos* (México: Fondo de Cultura Económica, 1984), 183–198. Originally published in *Revista de la Universidad de México* in 1958. Pagination in brackets refers to the 1984 edition.

11. We believe that Portilla meant to refer to the article "The Living Spirit" from the same year and which treats the same topics that Portilla references here. Please refer to Thomas Mann, "The Living Spirit," *Social Research* 4, no. 3 (1937): 265–272—Translators.

Bibliography

Allen, Frederick E. "September 11 and American Innocence: What Really Happened to US?" *Forbes*, September 9, 2011.

Althusser, Louis. *Lenin and Philosophy and Other Essays*. Translated by Ben Brewster. New York: Monthly Review Press, 1971.

———. *On Ideology*. Translated by Ben Brewster. London: Verso, 2008.

Anzaldúa, Gloria. *Borderlands/La Frontera*. San Francisco: Aunt Lute, 1987.

Aquinas, Thomas. *Selected Writings*. Edited by Ralph McInerny. New York: Penguin Classics, 1999.

Bailey, Beth. "From panty raids to revolution: Youth and authority, 1950–1970." In *Generations of Youth: Youth Cultures and History in Twentieth-Century America*, edited by Joe Alan Austin and Michael Willard, 187–204. New York: New York University Press, 1998.

Beauvoir, Simone de. *The Second Sex*. Translated by Constance Borde and Sheila Malovany-Chevallier. 1949. Reprint, New York: Vintage Books, 2011.

Becker, Ernest. *The Denial of Death*. New York: The Free Press, 1973.

Bell, Daniel. *The Winding Passage: Sociological Essays and Journeys*. New Brunswick, NJ: Transaction Publishers, 1991.

Blattner, William. *Heidegger's* Being and Time: *A Reader's Guide*. London: Continuum, 2006.

Brenner, Anita. *Idols Behind Altars: The Story of the Mexican Spirit*. New York: Beacon Press, 1970.

Castellanos, Rosario. "On Feminine Culture." Translated by Carlos Alberto Sánchez. In *Mexican Philosophy in the 20th Century: Essential Readings*, 206–215. Oxford: Oxford University Press, 2017.

Cavarero, Adriana. *Horrorism: Naming Contemporary Violence*. Translated by William McCuaig. New York: Columbia University Press, 2009.

Chomsky, Aviva. *"They Take Our Jobs!" And 20 Other Myths About Immigration*. Boston: Beacon Press, 2007.

Cohn, Deborah. "The Mexican Intelligentsia, 1950–1968: Cosmopolitanism, National Identity, and the State." *Mexican Studies/Estudios Mexicanos* 21, no. 1 (2005): 141–182.

Contâncio, João. "Nietzsche and Schopenhauer: On Nihilism and the Ascetic 'Will to Nothingness.'" In *The Palgrave Schopenhauer Handbook*, edited by Sandra Shapshay, 425–446. London: Palgrave McMillan, 2017.

Coriat, Isador H. *What is Psychoanalysis?* Abingdon, UK: Routledge, Trench, Troubner & Co., 1919.

Dial, Eleanore Maxwell. "Drama Critics in Search of an Identity in Mexico in the 1950s." *Latin American Literary Review* 2, no. 4 (1974): 113–125.

DiAngelo, Robin. "White Fragility." *International Journal of Critical Pedagogy* 3, no. 3 (2011): 54–70.

Domínguez Michael, Christopher. *Octavio Paz en su siglo*. Mexico City: Aguilar, 2015.

Dreyfus, Hubert, and Sean Kelly. *All Things Shining: Reading the Western Classics to Find Meaning in a Secular Age*. New York: Simon and Schuster, 2011.

Emerson, Ralph Waldo. *The Journals and Miscellaneous Notebooks: Volume XIII, 1852–1855*. Edited by Ralph H. Orth and Alfred Ferguson. Cambridge: Harvard University Press, 1977.

———. "Self-Reliance." In *The Works of Ralph Waldo Emerson: Essays, Lectures, Poems, and Orations*. London: George Bell and Sons, 1883.

Femenías, María Luisa, and Amy Oliver. *Feminist Philosophy in Latin America and Spain*. New York: Rodopi, 2007.

Freud, Anna. *The Ego and the Mechanisms of Defense*. 1936. Reprint, London: Routledge, 1992.

Freud, Sigmund. *Beyond the Pleasure Principle*. Translated by J. Strachey. New York: Hogarth Press, 1950.

Fricker, Miranda. *Epistemic Injustice: Power and the Ethics of Knowing*. Oxford: Oxford University Press, 2007.

Gallegos, Francisco. "Seriousness, Irony, and Cultural Politics: A defense of Jorge Portilla." *APA Newsletter on Hispanic/Latino Issues in Philosophy* 13, no. 1 (2013): 11–18.

———. "Surviving Social Disintegration: Jorge Portilla on the Phenomenology of Zozobra." *APA Newsletter on Hispanic/Latino Issues in Philosophy* 17, no. 2 (2018): 3–6.

Gargallo, Francesca. *Las ideas feministas latinoamericanas*. Mexico City: UACM, 2006.

Gilroy, Paul. *"There Ain't No Black in the Union, Jack": The Cultural Politics of Race and Nation*. Chicago: University of Chicago Press, 1991.

Gracia, Jorge J. E., ed. *Latin American Philosophy in the Twentieth Century*. Buffalo: Prometheus, 1986.

———. "What Is Latin American Philosophy?" In *Philosophy in Multiple Voices*, edited by George Yancey. New York: Rowman & Littlefield, 2007.

Greenwald, Glenn. *A Tragic Legacy: How a Good vs. Evil Mentality Destroyed the Bush Presidency*. New York: Three Rivers Press, 2007.

Grillo, Ioan. "The Paradox of Mexico's Mass Graves." *New York Times*, July 19, 2017, www.nytimes.com/2017/07/19/opinion/mexico-mass-grave-drug-cartel.html.

Hegel, G. W. F. *Lectures on the Philosophy of Religion*. Translated by P. G. Hodgson. Berkeley: University of California Press, 1988.

Heidegger, Martin. *Being and Time*. Translated by John Macquarrie and Edward Robinson. 1927. Reprint, New York: Harper & Row, 1962.

Herman, Judith. *Trauma and Recovery: The Aftermath of Violence—From Domestic Abuse to Political Terror*. London: Hachette UK, 2015.

Horkheimer, Max. *Eclipse of Reason*. New York: Bloomsbury Academic, 2013.

Ibargüengoitia, Antonio. *Filosofía mexicana: en sus hombres y en sus textos*. Mexico City: Porrúa, 1967.

Jaffary, Nora, Edward Osowski, and Susie Porter, eds. *Mexican History: A Primary Source Reader*, 361–373. Philadelphia: Westview Press, 2010.

James, William. "The Will to Believe." In *The Will to Believe and Other Essays in Popular Philosophy, Vol. 6*. Cambridge, MA: Harvard University Press, 1979.

Jameson, Fredric. *The Prison House of Language: A Critical Account of Structuralism and Russian Formalism*. Princeton: Princeton University Press, 1972.

Kinsey, Alfred, Wardell Pomeroy, and Clyde Martin. *Sexual Behavior in the Human Male*. Philadelphia: Saunders, 1948.

Kinsey, Alfred, Wardell Pomeroy, Clyde Martin, and Paul Gebhard. *Sexual Behavior in the Human Female*. Philadelphia: Saunders, 1953.

Knight, Alan. "Mexican Revolution: Interpretations." In *Encyclopedia of Mexico*, vol. 2. Chicago: Fitzroy Dearborn, 1997.

Koh, Harold H. *On American Exceptionalism*. New Haven: Yale Law School Legal Repository, 2013.

Krauze, Rosa. "Sobre la *Fenomenología del relajo*." *Revista de la Universidad de México* 20, no. 8 (1966): 9–14.

Kurzke, Hermann. *Thomas Mann: Life as a Work of Wrt: A Biography*. Translated by Leslie Willson. Princeton, NJ: Princeton University Press, 2002.

Lear, Jonathan. *Radical Hope: Ethics in the Face of Cultural Devastation*. Cambridge, MA: Harvard University Press, 2006.

Levinas, Emmanuel. *Time and the Other*. Translated by Richard A. Cohen. Pittsburgh: Duquesne University Press, 1987.

Lomnitz, Claudio. *Death and the Idea of Mexico*. New York: Zone Books, 2005.

López, Rick. *Crafting Mexico: Intellectuals, Artisans, and the State after the Revolution*. Durham, NC: Duke University Press, 2010.

Madsen, Deborah L. *American Exceptionalism*. Jackson: University of Mississippi Press, 1998.

Mann, Thomas. "The Living Spirit." *Social Research* 4, no. 3 (1937): 265–272.

Matysik, Tracie. *Reforming the Moral Subject: Ethics and Sexuality in Central Europe 1890–1930*. Ithaca, NY: Cornell University Press, 2008.

Mendieta, Eduardo. "Is There Latin American Philosophy?" *Philosophy Today*, 43 (Supplement, 1999): 50–61.

———, ed. *Latin American Philosophy: Currents, Issues, and Debates*. Bloomington: Indiana University Press, 2003.

Mendoza, Jose Jorge. "Illegal: White Supremacy and Immigration: Core Issues and Emerging Trends." In *The Ethics and Politics of Immigration: Core Issues and Emerging Trends*, ed. Alex Sager, 201–220. London: Rowman & Littlefield International, 2016.

Merleau-Ponty, Maurice. *Phenomenology of Perception*. Translated by Donald Landes. 1945. Reprint, New York: Routledge, 2012.

Meyer, Jean A. *The Cristero Rebellion: The Mexican People Between Church and State, 1926–1929*. Cambridge: Cambridge University Press, 1976.

Niblo, Stephen R. *Mexico in the 1940s: Modernity, Politics, and Corruption*. Washington, DC: Scholarly Resources Inc., 1991.

Niebuhr, Reinhold. *The Irony of American History*. Chicago: University of Chicago Press, 1952.

Nuccetelli, Susana. *Latin American Thought: Philosophical Problems and Arguments*. Boulder, CO: Westview Press, 2001.

Nuccetelli, Susana, and Gary Seay, eds. *Latin American Philosophy: An Introduction with Readings*. Upper Saddle River, NJ: Prentice Hall, 2003.

Nuccetelli, Susana, Ofelia Schutte, and Otávio Bueno, eds. *A Companion to Latin American Philosophy*. Malden, MA: Wiley-Blackwell, 2010.

Ortega, Mariana. *In-Between: Latina Feminist Phenomenology, Multiplicity, and the Self*. Albany: State University of New York Press, 2016.

Owen, David S. "Towards a Critical Theory of Whiteness." *Philosophy and Social Criticism* 33, no. 2 (2007): 203–222.

Patterson, Orlando. *Slavery and Social Death*. Cambridge, MA: Harvard University Press, 1982.

Paz, Octavio. *The Labyrinth of Solitude and Other Writings*. Translated by Lysander Kemp. New York: Grove Press, 1985.

Peale, Norman Vincent. *Not Death At All*. New York: Prentice Hall, 1949.

Pitts, Andrea. "Carlos Alberto Sánchez: *Contingency and Commitment: Mexican Existentialism and the Place of Philosophy*," *Human Studies* 39, no. 4 (2016): 645–652.

———. "Toward an Aesthetics of Race: Bridging the Writings of Gloria Anzaldúa and José Vasconcelos." *Inter-American Journal of Philosophy* 5, no. 1 (2012): 80–100.

Portilla, Jorge. *La fenomenología del relajo y otros ensayos*. Mexico City: Fondo de Cultura Económica, 1984.

———. "Phenomenology of Relajo." In *The Suspension of Seriousness*, by Carlos Alberto Sanchez. Albany: State University of New York Press, 2012.

Ram, Kalpana, and Christopher Houston. *Phenomenology in Anthropology: A Sense of Perspective*. Bloomington: Indiana University Press, 2015.

Rancher, Shoni. "The Political Relevance of Kierkegaardian Humor in Jorge Portilla's *Fenomenología del relajo.*" *APA Newsletter on Hispanic/Latino Issues in Philosophy* 18, no. 1 (2018), 12–16.

Ratcliffe, Matthew. *Feelings of Being: Phenomenology, Psychiatry, and the Sense of Reality*. Oxford: Oxford University Press, 2008.

Reyes, Juan José. *El péndulo y el pozo*. Mexico City: Consejo para la cultura nacional, 2004.

Rivera Berruz, Stephanie, and Leah Kalmanson, eds. *Comparative Studies in Asian and Latin American Philosophies: Cross-Cultural Theories and Methodologies*. New York: Bloomsbury, 2018.

Romanell, Patrick. *The Making of the Mexican Mind*. Lincoln: University of Nebraska Press, 1952.

Romero, Robert Chao. *The Chinese in Mexico, 1882–1940*. Tucson: University of Arizona Press, 2010.

RT News. "Estrategia fallida: 250.000 asesinatos en México desde el inicio de la 'guerra contra el narco.'" May 24, 2018, https://actualidad.rt.com/actualidad/272788-mexico-llega-250000-asesinatos-inicio-guerra-narcotrafico.

Salles, Arlene, and Elizabeth Millán, eds. *The Role of History in Latin American Philosophy: Contemporary Perspectives*. Albany: State University of New York Press, 2005.

Sánchez, Carlos Alberto. *Contingency and Commitment: Mexican Existentialism and the Place of Philosophy*. Albany: State University of New York Press, 2016.

———. "Death and the Colonial Difference: An Analysis of a Mexican Idea." *Journal of Philosophy of Life* 3, no. 3 (2013): 168–189.

———. "The Gift of Mexican Historicism." *Continental Philosophy Review* 51, no. 3 (2018): 439–457.

———. "On Emilio Uranga's *Análisis del ser del mexicano*: Decolonizing Pretensions, Recolonizing Critiques," *Southern Journal of Philosophy* 57, no. S1 (2019): 63–89.

———. "Serious Subjects: On Values, Time, and Death." *Spaziofilosofico* 18 (2017): 463–473.

———. *The Suspension of Seriousness: On the Phenomenology of Jorge Portilla*. Albany: State University of New York Press, 2012.

Sánchez, Carlos Alberto, and Robert Eli Sanchez. "Introduction" to *Mexican Philosophy in the 20th Century: Essential Readings,* ed. Sánchez and Sanchez. New York: Oxford University Press, 2017.

Sanchez, Robert Eli, Jr., ed. *Latin American and Latinx Philosophy: An Introduction*. London: Routledge, 2019.

Santos Ruiz, Ana. *Los hijos de los dioses: El "Grupo Filosófico Hiperión" y la filosofía de lo mexicano*. Mexico City: Bonilla Artigas Editores, 2016.

Sartre, Jean-Paul. *Being and Nothingness*. Translated by Hazel Barnes. New York: Washington Square Press, 1956.

Schmid, Hans B. *Plural Action: Essays in Philosophy and Social Science*. Dordrecht, Netherlands: Springer Science & Business Media, 2009.

Schmitt, Carl. *The Concept of the Political*. Translated by George Schwab. Chicago: University of Chicago Press, 2007.

Schutte, Ofelia. "Continental Philosophy and Postcolonial Subjects," in *Latin American Philosophy: Currents, Issues, Debate*, edited by Eduardo Mendieta, 150–164. Bloomington: Indiana University Press, 2003.

———. *Cultural Identity and Social Liberation in Latin American Thought*. Albany: State University of New York Press, 1993.

———. "Toward an Understanding of Latin American Philosophy." *Philosophy Today* 31, no. 1 (1987): 21–34.

Southern Poverty Law Center. "Anti-Immigrant." Accessed January 23, 2020, www.splcenter.org/fighting-hate/extremist-files/ideology/anti-immigrant.

Spielvogel, Jackson. *Hitler and Nazi Germany: A History*. London: Routledge, 2004.

Sullivan, Shannon. "*White Innocence: Paradoxes of Colonialism and Race* by Gloria Wekker," *philoSOPHIA: A Journal of Continental Feminism* 7, no. 2 (2017): 363–367.

Uhlmann, E. L., T. A. Poehlman, D. Tannenbaum, and J. A. Bargh. "Implicit Puritanism in American moral cognition," *Journal of Experimental Social Psychology* 47 (2011): 312–320.

Uranga, Emilio. "Essay on the Ontology of the Mexican (1951)." Translated by Carlos Alberto Sánchez. In *Mexican Philosophy in the 20th Century: Essential Readings*, 165–177. New York: Oxford University Press, 2017.

———. "El tema de la muerte en la filosofía contemporánea." *México en la cultura*, October 29, 1950.

Vargas, Manuel. "Lessons from the Philosophy of Race in Mexico." *Philosophy Today* 44 (*SPEP Supplement* 26, 2000): 18–29.

Villaurrutia, Xavier. "Décima Muerte." 1933. Accessed December 12, 2008, http://amediavoz.com/villaurrutia.htm.

Villegas, Abelardo. *La filosofía de lo mexicano*. Mexico City: Universidad Autonoma de México, 1979.

West, Cornel. *The Cornel West Reader*. New York: Civitas Books, 2000.

Young, Julian. *German Philosophy in the 20th Century: Weber to Heidegger*. London: Routledge, 2018.

Zea, Leopoldo. *Filosofía latinoamericana como filosofía sin mas*. Mexico City: Siglo XXI, 1969.

Index

accidentality, 53, 190

American exceptionalism, 2, 11, 77, 79, 87, 88, 92fn6, 94

apretado, 35–37, 39, 57–59, 63, 65, 105, 153–155, 157, 162fn14, 162fn15

brutality, 27, 126

Caso, Antonio, 9

Castellanos, Rosario, 9, 10

character type, 7, 19, 35, 37, 58, 59, 201

Christianity, 29, 114, 125, 148, 168, 195, 196, 199, 200–203

Colonialism, 11, 22, 27, 34, 46, 50–52, 65, 133–134

community, 1, 2, 5, 6, 9, 10, 18, 21–23, 26, 30, 31, 38, 45–56, 66fn7–8, 82, 104, 105, 114, 116, 128, 152, 154, 156, 158, 165–167, 184, 186

consmopolitanism, 22–25, 38–39, 40fn13

culture, 1, 8, 8, 11, 18, 21, 23, 25, 26, 28, 28, 31, 35, 36, 38, 39, 40fn6, 43, 49, 63, 71, 73, 74, 77–79, 81, 87–91, 94, 100, 101, 114, 126, 128, 129, 131, 140, 141, 145, 167–169,

176, 178, 186, 189, 191, 196, 199, 204, 205

death, 4, 7, 11, 12, 13, 21, 27, 30, 31, 40, 44, 76, 87, 93, 94, 96, 107, 108–111, 114, 116, 118, 123–145, 147, 148, 159, 177, 181, 183, 192, 194, 196–198, 206

defense mechanism, 41fn34, 55–57, 61, 64–65, 94, 98–99, 111, 118fn24, 155, 157–159, 187–189

diversity, 8, 11, 62–64, 78, 95, 105, 113

duty, 32–34, 204

el grupo Hiperión, 4, 13fn6–7, 62, 101, 131, 132, 137, 190

Emerson, Ralph Waldo, 11, 83–84, 86, 88

enemies, 20, 23, 30, 32, 33, 39, 81, 87, 107, 143, 171, 189

ethics, 39, 86, 128, 137, 149, 181

fear, 4, 6, 11, 27, 28, 31, 43, 52, 55, 78, 84, 85, 90, 103, 106, 117, 128, 13, 134, 138, 154, 161, 188, 191

friends, 4, 20, 23, 30, 87, 107

Gaos, Jose, 8, 9, 190

gender, 8, 9, 44, 68fn30, 118fn25

hate, 6, 7, 38, 89, 130, 161fn5, 201
Hegel, G. W. F., 5, 11, 55, 56, 127, 141, 177, 195
Heidegger, Martin, 44, 46, 65, 66, 103, 106, 107, 108, 109, 117, 129
historicism, 7

ideology, 6, 18, 19, 22, 24, 25, 27, 30, 32–34, 37, 39fn3, 40fn13, 75–78, 82–91, 127, 198, 202
intentionality, 129

Krauze, Rosa, 9, 10

Levinas, Emmanuel, 12, 137–138
lo mexicano, 5, 17, 18, 22, 24, 25, 27, 39, 62
love, 18, 19, 20, 38, 39, 107, 128, 148, 162fn15, 170, 173, 176, 178, 191, 194, 197–198, 203

Manichaeism, 10, 19–23, 38, 60, 173
Marxism, 6, 114
Merleau-Ponty, Maurice, 44, 65, 210
mestizaje, 8–9, 29–30, 168
metaphysics, 149
Mexican Revolution, 17, 20, 22, 24, 27, 32, 40fn6, 40fn10, 53, 56, 118, 124, 142fn23, 195, 202–204
Mexicanidad, 13fn6
mood, 11–13, 19–22, 44, 52, 62–64, 114–115, 117fn21, 149–150, 154–155, 158

National Socialism, 124, 129, 131, 145–146, 198–199, 201–202, 204
Nazism, 2, 9, 11, 145, 147, 199
negation, 18, 27, 28, 124, 154, 167, 168, 171
Niebuhr, Reinhold, 83, 101, 185–187

Nietzsche, Freidrich, 123–127, 129, 139, 141fn1, 145, 148, 182, 191, 193, 195, 198–204
nihilism, 1, 6, 11, 17, 53, 123, 124, 128, 153, 159, 204

oppression, 9–10, 32, 34, 51, 78, 87, 172
Ortega y Gasset, Jose, 125, 129

Paz, Octavio, 4, 13fn7, 22–26, 40fn12, 131–134, 137, 140, 142fn12, 142fn18, 166, 172
phenomenology, 2, 3, 8, 11, 44, 45, 51, 65fn2, 95, 99, 100, 101, 103, 104, 112, 148, 149
poetry, 17, 132, 137
pragmatism, 82–83, 98, 116fn4, 179, 183–185, 188–189, 196
puritanism, 10, 75, 77, 94, 116fn7, 180

race, 19, 26, 28–30, 33, 37, 87, 115, 168, 196, 202
Ramos, Samuel, 8, 190
relajo, 4, 5, 6, 8, 12fn1, 17, 18, 30, 35, 36, 123, 126–128
responsibility, 29, 33, 59, 60, 74, 84, 85, 90, 91, 126–129, 138, 153

Sartre, Jean-Paul, 37
Schmitt, Carl, 20
Schopenhauer, Arthur, 123, 125–126, 139, 141fn1, 145, 148, 193, 195–199, 202, 204
seriousness, 5, 18, 35, 59, 123, 126–127, 129, 135, 151, 153
socialism, 6, 148, 201–204
suspension, 18, 30, 123, 129, 153, 154, 157, 161

terrorism, 19, 25, 31–37, 41fn21, 141, 170

universality, 27, 28, 168, 169
Uranga, Emilio, 4, 8, 20, 21, 39, 40, 53, 67, 131–138, 140

Villoro, Luis, 4, 8
violence, 11, 12, 31, 41, 124, 126, 130, 154, 161, 180, 185, 199

West, Cornel, 114, 148

Whiteness, 11, 71–72, 81–82, 87, 89, 91, 91fn2, 95, 114–115, 118fn24, 119fn35, 182

xenophile, 43, 60, 166–168
xenophobia, 12, 18, 20, 27, 72

Zea, Leopoldo, 4, 8, 38, 134, 190
zozobra, 12fn4, 43, 52–64, 105, 114, 156